Self-Regulated Learning

SELF-REGULATED LEARNING
From Teaching
to Self-Reflective Practice

Edited by
DALE H. SCHUNK
BARRY J. ZIMMERMAN

THE GUILFORD PRESS
New York   London

©1998 The Guilford Press
A Division of Guilford Publications, Inc.
72 Spring Street, New York, NY 10012
http://www.guilford.com

Printed in the United States of America

This book is printed on acid-free paper.

Last digit is print number: 9 8 7 6 5 4 3 2 1

Library of Congress Cataloging-in-Publication Data

Self-regulated learning: from teaching to self-reflective practice /
  Dale H. Schunk and Barry J. Zimmerman, editors.
      p.   cm.
  Includes bibliographic references and indexes.
  ISBN 1-57230-306-9
  1. Learning. 2. Self-control. 3. Study skills. 4. Students—
Self-rating of. I. Schunk, Dale, H. II. Zimmerman, Barry J.
LB1060.S42 1998
370.15'23—dc21   97-46438
                                                               CIP

We dedicate this book to Ted Rosenthal, whose intellectual influence on the scope and direction of social-cognitive research and self-regulation theory was seminal. At a time when stage conceptions dominated views of cognitive development, Ted demonstrated that young children readily induce fundamental concepts about the physical and social worlds around them, through observation of such models as parents, teachers, and peers, as they self-regulate their immediate environment. His work expanded theoretical conceptions of what children and youth can abstract from vicarious experiences, and it foreshadowed current theoretical interest in contextualism and the social nature of human thought. Ted also conducted extensive research on the social and self-regulatory processes that foster therapeutic change across a broad spectrum of personal dysfunctions including anxiety, stress, and fears. He wrote about the important role that self-confident models could play in dispelling unfortunate self-beliefs and instilling effective courses of self-corrective action. Ted's wit, command of the written word, and selfless dedication to his students and patients were legendary. His untimely death was a tragic loss not only to those who knew him personally but also to our field, which he so illustriously graced.

Contributors

Phillip J. Belfiore, PhD, Education Division, Mercyhurst College, Erie, Pennsylvania

Andrew Biemiller, PhD, Institute of Child Study/Department of Human Development and Applied Psychology, University of Toronto, Toronto, Ontario, Canada

Rachel Brown, PhD, London, England

Deborah L. Butler, PhD, Educational Psychology and Special Education, Faculty of Education, University of British Columbia, Vancouver, British Columbia, Canada

Pamela Beard El-Dinary, PhD, Montgomery County, Maryland, Public Schools, Rockville, Maryland

Steve Graham, EdD, Department of Special Education, University of Maryland, College Park, Maryland

Karen R. Harris, EdD, Department of Special Education, University of Maryland, College Park, Maryland

Barbara K. Hofer, PhD, Center for Human Growth and Development, University of Michigan, Ann Arbor, Michigan

Rebecca S. Hornyak, Education Division, Mercyhurst College, Erie, Pennsylvania

Alison Inglis, MA, Department of Human Development and Applied Psychology, University of Toronto, Toronto, Ontario, Canada

William Y. Lan, PhD, Division of Educational Psychology and Leadership, College of Education, Texas Tech University, Lubbock, Texas

Donald Meichenbaum, PhD, Department of Psychology (emeritus), University of Waterloo, Waterloo, Ontario, Canada

Paul R. Pintrich, PhD, Combined Program in Education and Psychology, University of Michigan, Ann Arbor, Michigan

Michael Pressley, PhD, Department of Psychology, University of Notre Dame, Notre Dame, Indiana

Dale H. Schunk, PhD, Department of Educational Studies, Purdue University, West Lafayette, Indiana

Michal Shany, PhD, Beit Berl Teachers College, Kfar Saba, Israel

Denise B. Stockley, MA, Faculty of Education, Simon Fraser University, Burnaby, British Columbia, Canada

Gary A. Troia, MS, Department of Special Education, University of Maryland, College Park, Maryland

Ruth Wharton-McDonald, PhD, Department of Education, University of New Hampshire, Durham, New Hampshire

Philip H. Winne, PhD, Faculty of Education, Simon Fraser University, Burnaby, British Columbia, Canada

Shirley L. Yu, PhD, Department of Educational Psychology, University of Houston, Houston, Texas

Barry J. Zimmerman, PhD, Doctoral Program in Educational Psychology, Graduate School and University Center, City University of New York, New York, New York

Preface

National and international recognition of the educational importance of self-regulation has increased dramatically in recent years. Theoretical accounts of learning, motivation, and performance have placed greater emphasis on the active role of students as seekers, generators, and processors of information, and less emphasis on the notion that students are passive recipients of information from the environment. *Self-regulated learning* refers to learning that occurs largely from the influence of students' self-generated thoughts, feelings, strategies, and behaviors, which are oriented toward the attainment of goals.

Educators generally accept the important role in behavior played by students' self-regulatory activities, but they often do not know how to teach students self-regulatory skills or how to otherwise enhance students' use of self-regulation principles in classrooms or other learning settings. This lack of knowledge stems from several sources. Teacher education programs typically emphasize content-area knowledge and mastery of pedagogical methods, and focus less on principles of learning, development, and motivation. Second, teachers typically feel overwhelmed with the sheer amount of material they are expected to cover, which leads them to forgo teaching self-regulation and other topics that are not required. Finally, few students and parents realize that self-regulation can be taught as a skill, and as a result these groups put little pressure on schools to offer self-regulation instruction as part of the curriculum.

The present volume represents the third in a series in which our overall goal is to provide readers with theoretical principles, research findings, and practical applications of self-regulation concepts and principles in learning settings. In the initial volume (Zimmerman & Schunk, 1989), we organized chapters around different theoretical perspectives. This format was useful for introducing and explaining the phenomenon of academic self-regulation in terms of prominent existing perspectives. The second volume (Schunk & Zimmerman, 1994) provided a conceptual framework for studying self-regulation, which detailed four areas in which students could exercise self-regulation: motives, methods, performance outcomes, and environmental and social resources. Two or more chapters were included for each area; authors discussed theory, research, and applications of self-regulation principles.

Moving beyond fundamental theories and the basic research identifying key self-regulation attributes and processes, the present volume considers larger-scale interventions whose effects are broader in scope and are assessed over lengthy periods of time. The *primary objectives* of this book are (1) to provide suggestions for teaching self-regulatory skills that are firmly derived from principles of self-regulation and (2) to discuss detailed applications of self-regulation principles in classrooms and other learning settings. The chapters in this book detail collaborations between researchers and practitioners for the purpose of integrating self-regulation instruction into the regular curriculum. The research was designed to promote long-term maintenance and generalization of instructional effects. Although most of the instructional models are in the early stages of development, the results are very promising.

The introductory chapter provides an overview of the book and discusses the key self-regulation processes and concepts inherent in various instructional models. The concluding chapter provides a critical analysis of the field of self-regulation and makes suggestions about where we go from here. The remaining chapters discuss self-regulation interventions.

To ensure uniformity in presentation across the intervention chapters, we asked authors to follow a five-step format: First, briefly introduce the chapter topic and provide a detailed description of the target students to whom the ideas were applied. Second, present a conceptualization of the intervention program to include relevant theory and research on which it is based. Third, describe the program's implementation. Fourth, discuss its results in terms of how well students acquired self-regulation principles and were able to apply them to enhance learning. And lastly, discuss how *self-reflective practice* enters into their program, and especially how it is an integral part of long-term maintenance.

In addition to being a resource for educational researchers and practitioners, this book is designed for use by graduate students—many of whom will be educational professionals (e.g., teachers)—and by advanced undergraduates who have a minimal course background in education and psychology. The book is appropriate for any course where self-regulation is addressed in some depth, such as in introductory courses in learning, development, instructional design, and educational psychology, as well as for specialty courses in learning, development, motivation, cognition, and instruction. Although we assume that students will possess some familiarity with psychological concepts and research methods, the text is written for general audiences and contains minimal references to statistical analyses.

ACKNOWLEDGMENTS

We want to acknowledge many individuals for their assistance during the various phases of this project. Our special thanks go to our contributors who, despite hectic schedules, worked diligently, met deadlines, and made our editorial work professionally satisfying. We express our appreciation to many colleagues and students with whom we have had rewarding professional interactions. In particular, we have benefited greatly from our association with colleagues who are members of the American Educational Research Association and Division 15 (Educational Psychology) of the American Psychological Association. Chris Jennison, our editor at The Guilford Press, was especially supportive of this project and provided needed editorial guidance. Finally, we express our deepest appreciation to our wives, Caryl Schunk and Diana Zimmerman, and to our daughters, Laura Schunk, Kristin Zimmerman Scott, and Shana Zimmerman, for their continuous encouragement and love.

REFERENCES

Schunk, D. H., & Zimmerman, B. J. (Eds.). (1994). *Self-regulation of learning and performance: Issues and educational applications*. Hillsdale, NJ: Erlbaum.

Zimmerman, B. J., & Schunk, D. H. (Eds.). (1989). *Self-regulated learning and academic achievement: Theory, research, and practice*. New York: Springer-Verlag.

Contents

1. Developing Self-Fulfilling Cycles of Academic Regulation: 1
   An Analysis of Exemplary Instructional Models
   Barry J. Zimmerman

2. Writing and Self-Regulation: Cases from the 20
   Self-Regulated Strategy Development Model
   Steve Graham, Karen R. Harris, and Gary A. Troia

3. Transactional Instruction of Comprehension Strategies 42
   in the Elementary Grades
   Michael Pressley, Pamela Beard El-Dinary,
   Ruth Wharton-McDonald, and Rachel Brown

4. Teaching College Students to Be Self-Regulated Learners 57
   Barbara K. Hofer, Shirley L. Yu, and Paul R. Pintrich

5. Teaching Self-Monitoring Skills in Statistics 86
   William Y. Lan

6. Computing Technologies as Sites for Developing 106
   Self-Regulated Learning
   Philip H. Winne and Denise B. Stockley

7. Teaching Elementary Students to Self-Regulate Practice 137
   of Mathematical Skills with Modeling
   Dale H. Schunk

8. A Strategic Content Learning Approach to Promoting 160
   Self-Regulated Learning by Students with
   Learning Disabilities
   Deborah L. Butler

xi

 9. **Operant Theory and Application to Self-Monitoring**   **184**
    in Adolescents
    Phillip J. Belfiore and Rebecca S. Hornyak

10. **Factors Influencing Children's Acquisition and**   **203**
    Demonstration of Self-Regulation on Academic Tasks
    Andrew Biemiller, Michal Shany, Alison Inglis,
    and Donald Meichenbaum

11. **Conclusions and Future Directions**   **225**
    for Academic Interventions
    Dale H. Schunk and Barry J. Zimmerman

    Author Index   **236**

    Subject Index   **242**

CHAPTER 1

Developing Self-Fulfilling Cycles of Academic Regulation: An Analysis of Exemplary Instructional Models

Barry J. Zimmerman

Research on academic self-regulation has grown out of an interest in explaining how students become masters of their own learning processes (Zimmerman, 1989). There are many biographies of inspiring figures, such as Benjamin Franklin, Abraham Lincoln, and George Washington Carver, who despite humble origins and limited access to high-quality instruction, educated themselves through reading, studying, and self-disciplined practice. Contemporary accounts of less famous but similarly dedicated learners continue to reveal the benefits of academic self-regulation, such as recent immigrant groups from Indochina (Caplan, Choy, & Whitmore, 1992). These Asian youngsters have succeeded academically despite many disadvantages, such as a lack of fluency in English, poorly educated parents, and attending inner city schools with few resources and large numbers of low-achieving classmates. Self-regulated learners, whether historic or contemporary, are distinguished by their view of academic learning as something they do for themselves rather than as something that is done to or for them. They believe academic learning is a proactive activity, requiring self-initiated motivational and behavioral processes as well as metacognitive ones (Zimmerman, 1986). For example, self-regulated students stand out from classmates by the goals they set for themselves, the accuracy of their behavioral self-monitoring, and the resourcefulness of their strategic thinking (e.g., Schunk & Zimmerman, 1994). These and other self-initiated processes enable these students to become controllers rather than victims of their learning experiences.

Academic self-regulation is not a mental ability, such as intelligence, or an academic skill, such as reading proficiency; rather, it is the self-directive process through which learners transform their mental abilities into academic skills. What is this process, and how can students become more self-regulatory? In this chapter, I present a cyclical phase analysis of self-regulation, identify key self-regulatory processes used during each phase, and compare how skillful self-regulators differ from their classmates in the use of these processes. I also describe the social, environmental, and personal conditions from which self-regulation emerges and analyze exemplary instructional models that have been used to develop students' self-regulatory skill. These educational models will be discussed in subsequent chapters of this volume.

SELF-REGULATED LEARNING CYCLE PHASES

Most self-regulation theorists view learning as a multidimensional process involving personal (cognitive and emotional), behavioral, and contextual components (Zimmerman, 1986, 1989). For an academic skill to be mastered, learners must behaviorally apply cognitive strategies to a task within a contextually relevant setting. This usually requires repeated attempts to learn because mastery involves coordinating personal, behavioral, and environmental components, each of which is separately dynamic as well as jointly interactive. For example, no single cognitive learning strategy will work equally well for all students, and few, if any, strategies will work optimally on all academic tasks. The effectiveness of a strategy will even change as a skill develops, such as when a novice science student shifts from a key word strategy for memorizing basic terms in a text passage to an organizational strategy for enhancing integration of the knowledge. As a result of these diverse and changing interpersonal, contextual, and intrapersonal conditions, self-regulated learners must constantly reassess their effectiveness.

Self-regulation theorists view learning as an open-ended process that requires cyclical activity on the part of the learner that occurs in three major phases: forethought, performance or volitional control, and self-reflection (see Figure 1.1). The *forethought* phase refers to influential processes and beliefs that precede efforts to learn and set the stage for such learning. The second self-regulatory phase, *performance* or *volitional control*, involves processes that occur during learning efforts and affect concentration and performance. The third self-regulatory phase, *self-reflection*, involves processes that occur after learning efforts and influence a learner's reactions to that experience. These self-reflections, in turn, influence forethought regarding subsequent learning efforts, thus completing the self-regulatory cycle.

Five types of forethought processes and beliefs have been studied in research on academic self-regulation to date (see Table 1.1). *Goal setting*

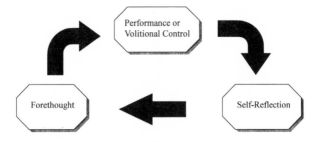

FIGURE 1.1. Academic learning cycle phases.

refers to deciding on specific outcomes of learning (Locke & Latham, 1990), and *strategic planning* refers the selection of learning strategies or methods designed to attain the desired goals (Zimmerman & Martinez-Pons, 1992). These goal-setting and strategic-planning processes are affected by a number of personal beliefs, such as a learner's self-efficacy, goal orientations, and intrinsic interest in or valuing of the task. *Self-efficacy* refers to personal beliefs about one's capability to learn or perform at certain designated levels (Bandura, 1986). For example, students who are self-efficacious set higher goals for themselves (Zimmerman, Bandura, & Martinez-Pons, 1992) and are more likely to choose effective learning strategies than classmates who lack efficacy (Zimmerman & Bandura, 1994). Students displaying a learning *goal orientation* tend to focus on learning progress rather than competitive outcomes and tend to learn more effectively than students with performance goals (Ames, 1992). Learners who have an *intrinsic interest* in a task will continue learning efforts, even in the absence of tangible rewards (Deci, 1975).

Three types of performance or volitional control processes have been studied in research on academic self-regulation (see Table 1.1). These processes help learners to focus on the task and optimize their performance. With regard to *attention focusing,* volition theorists, such as Kuhl (1985), Heckhausen (1991), and Corno (1993), emphasize the need for learners to protect their intention to learn from distractions and from competing intentions. Low achievers are more easily diverted from the task and tend to ruminate more about prior decisions and mistakes than high achievers. Kuhl (1985) calls this type of volitional dysfunctioning "state" controlled rather than "action" controlled, and he believes the self-regulatory processes that learners use during the volitional control or performance phase are distinct from those used initially to plan and motivate the learning effort. Heckhausen and Corno have used Caesar's "Rubicon" (river of no return) as a metaphor to emphasize the need to protect performance phase processes from competing forethought phase processes.

A second group of performance or volitional control phase processes affect students' implementation of strategic or other learning methods, such as self-instructions or imaginal guidance. *Self-instruction* refers to telling oneself how to proceed during a learning task, such as solving a mathematics problem, and research shows that it can improve students' learning (Schunk, 1982). Meichenbaum and colleagues (e.g., Biemiller, Shany, Inglis, & Meichenbaum, Chapter 10, this volume) have conducted numerous studies of students' self-verbalization during learning efforts, and Harris, Graham, and Troia (Chapter 2, this volume) use self-verbalization extensively in their approach to teaching disabled children to self-regulate more effectively. Pressley and Levin (Pressley, 1977; Pressley & Levin, 1977) have demonstrated the effectiveness of *imagery* (i.e., forming mental pictures) as a technique to enhance learning and recall, and Zimmerman and Rocha (1984, 1987) have used images of modeling sequences to assist very young children to learn and remember.

The third type of volition or performance control process involves *self-monitoring*. This is a vital yet problematic self-regulatory process because it informs learners about their progress (or lack thereof) but can interfere with strategic implementation processes (Winne, 1995). Many researchers studying self-monitoring, especially on motoric tasks, recommend limiting self-monitoring just to key processes or outcomes (Singer & Cauraugh, 1985). Self-monitoring is further complicated by the fact that as skills are acquired they require less intentional monitoring—a phenomenon called *automatization* or *routinization*. Many theorists assume students no longer need to monitor their academic performance as the learning process becomes routine, but Carver and Scheier (1981) suggest that students instead shift their self-monitoring to a more general level, such as from the action itself to the immediate environment and the outcomes of that action. For example, this occurs when a writer no longer has to worry about closely monitoring his or her grammar and can shift attention to the metaphorical qualities of created prose.

Four types of self-reflection processes have been studied in research on academic self-regulation to date (see Table 1.1). *Self-evaluation* is usually

TABLE 1.1. Cyclical Phases and Subprocesses of Self-Regulation

	Cyclical self-regulatory phases	
Forethought	Performance/volitional control	Self-reflection
Goal setting	Attention focusing	Self-evaluation
Strategic planning	Self-instruction/imagery	Attributions
Self-efficacy beliefs	Self-monitoring	Self-reactions
Goal orientation		Adaptivity
Intrinsic interest		

one of the initial self-reflective processes to occur during this phase. It involves comparing self-monitored information with some sort of standard or goal, such as judging feedback regarding missed test items according to the teacher's grading curve. Self-regulated learners want to evaluate how well they are doing promptly and accurately, and students will resort to comparing their performance to others when no formal standards are available (Festinger, 1954). Self-evaluations typically lead to *attributions* about the causal meaning of the results, such as whether a poor performance is due to one's limited ability or to insufficient effort (Weiner, 1979). These attributional processes are pivotal to self-reflection because attributions of errors to ability compel learners to react negatively and to give up trying to improve. Attributions are influenced by a variety of personal and contextual factors, such as one's goal orientation, accompanying task conditions, and how well others did on the task. Self-regulated learners tend to attribute failures to correctable causes and attribute successes to personal competence. These self-protective attributions lead to positive *self-reactions*, even during long stretches of performance with meager learning results. There is evidence that personal attributions of successes and failures to strategy use are directly related to positive self-reactions but that attributions of these outcomes to ability are related to negative self-reactions (Zimmerman & Kitsantas, 1997).

Strategic attributions not only enhance self-reactions, they assist in identifying the source of learning errors and adapting one's performance (Zimmerman & Martinez-Pons, 1992). Strategy attributions reinforce systematic variations in approach until learners finally discover the strategy that work best for them. For important academic skills, this *adaptation* process can take many practice cycles. In addition to their attributions, self-regulated learners are more adaptive because they evaluate their performance more appropriately. Favorable self-reactions cyclically enhance positive forethought about oneself as a learner such as greater self-efficacy about eventually mastering the academic skill, a stronger learning goal orientation (Dweck, 1988), and greater intrinsic interest in the task (Zimmerman & Kitsantas, 1997). These links between self-reflection and forethought processes complete the self-regulatory phase cycle. Because use of self-regulatory processes is inherently cyclical, the phases tend to be self-sustaining in the sense that each phase creates inertia that can facilitate or undermine learning during subsequent phases.

In summary, the forethought phase of self-regulation prepares the learner for and influences the effectiveness of the performance or volitional control phase processes, which in turn affect processes used during the self-reflection phase. These self-reflective processes influence subsequent forethought and prepare the learner for further efforts to achieve mastery.

COMPARING SKILLFUL AND NAIVE
SELF-REGULATED LEARNERS

All learners try to self-regulate their academic learning and performance in some way, but there are dramatic differences in methods and self-beliefs among students. From the perspective of self-regulatory phase processes, how do naive or unsophisticated learners differ from skillful or knowledgeable learners? These differences in processes are presented in Table 1.2.

Naive learners do not lack goals but instead are handicapped by the low quality of their goals. These goals tend to be nonspecific and distal and, as such, lead to poor performance or volitional control and limited forms of self-reflection. By contrast, skillful or knowledgeable self-regulated learners form a graduated system of specific, proximal goals that are linked to distal goals in a hierarchy (Bandura, 1991). By forming their goals into hierarchies that are sequenced according to their achievability, self-regulated learners ensure the continued availability of challenging but achievable goals to guide them. Goal hierarchies also provide skillful learners with a personally relevant self-standard for evaluating their personal progress that neither depends on external feedback from others nor delays positive self-reactions until distal goal attainment. Naive self-regulators remain dependent on others or must generate extraordinary personal motivation to delay gratification until distal goals are achieved because these standards convey little feedback of proximal success. As a result of this impoverished feedback, the self-evaluations of naive self-regulators invariably decline over time. On the other hand, the completion of hierarchical subgoal standards by skillful self-regulated learners conveys explicit

TABLE 1.2. Self-Regulatory Subprocesses of Naive and Skillful Learners

Self-regulatory phases	Classes of self-regulated learners	
	Naive self-regulators	Skillful self-regulators
Forethought	Nonspecific distal goals	Specific hierarchical goals
	Performance goal orientation	Learning goal orientation
	Low self-efficacy	High self-efficacy
	Disinterested	Intrinsically interested
Performance/ volitional control	Unfocused plan	Focused on performance
	Self-handicapping strategies	Self-instruction/imagery
	Outcome self-monitoring	Process self-monitoring
Self-reflection	Avoid self-evaluation	Seek self-evaluation
	Ability attributions	Strategy/practice attributions
	Negative self-reactions	Positive self-reactions
	Nonadaptive	Adaptive

feedback of proximal success and enhances their self-evaluations (Earley, Connolly, & Ekegren, 1989).

Skillful self-regulated learners also report having a learning or mastery goal orientation whereas naive learners adopt a performance or ego-related goal orientation (Pintrich & DeGroot, 1990). This is not surprising in light of Dweck's (1988) conclusion that performance goal orientations are predicated on fixed conceptions of intelligence, but learning or mastery goal orientations are based on incremental conceptions. Naive self-regulators view learning episodes as personally threatening experiences during which their performance will be evaluated and their intelligence may be compared unfavorably with others, which leads to devaluing and avoiding learning opportunities. In contrast, skillful self-regulators view learning episodes as opportunities to enhance their abilities further, and, as a result, these experiences are valued in their own right.

Skillful self-regulated learners also perceive themselves to be more self-efficacious than do naive learners. Self-efficacy beliefs instill not only greater motivation to learn (Schunk, 1984) but also greater motivation to self-regulate one's learning. For example, self-efficacious learners are more likely to set high goals for themselves, to self-monitor accurately, and to self-react in a positive manner than learners who lack self-efficacy (Zimmerman, 1995). Students who are low in self-efficacy tend to be more anxious about learning (Meece, Wigfield, & Eccles, 1990) and to avoid learning opportunities when they arise (Zimmerman & Ringle, 1981). Positive self-reaction to prior learning efforts is a key cyclical source of self-efficacy for skillful self-regulators (Zimmerman, 1989).

In contrast to naive learners, skillful self-regulated learners report significantly greater intrinsic interest in learning tasks (Pintrich & DeGroot, 1990; Zimmerman & Kitsantas, 1997). Intrinsically interested students not only rate the learning task as more interesting, but they also are more likely to select it during free choice opportunities, to exert effort when learning it, and to continue learning efforts despite the presence of obstacles (Bandura, 1986). These students see interests as something that they develop themselves by engaging in the task, such as developing an interest in the Civil War or baseball by reading about them. Naive self-regulators have trouble developing an interest in a topic or skill because they attribute their lack of intrinsic interest to outside factors, such as to uninspiring teachers or inherently boring tasks. Intrinsic motivation theorists claim such learners are more dependent on external social influences and rewards to learn (Deci, 1975).

Turning to performance or volitional control processes, skillful self-regulators are able to concentrate their attention on their learning performance whereas naive self-regulators are easily distracted by diversions or competing thoughts, such as ruminations about errors. Students report that sustaining attention and motivation during learning are usually the most difficult tasks involved in self-regulating academic learning (e.g., Zimmerman & Bandura, 1994; Zimmerman & Martinez-Pons, 1986). Volition researchers (Corno, 1993; Kuhl, 1985) suggest that the attention of naive self-regulators is drawn to their emotional states or the surrounding conditions whereas knowledgeable self-regulators are better able to remain focused on their learning performance.

Skillful self-regulators are also more likely to use systematic guides or techniques, such as self-instructions or imaginal guidance, to implement their methods or strategies of learning. Self-guiding verbalizations can play a variety of performance control functions such as concentrating one's attention, following each step of a strategy sequentially, and praising oneself to sustain motivation. Vygotsky (1978) and his students emphasized the mediating role that self-instruction can play with young children in assisting to internalize the learning methods of others, such as parents or teachers. In contrast, naive self-regulators seldom verbalize (Biemiller et al., Chapter 10, this volume), and when they do, it is often negatively self-directive. Many sport psychologists specifically teach athletes to avoid making negative self-statements regarding their performance because such utterances are self-defeating, and instead encourage athletes to make self-encouraging statements (Garfield & Bennett, 1985). Skillful self-regulators also employ vivid imagery to enhance implementation of strategic methods of learning. For example, novelists will often imagine a scene in vivid detail before trying to capture it in prose (Zimmerman & Risemberg, 1997). Watching an expert perform a learning task before trying it oneself can provide useful modeling imagery when it cannot be easily self-generated (Rosenthal & Zimmerman, 1978; Zimmerman & Rocha, 1984, 1987). Naive self-regulators are unaware of the importance of imagery as a guide and instead tend to rely on the results from trial-and-error experiences to implement new methods of learning. There is some evidence (Garcia & Pintrich, 1994) that in extreme cases naive self-regulators may intentionally create obstacles to success in order to maintain favorable self-reactions, such as deliberately exerting low effort, spreading oneself too thin, or procrastinating until it is too late to succeed. Under these mitigating circumstances, poor academic performance cannot be attributed to low ability. These unfortunate learning techniques or *self-handicapping strategies* are adopted to preclude adverse self-reactions.

Perhaps the most important performance control process that distinguishes skillful from naive self-regulators is self-monitoring (Zimmerman & Paulsen, 1995). This process involves keeping track of key indicators of personal effectiveness as one performs. Skillful self-monitors know when they are performing well and when they are not, and they use this vital information to alter their performance without waiting for social assistance from others or for adverse external outcomes to eventuate. In contrast, naive self-regulators fail to monitor their performance systematically but rather rely on general awareness or fragmentary information to keep them apprised of ongoing efforts. There is growing evidence (Ghatala, Levin, Foorman, & Pressley, 1989) that many students fail to self-monitor their learning progress accurately and tend to overestimate their level of success. This leads to misplaced optimism, substantial understudying, and, ultimately, low test scores.

Among processes used during the self-reflection phase, skillful self-regulators seek out opportunities to self-evaluate their learning efforts whereas naive self-regulators are oblivious to them or actively avoid these opportunities. To skillful self-regulators, favorable self-evaluations stem directly from their goal-setting and self-monitoring efforts. They prefer to compare the results of current learning efforts with earlier efforts (which are typically favorable). In contrast, naive self-regulators, having set their goals distally and self-monitored haphazardly, find it difficult to self-evaluate on any basis other than social comparisons with others (which are often unfavorable). Because naive self-regulators have a tendency to think in terms of normative comparisons of their performance with others, they often experience ego-threatening self-reactions (Nicholls, 1984).

Skillful self-regulators attribute negatively evaluated outcomes mainly to strategy use, learning method, or insufficient practice whereas naive self-regulators tend to attribute them to ability limitations (Zimmerman & Kitsantas, 1997). Attributions of unfavorable results to limited ability lead to negative self-reactions and undermine further adaptive efforts because personal ability is viewed as fixed (Weiner, 1979). Students' attributions of favorable results to ability will lead to positive self-reactions but may still discourage future learning efforts because these are viewed as unnecessary.

Naive self-regulators are unsystematic about their methods of adaptation and often rely on intuition or guessing to make corrections because they lack more complete information or misinterpret their results. By contrast, skillful self-regulators systematically adapt their performance on the basis of previously set hierarchical goals, accurate self-monitoring, and appropriate self-evaluation. These learners also tend to attribute negative outcomes to ineffective strategies, which staves off adverse self-reactions and fosters systematic variations in approach until they finally discover an effective one. In this way, the attributions of skillful self-regulators lead to different self-reactions and types of adaptation. Skillful self-regulators also take into account contextual factors that can adversely affect the success of the strategy or learning method, such as variations in task and setting. Adaptation and optimization of one's academic learning method usually requires repeated trials for important academic skills because of their hierarchical complexity, and thus strong motivation to continue the learning cycle is essential for eventual mastery. Skillful self-regulators possess this motivation because they have optimized other self-reflection processes, namely favorable self-evaluation, appropriate attributions, and positive self-reactions.

These self-reflection phase processes influence forethought phase processes positively for skillful learners and negatively for naive learners. For skillful self-regulated learners, self-reflective thoughts strengthen or preserve forethought beliefs, such as (1) self-efficacy about eventually mastering the academic skill, (2) a learning goal orientation (Dweck, 1988), and (3) intrinsic interest in the task (Zimmerman & Kitsantas, 1997). Furthermore, self-reflection processes of attribution and adaptation directly affect goal-setting and strategic-planning processes involved in forethought. Conversely, the self-reflective processes of naive self-regulators undermine forethought by reducing their perceptions of self-efficacy, intrinsic interest, learning goal orientation, and efforts to be strategic. Thus, students' level of self-regulatory skill ultimately determines whether their learning experiences will become self-destructive or self-fulfilling. Once in place, personal cycles of self-regulation, whether skillful or naive, are resistant to change without employing interventions that address their inherently cyclical qualities. By conveying this self-regulatory learning cycle to students, teachers can help them to understand the self-fulfilling qualities of skillful self-regulated learning and avoid the descending cycle of self-reactions and self-efficacy that can result from naive learning efforts (Zimmerman, Bonner, & Kovach, 1996). Awareness of the importance of this learning cycle is the foundation for students' assuming the responsibility for their own academic achievement.

THE DEVELOPMENT OF ACADEMIC SELF-REGULATION

What are the personal, social, and environmental conditions that lead students to become skillful rather than naive self-regulators of their academic learning? Schunk and Zimmerman (1996) have suggested that self-regulation emerges from two essential sources: social and self-directed experiences. Social sources include adults (e.g., parents, coaches, and teachers) and peers (e.g., siblings, friends, and classmates). Most of these purveyors of self-regulatory knowledge and skill rely on a range of techniques, such as modeling, verbal tuition, physical guidance, corrective feedback, social structuring, supervision and monitoring, peer teaching, cooperative learning, and reciprocal teaching. Some social influences involve formal efforts to convey specific self-regulatory techniques, such as a teacher showing students a strategy for multiplying fractions in arithmetic. Other social influences are informal and subtle, such as parents' expectations that their children will assume responsibility for completing homework assignments without prodding.

Although research on self-regulation in naturalistic contexts is very limited to date, it is unlikely that this capability emerges directly from formal instruction. Rather, it appears to have its origins in a combination of parents' expectations and indirect support for their children's studying and achievement, teachers' assignment of homework that requires students to learn outside of classroom settings, and cooperative learning with peers. Recent research on out-of-school influences on academic learning (Steinberg, 1996) has shown that parents of high-achieving students have strong expectations regarding high grades and monitor their children closely. High-achieving students also seek help from teachers and peers more often and more effectively than low achievers (Newman, 1990). Clearly high-achieving students are not social isolates but rather self-regulate their reliance on others when information and support is needed (Newman, 1994).

But for academic learning techniques to become fully *self*-regulated, students also need opportunities to rehearse and develop them on their own. Academic expertise, such as math problem-solving skill, reading comprehension, and writing, requires countless hours of practice. As was noted in prior conceptual analyses (Zimmerman, 1994), students cannot develop or display their self-regulatory skill in settings where they cannot exercise personal choice or control. Although students' learning in school settings is largely constrained by teachers, there is much opportunity for self-regulation during homework and studying, which students must schedule, organize, and complete out of their instructor's presence. Homework is invaluable because it provides students with the practice necessary to routinize a study skill.

Ericsson and Charness (1994) estimate that youthful experts across a wide variety of disciplines typically spend at least 10,000 hours in what is called "deliberate practice," and these researchers concluded that practice is as crucial to the development of expertise as talent and high-quality instruction. They found that the practice sessions of prodigies are seldom an autonomous affair, but, rather, are structured, scheduled, and supported by parents or coaches. These parents or their surrogates help their offspring to set aside time for practice sessions, eliminate competing demands, and monitor and reinforce students for small improvements in skill. By planning practice as a regular part of these youngsters' daily schedule, their parents foster routinization of the skill and convey the importance of effort and extended practice to eventual mastery, or as it is inelegantly expressed in popular vernacular, "No pain, no gain!" Thus, optimal self-regulatory development appears to take root in socially supportive environments that provide extensive opportunities for self-directed practice.

The issue of how social support and self-directed practice opportunities are arranged to maximize students' self-regulatory development is not yet clear. These two sources of personal development figure prominently in virtually all theories of academic self-regulation (Zimmerman & Schunk, 1989), and experimental efforts to test various types of social training and practice processes have produced encouraging results (Schunk & Zimmerman, 1994). On the basis of these research findings, a number of educators have begun to develop instructional models to teach self-regulated learning skills to students in school settings.

INSTRUCTIONAL MODELS OF ACADEMIC SELF-REGULATION

In the chapters that follow, a variety of instructional models for developing academic self-regulation skills are described that involve teaching as well as self-directed practice components. The authors of these models often adapted existing forms of instruction that provide important opportunities for self-directed learning, such as computer-assisted instruction, tutoring, and homework exercises, to emphasize self-regulatory processes. These adaptations were guided by a variety of theories of academic self-regulation, ranging from operant to metacognitive perspectives. Despite these differences in theoretical origin and choice of instructional vehicle, these authors incorporate a core set of social and self-directed experiences such as modeling, strategy training, verbal tuition, and academic practice. Several instructional models develop self-regulatory skill in a planned sequence of stages or steps, whereas other models provide teachers with basic principles or specific tools to guide their efforts. However, all of these authors view self-regulation of academic learning as an inherently cyclical activity involving forethought, performance or volitional control, and self-reflection processes.

In Chapter 2, Graham et al. describe their self-regulated strategy development (SRSD) model, which organizes interactive learning between teachers and students into seven stages of a "metascript" for students. This model is derived from Meichenbaum's (1977) cognitive-behavior modification views; the Soviet theorists Vygotsky (1978), Luria (1982), and Sokolov's (1975) work on verbal self-regulation; Brown, Campione, and Day's (1981) views of self-control instruction; and Deshler and Schumaker's (1986) learning strategies model. During stage 1, the teacher helps students develop necessary "preskills" for understanding and executing the target strategy, such as for writing a brief essay. In stage 2, the teacher and students examine previously used writing strategies for their impact on performance in the academic content area, and in stage 3, the teacher describes the target strategy, its purpose, and how to use it. The teacher models the strategy along with appropriate instructions during stage 4, and then it is memorized during stage 5. The sixth stage involves collaborative practice of the strategy by the teacher and student, which shifts to independent practice by the student during the seventh and last stage in self-regulatory instruction. The SRSD model has been introduced as a separate instructional module in special education classes.

In Chapter 3, Pressley, El-Dinary, Wharton-McDanold, and Brown describe a transactional strategies instructional model, which grew out of experimental research on good strategy users (Pressley, Borkowski, & Schneider, 1987) and observational research on exemplary teaching at Benchmark and other schools. The transactional strategies model embodies seven features. First, strategy instruction recurs repeatedly throughout the school year and during subsequent years. A second feature is that teachers convey a limited number of powerful strategies to students through explanation and modeling, and thirdly, students are coached as they need it about using the strategies. Fourth, teachers and students are engaged in reciprocal modeling of strategies while thinking aloud (i.e., verbally mediating) as they perform. Fifth, teachers emphasize the usefulness of strategies repeatedly throughout instruction and specify the context where each strategy is most effective. The sixth feature involves using strategies as vehicles for discussing academic work such as text passages, and the seventh feature is variegated practice while thinking aloud to enhance the implementation of these strategies. The transactional strategies model of self-regulatory development has been implemented as general approach to instruction in elementary school classrooms.

Chapter 4 describes Learning to Learn, a course that grew out of previous research by Pintrich and colleagues (Garcia & Pintrich, 1994; McKeachie, Pintrich, & Lin, 1985; Pintrich & DeGroot, 1990) on learning and motivation strategies at the University of Michigan. Examples of motivational strategies that have been taught are attributional styles, self-affirmation, self-handicapping, and defensive pessimism; examples of cognitive strategies include rehearsal, elaboration, and organization of information. In addition to providing instruction about these strategies, the instructors give the Motivated Strategies for Learning Questionnaire to inform students about their current strategy use, and the teachers describe how to use this information to guide further strategy learning. A variety of instructional vehicles is used, such as a research project and an academic journal as well as textbook material, to convey the effectiveness of these methods of learning. Finally, Learning to Learn classroom instruction focuses on conveying conditional knowledge about the circumstances under which these motivational and cognitive strategies are most effective.

In Chapter 5, Lan describes a self-monitoring instructional model that focuses on the impact of this self-regulatory process during a statistics course at Texas Tech University. His self-regulatory instructional techniques were derived from metacognitive views of self-monitoring, operant views of record keeping, and social-cognitive views of self-efficacy. First, Lan provided students with specific instructional goals that were expected to be learned during the statistics course, such as distinguishing continuous and discrete variables. Students were shown how to use special protocols to record the frequency and duration of their learning activities related to each goal. These self-monitoring activities included listening to lectures, reading texts, completing assignments, participating in discussions, and receiving tutoring. On the protocol, the students were also asked to write the frequencies and time devoted to learning each goal and to rate their self-efficacy regarding attaining the goal. In addition to providing detailed feedback about their level of understanding, self-monitoring experiences were designed to enhance students' self-efficacy beliefs and motivation to continue studying until each goal concept was mastered.

In Chapter 6, Winne and Stockley describe the STUDY instructional tool for developing self-regulated learning within a prototypic computerized environment. This formulation was derived from information processing and metacognitive theories of self-regulation. The STUDY computing environment was designed to provide various types of self-regulatory support on a menu-driven basis for learning a variety of topics. A key feature of the STUDY software is the ability of the learner to access certain computerized adjuncts for self-regulation as they are needed and to eliminate them after they are no longer necessary. The computerized environment offers students opportunities to set specific goals for themselves, to use certain strategies to attain those goals, and to self-monitor their performance efforts using computer-recorded and -analyzed data. Computer-assisted forms of self-regulatory support have the advantage of providing very accurate performance information for the learner and being able to transform those data into personal learning profiles for better interpretation. STUDY thus has the potential to enhance self-reflection processes through the use of a technological tool that can greatly extend human capabilities.

In Chapter 7, Schunk describes a social-cognitive instructional model to teach self-regulatory skill through social modeling, corrective feedback, and practice using conventional homework materials. The model is derived from Bandura's (1986) social-cognitive view of human self-regulation, which emphasizes (among other variables) the role of self-efficacy beliefs as both an outcome and as a motive to continue learning. When using the social-cognitive approach to teach basic arithmetic skills such as long division, the teacher/model demonstrates and explains solution strategies, provides hands-on experience with concrete manipulatives, and provides exercises for guided and independent practice of self-regulatory activities. The students' self-efficacy beliefs about learning the skill in question are assessed before learning, and self-efficacy to execute the skill in a variety of real-world situations is assessed afterward to help determine changes in this self-belief. The social-cognitive model of self-regulatory instruction can be used by teachers to teach virtually any type of academic skill and can be easily adapted to regular curriculum materials.

In Chapter 8, Butler presents a strategic content learning (SCL) instructional model for promoting self-regulated learning by students with learning disabilities. This formulation was developed from metacognitive theories as well as from Vygotskian notions of co-construction of knowledge. SCL does not attempt to teach preplanned learning strategies to students, but instead guides learners and instructors to create unique strategies collaboratively while engaged in difficult academic tasks. Butler's SCL model relies on a number of key instructional scaffolding principles. For example, students are supported as they tackle a meaningful task, and they are engaged in a cycle of cognitive processes to self-regulate their academic task engagement (e.g., analyzing tasks, selecting, adapting or inventing strategies, monitoring and modifying approaches). Self-regulatory support is geared to the student's individual needs and is increased or reduced as required. Finally, students and instructors engage in collaborative problem solving by means of interactive dialogues. The SCL approach relies on students' active role in guiding their own learning and constructing their own self-regulatory solutions, with the instructor assisting only when needed. The SCL instructional model was developed in tutoring situations with college-level students.

In Chapter 9, Belfiore and Hornyak describe their purposeful learning model of self-regulatory training, which has been used with adolescent students who are at risk for academic failure. This formulation was developed from operant theory and emphasizes the importance of self-reinforcement in academic self-regulation. The purposeful learning approach relies heavily on self-monitoring, which involves teaching a learner to discriminate a designated or "target" behavior and then recording its frequency or duration. Self-recording often produces self-reactivity, which consists of self-initiated efforts to control the target behavior, and, in these instances, self-recording is sufficient to bring an academic learning response under self-regulatory control. In cases where additional training is needed, instructors can help a student arrange their learning environments to enhance discriminative stimuli that control the response, such as placing a card with rules for solving a class of mathematics problems on the student's desk. A second type of instructional influence involves teaching self-instructions, such as verbalizing rule-governed steps as one solves new math problems. Self-reinforcement occurs when response increases in frequency after a learner's performance meets some sort of standard, such as when a math problem is correctly solved. The purposeful learning model is an individually oriented approach to self-regulatory training, but it is possible to use it in classroom settings with the teacher serving as a self-regulatory consultant to each student on an individualized basis.

In Chapter 10, Biemiller et al. present a verbal task regulation view of self-regulatory development. This approach was derived from cognitive-behaviorist (Meichenbaum, 1977) and Vygotskian theoretical traditions, and places primary emphasis on the role of self-instruction as a potent personal force in students' self-regulation of academic activities. These authors suggest that academic tasks make extensive use of verbal operations such as definitions and explanations, and the goal of the verbal task regulation instructional approach is bring these academic skills under active personal control via self-instruction. Biemiller et al. caution that efforts to compel students to verbalize as they learn new academic tasks can be problematic because verbalization occupies cognitive capacity and may supplant capacity needed for mental storage. Instead the authors recommend matching self-regulatory speech with the academic task demands and the student's prior achievement so that the learning demands do not preclude effective self-instruction. Biemiller et al. discovered that failure of middle- and low-achieving students to verbalize during classroom learning could be overcome if students were asked to help peers learn. Thus, peer teaching can serve as an instructional vehicle to enhance this verbal form of academic self-regulation.

CONCLUSIONS

These nine exemplary instructional models are predicated on the assumption that academic self-regulation is an acquired capability composed of phase-specific processes that students apply repeatedly during learning experiences. Reflecting on one's learning should not be an afterthought for students; rather, it should be a self-fulfilling phase of a cyclical process that is preceded by systematic forethought and performance or volitional control. Although academic self-regulation and its constituent forms of self-reflection are seldom taught in most schools, they can be learned through a core set of instructional and personal practice experiences by diverse students, ranging in age from elementary school to college and differing widely in ability. In the chapters that follow, the authors of these self-regulatory instructional models describe in detail how their methods empower students to develop self-fulfilling cycles of academic learning.

ACKNOWLEDGMENTS

I would like to thank Dale H. Schunk for his helpful comments on an initial draft of this chapter.

REFERENCES

Ames, C. (1992). Achievement goals and the classroom motivational climate. In D. H. Schunk & J. L. Meece (Eds.), *Student perceptions in the classroom* (pp. 327–348). Hillsdale, NJ: Erlbaum.

Bandura, A. (1977). Self-efficacy: Toward a unifying theory of behavioral change. *Psychological Review, 84*, 191–215.

Bandura, A. (1991). Self-regulation of motivation through anticipatory and self-reactive mechanisms. In R. A. Dienstbier (Ed.), *Perspectives on motivation: Nebraska symposium on motivation* (Vol. 38, pp. 69–164). Lincoln: University of Nebraska Press.

Brown, A. L., Campione, J. C., & Day, J. D. (1981). Learning to learn: On training students to learn from tests. *Educational Researcher, 10,* 14–21.

Caplan, N., Choy, M. H., & Whitmore, J. K. (1992, February). Indochinese refugee families and academic achievement. *Scientific American,* pp. 37–42.

Carver, C., & Scheier, M. (1981). *Attention and self-regulation: A control theory approach to human behavior.* New York: Springer-Verlag.

Corno, L. (1993). The best-laid plans: Modern conceptions of volition and educational research. *Educational Researcher, 22,* 14–22.

Deci, E. L. (1975). *Intrinsic motivation.* New York: Plenum Press.

Deshler, D. D., & Schumaker, J. B. (1986). Learning strategies: An instructional alternative for low-achieving adolescents. *Exceptional Children, 52,* 583–590.

Dweck, C. S. (1988). Motivational processes affecting learning. *American Psychologist, 41,* 1040–1048.

Earley, P. C., Connolly, T., & Ekegren, C. (1989). Goals, strategy development and task performance: Some limits on the efficacy of goal-setting. *Journal of Applied Psychology, 74,* 24–33.

Ericsson, A. K., & Charness, N. (1994). Expert performance: Its structure and acquisition. *American Psychologist, 49,* 725–747.

Festinger, L. (1954). A theory of social comparison processes. *Human Relations, 7,* 117–140.

Garcia, T., & Pintrich, P. R. (1994). Regulating motivation and cognition in the classroom: The role of self-schemas and self-regulatory strategies. In D. H. Schunk & B. J. Zimmerman (Eds.), *Self-regulation of learning and performance: Issues and educational applications* (pp. 127–53). Hillsdale, NJ: Erlbaum.

Garfield, C. A. & Bennett, Z. H. (1985). *Peak performance: Mental training techniques of the world's greatest athletes.* New York: Warner Books.

Ghatala, E. S., Levin, J. R., Foorman, B. R., & Pressley, M. (1989). Improving children's regulation of their reading PREP time. *Contemporary Educational Psychology, 14,* 49–66.

Heckhausen, H. (1991). *Motivation and action* (P. K. Leppmann, Trans.). Berlin: Springer-Verlag.

Kuhl, J. (1985). Volitional mediators of cognitive behavior consistency: Self-regulatory processes and action versus state orientation. In J. Kuhl & J. Beckman (Eds.), *Action control* (pp. 101–128). New York: Springer.

Locke, E. A., & Latham, G. P. (1990). *A theory of goal setting and task performance.* Englewood Cliffs, NJ: Prentice-Hall.

Luria, A. R. (1982). *Language and cognition.* New York: Wiley.

McKeachie, W. J., Pintrich, P. R., & Lin, T. G. (1985). Teaching learning strategies. *Educational Psychologist, 20,* 153–160.

Meece, J. L., Wigfield, A., & Eccles, J. S. (1990). Predictors of math anxiety and its influence on young adolescents' course enrollment intentions and performance in mathematics. *Journal of Educational Psychology, 82,* 60–70.

Meichenbaum, D. (1977). *Cognitive-behavior modification: An integrative approach.* New York: Plenum Press.

Newman, R. S. (1990). Children's help-seeking in the classroom: The role of motivational factors and attitudes. *Journal of Educational Psychology, 82,* 71–80.

Newman, R. S. (1994). Academic help-seeking: A strategy of self-regulated learning. In D. H. Schunk & B. J. Zimmerman (Eds.), *Self-regulation of learning and performance: Issues and educational applications* (pp. 283–301). Hillsdale, NJ: Erlbaum.

Nicholls, J. (1984). Achievement motivation: Conceptions of ability, subjective experience, task choice, and performance. *Psychological Review, 91*, 328–346.

Pintrich, P. R., & DeGroot, E. (1990). Motivational and self-regulated learning components of classroom academic performance. *Journal of Educational Psychology, 82*, 33–40.

Pressley, M. (1977). Imagery and children's learning: Putting the picture in developmental perspective. *Review of Educational Research, 47*, 586–622.

Pressley, M., Borkowski, J., & Schneider, W. (1987). Cognitive strategies: Good strategy users coordinate metacognition and knowledge. *Annals of Child Development, 4*, 89–129.

Pressley, M., & Levin, J. R. (1977). Task parameters affecting the efficacy of a visual imagery learning strategy in younger and older children. *Journal of Experimental Child Psychology, 24*, 53–59.

Rosenthal, T. L., & Zimmerman, B. J. (1978). *Social learning and cognition*. New York: Academic Press.

Schunk, D. H. (1982). Verbal self-regulation as a facilitator of children's achievement and self-efficacy. *Human Learning, 1*, 265–277.

Schunk, D. H. (1984). The self-efficacy perspective on achievement behavior. *Educational Psychologist, 19*, 199–218.

Schunk, D. H., & Zimmerman, B. J. (Eds.). (1994). *Self-regulation of learning and performance: Issues and educational applications*. Hillsdale, NJ: Erlbaum.

Schunk, D. H., & Zimmerman, B. J. (1996). Modeling and self-efficacy influences on children's development of self-regulation. In K. Wentzel & J. Juvonen (Eds.), *Social motivation: Understanding children's school adjustment* (pp. 154–180). New York: Cambridge University Press.

Singer, R. N., & Cauraugh, J. H. (1985). The generalizability effect of learning strategies for categories of psychomotor skills. *Quest, 37*, 103–119.

Sokolov, A. N. (1975). *Inner speech and thought*. New York: Plenum Press.

Steinberg, L. (1996). *Beyond the classroom*. New York: Simon & Schuster.

Vygotsky, L. S. (1978). *Mind in society: The development of higher psychological processes*. Cambridge, MA: Harvard University Press.

Weiner, B. (1979). A theory of motivation for some classroom experiences. *Journal of Educational Psychology, 71*, 3–25.

Winne, P. (1995). Inherent details in self-regulated learning. *Educational Psychologist, 30*, 173–187.

Zimmerman, B. J. (1986). Development of self-regulated learning: Which are the key subprocesses? *Contemporary Educational Psychology, 11*, 307–313.

Zimmerman, B. J. (1989). A social cognitive view of self-regulated academic learning. *Journal of Educational Psychology, 81*, 329–339.

Zimmerman, B. J. (1994). Dimensions of academic self-regulation: A conceptual framework for education. In D. H. Schunk & B. J. Zimmerman (Eds.), *Self-regulation of learning and performance: Issues and educational applications* (pp. 3–21). Hillsdale, NJ: Erlbaum.

Zimmerman, B. J. (1995). Self-efficacy and educational development. In A. Bandura

(Ed.), *Self-efficacy in changing societies* (pp. 202–231). New York: Cambridge University Press.

Zimmerman, B. J., & Bandura, A. (1994). Impact of self-regulatory influences on writing course attainment. *American Educational Research Journal, 31,* 845–862.

Zimmerman, B. J., Bandura, A., & Martinez-Pons, M. (1992). Self-motivation for academic attainment: The role of self-efficacy beliefs and personal goal setting. *American Educational Research Journal, 29,* 663–676.

Zimmerman, B. J., Bonner, S., & Kovach, R. (1996). *Developing self-regulated learners: Beyond achievement to self-efficacy.* Washington, DC: American Psychological Association.

Zimmerman, B. J., & Kitsantas, A. (1997). Developmental phases in self-regulation: Shifting from process to outcome goals. *Journal of Educational Psychology, 89,* 29–36.

Zimmerman, B. J., & Martinez-Pons, M. (1986). Development of a structured interview for assessing students' use of self-regulated learning strategies. *American Educational Research Journal, 23,* 614–628.

Zimmerman, B. J., & Martinez-Pons, M. (1992). Perceptions of efficacy and strategy use in the self-regulation of learning. In D. H. Schunk & J. Meece (Eds.), *Student perceptions in the classroom: Causes and consequences* (pp. 185–207). Hillsdale, NJ: Erlbaum.

Zimmerman, B. J., & Paulsen, A. S. (1995). Self-monitoring during collegiate studying: An invaluable tool for academic self-regulation. In P. Pintrich (Ed.), *New directions in college teaching and learning: Understanding self-regulated learning* (No. 63, Fall, pp. 13–27). San Francisco: Jossey-Bass.

Zimmerman, B. J., & Ringle, J. (1981). Effects of model persistence and statements of confidence on children's self-efficacy and problem solving. *Journal of Educational Psychology, 73,* 485–493.

Zimmerman, B. J., & Risemberg, R. (1997). Becoming a self-regulated writer: A social cognitive perspective. *Contemporary Educational Psychology, 22,* 73–101.

Zimmerman, B. J., & Rocha, J. (1984). Influence of a model's verbal description of toy interactions on kindergarten children's associative learning. *Journal of Applied Developmental Psychology, 5,* 281–291.

Zimmerman, B. J., & Rocha, J. (1987). Mode and type of toy elaboration strategy training on kindergartners' retention and transfer. *Journal of Applied Developmental Psychology, 8,* 67–78.

Zimmerman, B. J., & Schunk, D. H. (Eds.). (1989). *Self-regulated learning and academic achievement: Theory, research, and practice.* New York: Springer-Verlag.

CHAPTER 2

Writing and Self-Regulation: Cases from the Self-Regulated Strategy Development Model

Steve Graham
Karen R. Harris
Gary A. Troia

In describing their writing habits, many professional authors indicate they use a variety of self-regulation strategies such as planning, revising, organizing, environmental structuring, and evaluating to help them manage their writing behavior, the composing task, and the writing environment (Graham & Harris, 1994; Plimpton, 1967; Zimmerman & Risemberg, 1997). Before writing *Setting Free the Bears* and *Cider House Rules*, for example, John Irving invested a considerable amount of time planning, gathering information, making notes, seeing, witnessing, observing, and studying (Plimpton, 1989). Susan Sontag, the author of *On Photography*, revised so much that she would often have 30 or 40 drafts of each page (Burnham, 1994). Joseph Heller, author of *Catch-22*, kept 3" × 5" index cards in his wallet so that he could write down ideas whenever or wherever they occurred to him (Plimpton, 1967).

Personal anecdotes such as these are consistent with the view that writing is a difficult and demanding task, requiring extensive self-regulation and attention control (Kellogg, 1996; McCutchen, in press). This view is acknowledged, either explicitly or implicitly, in most current models of composing (Beaugrande, 1984; Flower & Hayes, 1980; Grabowski, 1996; Hayes, 1996). It is also supported by three other lines of evidence. First, the extensive literature on expertise, including research on writing (Scardamalia & Bereiter, 1986), suggests that the acquisition of strategic knowledge plays a critical role in learners' progress from naivete to competence to expertise (Alexander, in press). Second, systematic observations of skilled writers by

Hayes and Flower (1986) are consistent with personal anecdotes from professional authors showing that they use a variety of self-regulatory strategies when writing. Third, there is a growing body of research that the writing performance of nonprofessional writers can be enhanced by explicitly teaching them self-regulated writing strategies (Graham & Harris, 1996; Harris & Graham, 1996; Zimmerman & Risemberg, 1997).

This is not to say that writing always requires a high degree of self-regulation or effort. Writing about a personal experience, for instance, may make fewer demands on cognitive processes, diminishing the need to self-regulate, as content is readily available and organized in memory (Graham & Harris, 1997b; Scardamalia & Bereiter, 1986). Similarly, many writing tasks that occur as a part of everyday life, such as jotting down a reminder to do something, can usually be done with little effort and without having to resort to high-level, goal-directed behavior. This does not diminish the importance of self-regulation in writing, however, as growth in writing is advanced by the development and use of these processes (Graham & Harris, 1994; Zimmerman & Riesemberg, 1997). Furthermore, employing self-regulation procedures such as planning and revising can transform and greatly enhance writing not only about unfamiliar topics (see MacArthur, Schwartz, Graham, Molloy, & Harris, 1996), but more familiar ones as well. Writing an autobiography, for example, by simply drawing information from memory, either sequentially or randomly, is likely to result in a boring and uninspiring manuscript. Planning in advance what points or lessons are to be highlighted, what experiences are to be shared, and how it will all be organized is much more likely to result in a paper worthy of reading.

KNOWLEDGE TELLING

In a recent *Peanuts* cartoon, Snoopy is sitting on top of his dog house, typewriter at paw. He types a sentence: The light mist turned to rain. He types the next sentence: The rain turned to snow. Before typing a third sentence, he rips the paper out of the typewriter and throws it away, muttering that the story turned boring.

His strategy for writing reminds us of the approach many children, including some college students, use when composing. They convert writing tasks into tasks of telling what one knows—that is, writing-as-remembering or writing-by-pattern (Scardamalia & Bereiter, 1986). Any information that is somewhat appropriate is retrieved from memory and written down, with each new phrase or sentence stimulating the generation of the next idea. Little attention is directed at the needs of the audience, the constraints imposed by the topic, the organization of the text, or the development of rhetorical goals. The role of planning, revising, and other self-regulation processes is minimized; this retrieve-and-write process typically functions like an automated and encapsulated program, operating largely without metacognitive control (McCutchen, 1988). This is not to suggest that this approach to writing is necessarily thoughtless; rather, it is mostly forward moving, with little recursive interplay between composing processes (Scardamalia & Bereiter, 1986).

This approach to writing appears to be especially prominent among students who find writing and learning challenging. In a study by Graham (1990), for instance, children with learning disabilities typically converted the writing task into a question-and-answer task, quickly telling whatever came to mind and then abruptly ending their response. They spent approximately 6 minutes writing, beginning their essays with a simple "yes" or "no" in response to the assigned topic, followed by the generation of a couple of reasons and elaborations.

An important goal in writing instruction for students who find writing and learning challenging, therefore, is to help them incorporate additional self-regulatory processes into their writing, so that they become more goal oriented, resourceful, and reflective. One means for accomplishing this goal is to tackle the problem head-on by explicitly teaching them how to use these procedures. Much of our research (Graham & Harris, 1993, 1996; Harris & Graham, 1996) has examined the effectiveness of this method, that is, teaching children with writing and learning problems the same kinds of strategies and processes that more skilled writers use when they compose.

In this chapter, we examine a theoretically and empirically based instructional approach for developing writing and self-regulation strategies among students. We refer to this approach as self-regulated strategy development (SRSD). With SRSD, children are collaboratively and explicitly taught how to use task-specific strategies for composing, such as planning and revising. These strategies are taught in combination with procedures for regulating the use of these strategies, the writing process, and behaviors (such as negative self-talk or impulsivity) that may impede performance.

Most of the students who have been taught writing strategies using SRSD are children with learning disabilities in fourth through eighth grade. The typical child scores in the normal range on a test of intelligence, experiences difficulty with writing on standardized tests and in the classroom, and performs 2 or more years below grade level in reading or math, or both. SRSD has also been used to teach writing strategies to normally achieving students (Danoff, Harris, & Graham, 1993) and students with learning disabilities who score above and below the normal range on a test of intelligence (De La Paz & Graham, 1997a). The two case studies presented in this chapter focus on the use of SRSD with children with learning disabilities.

SELF-REGULATED STRATEGY DEVELOPMENT

SRSD is designed to help students master the higher-level cognitive processes involved in composing; develop autonomous, reflective, self-regulated use of effective writing strategies; increase knowledge about the characteristics of good writing; and form positive attitudes about writing and their capabilities as writers (Harris & Graham, 1996).

These goals are achieved through various forms of support integrated throughout the model. One form of support is inherent in the writing strategies students are taught—a strategy provides structure that helps one organize and sequence behavior. A second form of support involves helping children acquire the self-regulation skills needed to use the target writing strategy successfully, manage the writing process, and replace unproductive behaviors with constructive ones. This includes teaching students to use self-regulatory procedures such as self-assessment, goal setting, and self-instruction.

Additional support is provided through the methods used to teach the writing strategy and accompanying self-regulation procedures. As students initially learn to use these processes, the teacher provides considerable assistance by modeling, explaining, reexplaining, and assisting when necessary. This scaffolding is gradually withdrawn, as students become more able to use these processes independently. Cognitive resources are further strengthened by increasing students' knowledge about themselves, writing, and the writing process. Model compositions are used to familiarize students with the characteristics of good writing. Self-monitoring, goal setting, and teacher feedback help students acquire knowledge of their writing capabilities and how to regulate the composing process.

Stages and Characteristics of Instruction

Six instructional stages provide the framework for SRSD (Harris & Graham, 1992, 1996). The stages are presented in Table 2.1 and include *Develop Background Knowledge* (develop knowledge and skills needed to use writing strategies and self-regulation procedures), *Discuss It* (discuss the purpose and form of writing strategies and self-regulation procedures), *Model It* (model how to use writing strategies and self-regulation procedures), *Memorize It* (memorize procedural steps for using writing strategies and self-regulation procedures), *Support It* (provide temporary and adjusted assistance in applying writing strategies and self-regulation procedures), and *Independent Performance* (encourage independent use of writing strategies and self-regulation procedures). These stages represent a "metascript," providing a general guideline that can be reordered, combined, or modified to meet student and

TABLE 2.1. Instructional Stages of the SRSD Model

Develop Background Knowledge: The first stage of instruction involves helping students develop the preskills—including knowledge of the criteria for good writing—needed to understand, acquire, and execute the writing strategy and accompanying self-regulation procedures.

Discuss It: During the second stage, teacher and students examine and discuss current writing performance and strategies used to accomplish specific assignments. The writing strategy targeted for instruction is then introduced, and its purpose and benefits as well as how and when to use it are examined. Students are asked to make a commitment to learn the strategy and act as collaborative partners in this endeavor. Any negative or ineffective self-statements or beliefs students currently use may also be addressed at this point.

Model It: In the third stage, the teacher models how to use the writing strategy using appropriate self-instructions, including problem definition, planning, strategy use, self-evaluation, coping and error correction, and self-reinforcement statements. After analyzing the teacher's performance, teacher and students may collaborate on how to change the writing strategy to make it more effective. Students then develop and record personal self-statements they plan to use during writing.

Memorize It: During stage 4, the steps of the writing strategy, any mnemonic for remembering it, and personalized self-statements are memorized. Students are encouraged to paraphrase as long as the original meaning is maintained. This stage is primarily included for children who have severe learning and memory problems and is not needed by all students.

Support It: In stage 5, students and teachers use the strategy and self-instructions collaboratively to complete specific writing assignments. Self-regulation procedures, including goal setting and self-assessment, may be introduced at this time.

Independent Performance: During the final stage, students use the strategy independently. If students are still using self-regulatory procedures such as goal setting or self-assessment, they may decide to start fading them out. Students are also encouraged (if they are not already doing so) to say their self-statements covertly "in their heads."

---

teacher needs. Furthermore, some stages may not be needed by all students. For instance, some students may have already mastered the background knowledge (stage 1) needed to use the writing strategy and self-regulation processes targeted for instruction.

Characteristics of SRSD instruction, presented in Table 2.2, include interactive learning between teacher and students, individualization, criterion-based instruction, and ongoing strategy development. Furthermore, procedures for promoting maintenance and generalization, including the use of self-reflection, are integrated throughout the SRSD model. These procedures include identifying opportunities to use the writing strategy and self-regulation procedures, analyses of how these processes might need to be

TABLE 2.2. Characteristics of SRSD

Interactive learning: Interactive learning between teacher and students is emphasized in the SRSD model. Students are viewed as collaborators who work with their teacher and each other to determine the goals of instruction, complete the task, and implement, evaluate, and modify the strategy and strategy-acquisition procedures.

Individualization: Instruction is individualized so that the processes and skills targeted for instruction are designed to upgrade each child's current approach to writing. Teachers further individualize by providing personally tailored feedback and support, and may modify the basic stages of the model (adding, deleting, or rearranging) depending on the capabilities and needs of their students.

Criterion-based instruction: Instruction is criterion rather than time based. Students move through the instructional stages at their own pace and do not proceed to later stages until they have met initial criteria for doing so. Instruction is also not terminated until students have mastered the writing strategy, using it efficiently and effectively.

Developmental process: SRSD is meant to be an ongoing process in which new strategies are introduced and previously taught strategies are upgraded. In teaching a peer-revising strategy, for example, students may initially use only two criteria for evaluating each others' writing—for example, identifying places in text that are unclear and places where more detail is needed (see MacArthur, Schwartz, & Graham, 1991). The strategy may be upgraded later to include feedback on text structure and order (see Stoddard & MacArthur, 1993).

modified with other tasks and in new settings, and evaluation of the success of these processes during instruction and subsequent application. Other teachers might also be asked to prompt the student to use the writing strategy and self-regulation procedures in their classrooms.

To date, 20 studies using SRSD to teach writing strategies have been conducted; these include studies completed by ourselves (see Graham, Harris, MacArthur, & Schwartz, 1991; Harris & Graham, 1996) and replications by others (Collins, 1992; De La Paz, 1997; Tanhouser, 1994). The model has been used to teach a variety of planning and revising strategies including brainstorming (Harris & Graham, 1985), self-monitoring of productivity (Harris, Graham, Reid, McElroy, & Hamby, 1994), reading for information and semantic webbing (MacArthur et al., 1996), generating and organizing writing content using text structure (Graham & Harris, 1989a, 1989b; Sawyer, Graham, & Harris, 1992), goal setting (Graham, MacArthur, & Schwartz, 1995; Graham, MacArthur, Schwartz, & Voth, 1992) revising using peer feedback (MacArthur, Schwartz, & Graham, 1991), and revising for both mechanics and substance (Graham & MacArthur, 1988).

SRSD has led to changes and improvement in four aspects of students' performance: quality of writing, knowledge of writing, approach to writing, and self-efficacy (cf. Graham et al., 1991; Harris & Graham, 1996). Evaluations of SRSD by teachers and students have also been positive. As one teacher noted, she could "see light bulbs going on" as students learned to use writing strategies. The applicability of SRSD to teaching strategies for writing is illustrated next with two different planning strategies.

Case Study 1

Martin Anderson, a contemporary essayist, indicated that "an outline or some sharply defined conceptual map always precedes any of my serious writing" (Anderson, 1995, p. 10). In several studies (Graham & Harris, 1989b; Sexton, Harris, & Graham, in press), we examined whether teaching a somewhat similar strategy to students who find writing and learning challenging would help them write better opinion essays. The strategy involved a series of steps designed to help writers identify what they plan to accomplish, generate an initial content outline, and continue to expand and modify the outline while writing.

Setting and Participants

The first case study took place in an elementary school located just outside of the "Beltway" surrounding Washington, DC. The population of the school was diverse—62% of the children in the school were African American, 23% were Caucasian, 11% were Asian American, and 3% were Hispanic. Approximately 40% of these students received free or reduced-fee lunches.

The writing strategy was taught to six students identified as learning disabled by the school district. These fifth- and sixth-grade students were in general education classes all day, as the school employed an inclusion model for teaching students with special needs. Their multigrade writing class was team taught by a general and special education teacher. A process approach to writing instruction, Writers' Workshop, was used in the classroom (Atwell, 1987). Students continued to participate in Writers' Workshop while receiving instruction in the composition strategy in a small group.

These students were selected to receive SRSD instruction based on teachers' judgment that each had difficulty with writing, displayed a low level of motivation, and had maladaptive beliefs about the causes of writing success and failure. The teachers also wanted them to improve their essay-writing skills, as they perceived these to be important not only for upper elementary school, but for the coming middle and high school years as well.

Four of the six students were male, and five were African American (one was Caucasian). Their IQ scores on the Wechsler Intelligence Scale for Children—Revised ranged from 81 to 117. The three fifth-grade students and one of the sixth-grade students were reading at a third-grade level, while the other two sixth-grade students were reading at a fourth-grade level. On a standardized measure of writing, the Test of Written Language—2 (Hammill & Larsen, 1988), five of the six students scored below the mean for their age level. Although one student scored above the mean, teachers indicated that the test did not provide an accurate representation of her writing, particularly her essay writing. The essays she typically produced failed to include important information and often contained a considerable amount of irrelevant material. Despite the emphasis on planning in their writing class, none of the six students showed any evidence of advance planning when writing.

Instruction

The teacher began instruction by leading a discussion on what the students already knew about opinion essays, including the elements that are commonly found in such an essay (Develop Background Knowledge). This knowledge was considered to be an essential prerequisite to using the target writing strategy, as these elements served as prompts for generating information to include in the outline. The teacher and students discussed three types of common essay elements: premise, supporting reasons, and conclusion. Next, they identified examples of these elements in essays they were reading in class and essays written by other children. They then spent some time generating ideas for essay parts, using different topics.

Following this initial lesson, an individual conference was held with each student (Discuss It). The teacher and student talked about strategies or self-statements that the student currently used when writing. At this point, the teacher indicated that she would like to teach the student a strategy for writing essays. They talked about the goals for learning the strategy (to write better essays) and how including and expanding essay parts could improve writing. The teacher also introduced the concept of progress monitoring, indicating that self-assessment would allow the student to monitor the completeness of essays and the effects of using the strategy. Together, they counted and graphed the number of elements included in previously written essays. The teacher explained how the graph would continue to be used for self-monitoring as the child learned the writing strategy. Before completing the conference, the teacher emphasized the student's role as a collaborator, and they conjointly developed a written goal to learn the strategy.

After the individual conferences, teacher and students resumed their discussion of the writing strategy in a small group. Each student had a chart listing the steps of the strategy (see Table 2.3). The first step in the strategy involves identifying the intended audience and reasons for writing the paper. During the second step, students develop an outline for their essay. This includes establishing the premise for the paper, generating ideas to support

TABLE 2.3. Steps in the Writing Strategy

- **Think,** who will read this, and why am I writing it?
- **Plan** what to say using TREE.
  note **T**opic sentence
  note **R**easons
  then **E**xamine reasons
  note **E**nding
- **Write** and **say more.**

the premise, evaluating readers' reaction to each idea (and eliminating unsound ideas), noting a conclusion for the paper, and determining how the argument will be structured or sequenced. The third step is a reminder to continue revising and improving the outline while writing.

The teacher asked the students what they thought the reason for each step might be. The group then discussed how and when to use the strategy (e.g., whenever you are asked to give your opinion or tell what you believe). The teacher described the procedures for learning the strategy, stressing the importance of effort, because a strategy cannot work if it has not been mastered (this was meant to serve both attributional and goal-setting functions).

During a third lesson, the teacher modeled how to use the writing strategy, while thinking out loud (Model It). The students participated by helping her as she planned and as she wrote the first draft. Together they accepted and rejected possible ideas to support the teacher's premise and continued to modify the plan while writing the paper. Once a first draft was written, the teacher and students reread the paper and made revisions.

As she modeled the strategy, the teacher used a variety of self-instructions to help her manage the strategy, the writing process, and her behavior. These included problem definition (e.g., "What do I need to do?"), planning (e.g., "OK, first I need to. . . . "), self-evaluation (e.g., "Did I say what I really believe?"), and self-reinforcement statements (e.g., "Great, this is a good reason."). She attributed her success in writing the essay to effort and use of the strategy. (As noted earlier, these children had maladaptive beliefs about causes of writing success and failure.) Examples of attributional self-statements included the following: "If I work hard and follow the steps of the strategy, I'll write a good essay," and "I want to write a good essay, so I will try hard to use the strategy and include good essay parts."

After modeling how to use the writing strategy, the teacher and students discussed the importance of what we say to ourselves while we work (students volunteered examples of personal positive, and sometimes negative, self-statements they used when writing). They also identified the types of things the teacher said that helped her work better, stressing statements emphasizing the role of effort and strategy use. After discussing how these self-statements were helpful, each student generated and recorded on a small chart self-statements they would use to (1) manage the strategy and the writing process (e.g., "Slow down and take my time.") and (2) attribute success to effort and use of the strategy (e.g., "Work hard— Write better.").

Students worked on memorizing the strategy, the mnemonic TREE (see Table 2.3), and several self-statements they planned to use during a fourth lesson (Memorize It). Practice memorizing this information was done with a partner—students typically practiced by quizzing each other. These items were memorized easily by most students, but some needed more extended practice.

In subsequent lessons, students received assistance from the teacher as they applied the writing strategy and self-regulation procedures while writing essays (Support It). The goal during this stage of instruction was to support children's efforts as they were learning to use these procedures. The teacher adjusted and modified the level of support provided, reducing assistance as each child became increasingly adept at using these procedures.

At first, students received considerable support in developing a writing outline. Based on her previous experience with the students, the teacher thought that this part of the strategy would be challenging for them. Support initially involved the teacher acting as the lead collaborator during planning. As they planned together, the teacher intentionally committed a few errors, like forgetting a strategy step. This led to discussions about the impacts of and reasons for such errors. The teacher then modeled correcting the miscue, combining the correction with a positive attributional statement such as "I need to try to follow all of the strategy steps, so I can write a good essay." If students subsequently made mistakes in using the strategy, the possible consequences of the miscue were again examined and students were encouraged to redo the step while using a positive attributional statement.

The teacher's role as a planning collaborator was quickly replaced with less intrusive forms of assistance and scaffolding, including reminders to carry out a step or use self-statements, prompts to devote more attention to a specific process (e.g., generate more possible supporting reasons), and feedback on the use of the strategy and accompanying self-regulation procedures. In some instances, it was necessary for the teacher and a student to revisit the rationale underlying an individual step (e.g., the need to evaluate readers' reactions to each idea). Assistance also included helping students determine which self-statements were useful to them. Reference to the strategy chart or self-statement lists as a reminder was faded, and the teacher encouraged students to use their self-statements covertly.

As students worked on their essays, the teacher encouraged them to use goal setting and self-assessment (continuing the use of the graphs) in conjunction with the writing strategy and self-statements. Prior to planning an essay, students set a goal to include all of the parts in their papers. Once an essay was completed, the student reviewed the paper, determining if any parts were missing as well as counting and graphing the number of essay elements included. Students then shared their essays with each other, providing feedback on the strengths and weaknesses of each other's arguments.

After writing three or four essays, all students were able to use the writing strategy and self-regulation procedures without teacher support. At this point, students planned and wrote essays independently (Independent Performance). The teacher provided positive and constructive feedback as needed, and students continued to share their essays with each other. Some students still relied on their strategy charts and lists of self-statements as prompts or reminders, but were encouraged to work without them. Students were asked to continue using goal setting and graphing on at least two more essays. After that, they were told that use of these procedures was up to them.

In a group conference, students discussed how what they were learning could be used in other classes. Several students indicated that they now told themselves "to try harder" when writing or asked themselves if their paper "was good enough." Opportunities for using the writing strategy and self-regulation procedures in the future were identified by the students. Each student also evaluated the strategy and the instructional process. They all indicated that they enjoyed learning the strategy and that other students would benefit from learning it as well (e.g., "All schools should learn this."). When asked if they would change anything about instruction, the only recommendation was to give homework assignments to use the strategy.

A formal evaluation, using single subject methodology, indicated that instruction changed both how and what students wrote (Sexton et al., in press). Prior to SRSD instruction, when asked to write an essay they immediately started to write, generating essays of poor quality, which contained only two or three ideas. They typically started their essays by stating their position, following with a single supporting reason, and ending abruptly without a concluding statement. Following instruction, most papers were planned in advance, and the quality of the resulting essays improved (see Table 2.4). Papers became longer, the number of reasons supporting the premise increased, text was coherently ordered, and all of the basic elements of a good essay were present. They were generally more confident about their ability to write a good essay. Five of the students also became more positive about the role of effort, strategy use, or both in writing. Similar results were obtained in previous evaluations by Graham and Harris (1989b) and Tanhouser (1994).

TABLE 2.4. Example of Performance before and after SRSD Instruction for a Student in Case Study 1

Before instruction
Well yes and no. It depends if you have the kind of house that is right and you think you can take care of it. [In response to: Should children be allowed choose their own pets?]

After instruction
Yes, I think it is a good idea for children to learn a second language. When they go to other countries, they will know what the people are saying. And if they move there and have to go to school they will understand the teacher and what she is saying. So that is why it is best that children learn a second language now, so when their Mom wants to travel to different countries, they will be excited and they will think it is fun because where ever they go or move to, they will know the language. So that is why I think children should learn a second language. [In response to: Should children be required to learn a second language?]

Case Study 2

The second case also involved teaching students to develop an outline for their paper in advance of writing. The methods used to teach the writing strategy differed, however, in two important ways. Instead of first describing the strategy and asking students to reflect on the rationale and value of each step, the instructor modeled how to do several tasks (using goal setting, brainstorming, and organizing), and students derived or abstracted the essential features, rationale, and value of the processes used by the instructor. A mnemonic (STOP & LIST) was then introduced as a way to help students remember to carry out these processes not only when writing, but with other tasks involving planning as well. A second difference involved the use of "homework" to promote maintenance and generalization. For homework, students were asked to identify opportunities to apply the strategy to other tasks at home or school, and to specify how it would be helpful and what modifications were needed. After completing the homework assignment, students reflected on the consequence and relevance of their strategy use.

Participants

The writing strategy was taught individually to three fifth-grade students with learning disabilities by the third author of this chapter (Troia, Graham, & Harris, 1997). On the Test of Written Language—2 (Hammill & Larsen, 1988), each child scored 1 standard deviation or more below the mean, and the children's teachers indicated that writing problems were evident in the classroom as well.

Two of the students were male, and one was African American (the other two were Caucasian). Their IQ scores on the Wechsler Intelligence Scale for Children—III ranged from 98 to 104. Each student was reading 2 standard deviations below grade level. Each child's teacher used the process approach to writing instruction. Although some planning instruction did occur during the writing period, none of the students planned in advance when writing.

Instruction

Instruction began by reviewing and expanding what each child knew about opinion essays and stories (Develop Background Knowledge). The instructor believed that the impact of the strategy would be greater if each child was knowledgeable about the attributes of a good essay and story. The instructional activities for developing this knowledge were similar to those used in the first case and are not reiterated here.

Following this initial session, each student participated in three lessons where the instructor modeled how to do specific tasks using goal setting, brainstorming, and sequencing (the primary processes included in the strategy); the student abstracted and evaluated the essential processes applied; and the strategy was introduced as a reminder for employing these processes with writing and other tasks (Model It and Discuss It).[2]

In the first lesson, the instructor modeled, while thinking out loud, the use of these processes to read a chapter and write a story. In reading the chapter, the instructor first set a goal ("find out how plants fit into the food chain"), brainstormed or listed what he already knew, and sequenced his ideas by topics. As he read, he modified his outline by adding, deleting, changing, and rearranging both ideas and categories. Similarly, when writing a story, the instructor set a goal ("to write a good story to share with my creative writing class"), brainstormed ideas to include in the story, and sequenced the ideas he planned to use. While writing, he modified his outline, adding, changing, deleting, and rearranging ideas. While modeling both tasks, he provided a rationale for each thing he did and verbally reinforced himself on a job well done. When the instructor was generating and organizing ideas or later modifying the plan, the student was encouraged to assist him.

After the two tasks were modeled, the student was asked to take some time and think about what the instructor did. To help the child abstract the essential features, rationale, and value of the three processes used to accomplish the tasks, the instructor guided the student's thinking by asking a series of questions. Questions initially focused on what the instructor did that was similar when doing both tasks and what was different. All of the students identified goal setting, brainstorming, and sequencing as similar. The instructor then focused the questions more tightly, by asking the student to think about why he used each of these processes and how they helped him. Questioning then shifted to how the instructor's approach to writing a story differed from the child's own approach. The student was also asked to evaluate the possible use of each of the processes in his or her own writing.

Identical procedures were used in the next two lessons where the instructor modeled preparing a speech, planning a trip, and writing a story. The only difference was that the student was asked to think about what the instructor did that was similar and different when modeling in each lesson. This series of lessons ended with the instructor introducing a mnemonic to help the child remember to set goals, brainstorm, and sequence when writing and doing other tasks involving planning. A small chart was used to introduce the mnemonic STOP & LIST: Stop Think Of Purpose & List Ideas Sequence Them.

On the following day, discussion of STOP & LIST resumed with the student considering if and how goal setting, brainstorming, and sequencing might be helpful. A list was generated of when, where, and why the student used each of the three processes previously.At this point, the instructor indicated that he was inviting the child to learn how to use STOP & LIST and described the procedures for learning it. He indicated that the purpose for learning the strategy was to "write better stories and use it with other tasks." The student then generated what he or she would do to facilitate the learning process (e.g., "not give up"; "work hard").

During this lesson, the student briefly practiced memorizing the mnemonic and sentence it represented (Memorize It). This continued in succeeding lessons until the student could repeat it both easily and quickly.

In the next stage of instruction, students received assistance from the instructor in applying STOP & LIST when writing stories (Support It). The instructor collaboratively planned a story with each student and made sure the strategy and mnemonic were used appropriately. The chart with the mnemonic was used to remind students to set goals, brainstorm, and sequence. On subsequent stories, the instructor modified the amount of input and support provided to meet each child's needs. Assistance included prompting, providing guidance and feedback, and reexplanations. This scaffolding, including the use of the mnemonic chart, was faded as quickly as possible for each child.

After writing a story, students were asked to identify why they were successful, unsuccessful, or both; to assess the role of goal setting, brainstorming, and sequencing in writing the story; and to consider what else they could have done to write an even better story. Each student also identified an opportunity to apply STOP & LIST at home or school, indicating how it would be helpful and what modifications were needed to make it work. Examples of homework included planning a report, a trip, and supplies needed for school. At the start of the next lesson, they provided evidence (their outline or planning sheet) that the homework assignment had been successfully completed and assessed the role and value of the strategy in carrying out the task. Each child also described any other times goal setting, brainstorming, or sequencing had been used since the prior lesson. Examples generated by the children centered on the completion of writing assignments.

After writing two stories, each student was able to use STOP & LIST without instructor support. At this point, students planned and wrote stories independently (Independent Performance). The teacher provided positive and constructive feedback as needed. Students continued to do homework as well as reflect on the consequence and relevance of using the strategy.

Instruction was discontinued when a child could use the strategy independently to write a story and had completed two homework assignments successfully in a row. Once this goal was achieved, the student was asked to reconsider how the processes of goal setting, brainstorming, and sequencing were helpful when writing stories and completing homework assignments. They further discussed how STOP & LIST had to be modified for these tasks and identified opportunities for applying the strategy in the future (e.g., writing assignments, homework, shopping, and organizing their room).

A formal evaluation, using single subject methodology (Tawney & Gast, 1984) indicated that instruction changed both what and how students wrote (Troia et al., 1997). Prior to the start of SRSD instruction, the participating students did no planning in advance of writing their stories. Following instruction, however, they consistently used STOP & LIST to plan stories, and their papers became longer and more complete (see Table 2.5). These effects generalized to a second genre, the writing of opinion essays, and were maintained on writing probes administered almost a month after instruction was terminated. Students were also positive about the strategy and instructional processes, indicating it would help "me get better grades in school," "think of ideas I might not have," and "write good stories."

SELF-REFLECTIVE PRACTICES

Knowing how to apply a strategy does not guarantee that it will be used when the opportunity arises. As Salomon and Globerson (1987) noted, people frequently do not make good use of what they have mastered, failing to apply available strategies to new situations. They further argued that the gap between what people can do and what they actually do under normal conditions exists, in part, because people are often not very mindful, operating on the basis of a least-effort principle.

TABLE 2.5. Example of Performance before and after SRSD Instruction for a Student in Case Study 2

Before instruction
One day in July a man went on a balloon ride. And he went in a canyon and [tried] to go through it but it stop ahead. The man tried to go up but it was run out of time, so he put it down instead. Then he climbed the side and went home. The end.

After instruction
One morning in Lusby, Maryland, Christina, a babysitter, was watching Chris. Chris was only nine years old. Chris was a scientist. Christina ate something in his laboratory. Christina was getting fat. Steam came from her ears and from her mouth too. Christina was turning colors. Chris gave her a cure. It didn't work. Chris started to make a new cure, but it was too late. Christina broke through the wall and bounced down the street. Christina bounced off a small cliff and she bounced back up to a monster car rally. She crushed all of the cars. Chris ran after her and threw her the pill. She swallowed it. She went back to normal. She was glad to be 89 pounds and not 698,319 pounds. They went back home. Chris' mom, Sue, came home but did not use the door. She came through a hole in the wall. Christina said it was one of Chris' experiments. The end.

In the absence of a mindful approach, individuals are less likely to recognize when to deploy available strategies. Transfer involves recognizing when to apply the familiar to the less familiar. When more mindless processes are activated, transfer rests primarily on cues of similarity (Salomon & Globerson, 1987). There are at least two drawbacks to relying on coincidental appearance to recognize when to use available strategies. First, only those instances that have clear and salient similarity to already practiced ones are likely to be identified. Consequently, transfer is unlikely to travel very far. Second, even when surface features are similar, individuals may fail to recognize an opportunity, particularly when there is already an existing routine for carrying out the task. It requires mindful control to overcome entrenched habits, even when those habits are in need of improvement.

Transfer may also not occur because an individual does not value, or comes to devalue, available strategies. When a strategy is learned and carried out in a mindless fashion, opportunities to establish connections between strategically mediated success and more typical performance are diminished. As a result, the user may not realize that the strategy is worth owning or may underestimate its potency.

Even when a strategy is initially held in high regard, mindless involvement in its application can mar perceptions of value, leading to a decline or even a cessation in its use. Available strategies can be erroneously applied, for example, when surface features are used to identify transfer opportunities, as they do not always ensure a good match (Salomon & Globerson, 1987).

One child we observed spontaneously used the strategy in Case Study 1, TREE, to develop an outline for a story (Graham & Harris, 1989b). Because TREE was developed to generate content for an opinion essay, this application resulted in a poorly designed story. If the student had not applied the strategy in a mindless fashion, she might have been able to overcome the poor match. One of her classmates did just that. The basic principle underlying TREE (use the elements of the genre to prompt ideas for an outline) was abstracted, and the strategy was modified so that it was appropriate to story writing.

Clearly, how much thinking and self-reflection occurs when learning and using strategies influences the extent and depth of transfer (Harris & Graham, 1992; Wong, 1994). In the SRSD model, self-reflection and mindfulness is instigated during instruction because many of the children we work with, especially those experiencing difficulty with writing and learning, are not particularly mindful when left to their own devices (Harris, 1982). The two case studies presented here illustrate the range of self-reflective practices students may engage in when using SRSD. These are summarized in Table 2.6.

Including self-reflection and mindfulness as part of instruction does not ensure strategy transfer. It is a necessary, but not sufficient, condition. Even when all of the elements above are included, some children may still fail to generalize.

TABLE 2.6. Self-Reflective Practices Typically Used in SRSD Instruction

- Abstract the elements of performance that are candidates for learning and transfer.
- Deduce the principles underlying each element or strategy.
- Determine how the strategies are applicable to solving tasks during instruction and transfer.
- Monitor use of the strategies.
- Assess consequences of using the strategies during instruction and transfer.
- Compare prior strategic behavior and outcomes with performance and behavior when using inculcated strategies.
- Consider why difficulties were experienced prior to instruction, during instruction, and at transfer.
- Uncover what else could be done to improve task performance.
- Think about how strategies should be applied and modified during instruction and transfer.
- Search memory to identify prior applications of the strategies.
- Discover opportunities to apply the strategies in the near and far future.
- Identify behaviors that would facilitate strategy learning.
- Evaluate the instructional process.

CONCLUSIONS

In this chapter, we have focused on a specific approach for helping children incorporate additional self-regulatory processes, such as planning and revising, into their writing. This involves explicitly teaching them how to use such strategies. Although we believe that this is a crucial ingredient in an effective writing program (for students with and without writing problems), such instruction needs to occur in an environment in which students' skills in self-regulation can prosper and grow (such as a process-writing classroom). If children do not value writing or what they write, for instance, they may fail to utilize the resources at their disposal, including the specific self-regulation procedures taught in the classroom. Likewise, the development of self-regulation in writing may be inhibited if children are provided few opportunities for managing their own behavior (Zimmerman, 1989). If we expect them to become planful, reflective, and resourceful writers, they need to have plenty of opportunities to apply the self-regulation skills they are learning (as well the ones they develop on their own). This includes letting them exert strategic control over personal, behavioral, and environmental influences in the classroom.

It is also important to realize that there is no one correct approach to writing. Professional writers differ greatly in how they carry out the writing process (see Plimpton, 1967) and may vary their approach depending upon the subject or the task. When working on *Barbary Shore,* for example, Norman Mailer indicated that he did little planning in advance and "had no idea where it was going to move from day to day" (Kazin, 1967, p. 258). On *The Naked and the Dead,* in contrast, he planned extensively, generating a file full of notes, a long dossier on each character, and a chart showing which characters had not interacted with other characters. Children may fail to develop this same level of flexibility if they operate in an environment where experimentation and risk taking are discouraged. They are more likely to explore different approaches to writing, however, if the classroom environment is supportive, pleasant, and nonthreatening (Corno, 1992; Graham & Harris, 1988).

Finally, fostering the development of self-regulation is just one aspect of a good writing program for children. Although self-regulation is a key ingredient in skilled writing, it is not the only one (Graham, Berninger, Abbott, Abbott, & Whitaker, 1997). This was illustrated in a recent study by Graham (1997). Providing children with procedural support in carrying out the self-regulation processes that underlie revising resulted in several important improvements, including an increase in the number of changes rated as bettering text. A variety of problems still remained, however. Students were generally indifferent to the possible concerns of their audience, overemphasized form, and struggled with the separate elements of revising, including translating intended changes into acceptable written English. Efforts to improve revising (and other aspects of writing), therefore, need to focus on more than just self-regulation. It is important that we maintain a reasonable balance between process, meaning, and form (Harris & Graham, 1994). Writing programs that focus on only one or two of these factors run the risk of shortchanging young writers, as progression from naivete to competence to expertise is dependent on changes that occur in each of these areas (Alexander, in press; Graham & Harris, 1997a).

NOTES

1. In the state of Maryland a learning disability is established by demonstrating a discrepancy between a child's expected level of performance (established via an individually administered intelligence test) and observed level of performance (established via individually administered achievement tests).
2. The stages of instruction were reordered by the instructor.

REFERENCES

Alexander, P. (in press). Stages and phases of domain learning: The dynamics of subject-matter knowledge, strategy knowledge, and motivation. In C. Weinstein & B. McCoombs (Eds.), Strategic learning: Skill, will, and self-regulation. Hillsdale, NJ: Erlbaum.

Anderson, M. (1995). The writing life: The language of left and right. Book World: Washington Post, pp. 1, 10.

Atwell, N. (1987). In the middle: Reading, writing, and learning from adolescents. Portsmouth, NH: Heinemann.

Beaugrande, R. de (1984). Text production: Toward a science of composition. Norwood, NJ: Ablex.

Burnham, S. (1994). For writers only. New York: Ballantine Books.

Collins, R. (1992). Narrative writing of option II students: The effects of combining the whole-language techniques, writing process approach and strategy training. Unpublished master's thesis, State University of New York, Buffalo.

Corno, L. (1992). Encouraging students to take responsibility for learning and performance. Elementary School Journal, 93, 69–83.

Danoff, B., Harris, K. R., & Graham, S. (1993). Incorporating strategy instruction within the writing process in the regular classroom. Journal of Reading Behavior, 25, 295–322.

De La Paz, S. (1997). Strategy instruction in planning: Teaching students with learning and writing disabilities to compose persuasive and expository essays. Learning Disability Quarterly, 20, 227–248.

De La Paz, S., & Graham, S. (1997a). Strategy instruction in planning: Effects on the writing performance and behavior of students with learning difficulties. Exceptional Children, 63, 167–181.

De La Paz, S., & Graham, S. (1997b). The effects of dictation and advanced planning instruction on the composing of students with writing and learning problems. *Journal of Educational Psychology, 89,* 203–222.

Flower, L., & Hayes, J. (1980). The dynamics of composing: Making plans and juggling constraints. In L. Gregg & R. Steinberg (Eds.), *Cognitive processes in writing* (pp. 31–50). Hillsdale, NJ: Erlbaum.

Grabowski, J. (1996). Writing and speaking: Common grounds and differences toward a regulation theory of written language production. In M. Levy & S. Ransdell (Eds.), *The science of writing: Theories, methods, individual differences, and applications* (pp. 73–92). Mahwah, NJ: Erlbaum.

Graham, S. (1990). The role of production factors in learning disabled students' compositions. *Journal of Educational Psychology, 82,* 781–791.

Graham, S. (1997). Executive control in the revising of students with writing and learning difficulties. *Journal of Educational Psychology, 89,* 223–234.

Graham, S., Berninger, V., Abbott, R., Abbott, S., & Whitaker, D. (1997). Role of mechanics in composing of elementary school students: A new methodological approach. *Journal of Educational Psychology, 89,* 170–182.

Graham, S., & Harris, K. R. (1988). Instructional recommendations for teaching writing to exceptional students. *Exceptional Children, 54,* 506–512.

Graham, S., & Harris, K. R. (1989a). A components analysis of cognitive strategy instruction: Effects on learning disabled students' compositions and self-efficacy. *Journal of Educational Psychology, 81,* 353–361.

Graham, S., & Harris, K. R. (1989b). Improving learning disabled students' skills at composing essays: Self-instructional strategy training. *Exceptional Children, 56,* 201–214.

Graham, S., & Harris, K. R. (1993). Self-regulated strategy development: Helping students with learning problems develop as writers. *Elementary School Journal, 94,* 169–181.

Graham, S., & Harris, K. R. (1994). The role and development of self-regulation in the writing process. In D. Schunk & B. Zimmerman (Eds.), *Self-regulation of learning and performance: Issues and educational applications* (pp. 203–228). Hillsdale, NJ: Erlbaum.

Graham, S., & Harris, K. R. (1996). Self-regulation and strategy instruction for students who find writing and learning challenging. In M. Levy & S. Ransdell (Eds.), *The science of writing: Theories, methods, individual differences, and applications* (pp. 347–360). Mahwah, NJ: Erlbaum.

Graham, S., & Harris, K. R. (1997a). It can be taught, but it does not develop naturally: Myths and realities in writing instruction. *School Psychology Review, 26,* 414–424.

Graham, S., & Harris, K. R. (1997b). Self-regulation and writing: Where do we go from here? *Contemporary Educational Psychology, 22,* 102–114.

Graham, S., Harris, K. R., MacArthur, C., & Schwartz, S. (1991). Writing and writing instruction with students with learning disabilities: A review of a program of research. *Learning Disability Quarterly, 14,* 89–114.

Graham, S., & MacArthur, C. (1988). Improving learning disabled students' skills at revising essays produced on a word processor: Self-instructional strategy training. *Journal of Special Education, 22,* 133–152.

Graham, S., MacArthur, C., & Schwartz, S. (1995). The effects of goal setting and procedural facilitation on the revising behavior and writing performance of students with writing and learning problems. *Journal of Educational Psychology, 87,* 230–240.

Graham, S., MacArthur, C., Schwartz, S., & Voth, T. (1992). Improving the compositions of students with learning disabilities using a strategy involving product and process goal setting. *Exceptional Children, 58,* 322–335.

Hammill, D., & Larsen, S. (1988). *Test of Written Language—2.* Austin, TX: Pro-Ed.

Harris, K. R. (1982). Cognitive-behavior modification: Application with exceptional students. *Focus on Exceptional Children, 15,* 1–16.

Harris, K. R., & Graham, S. (1985). Improving learning disabled students' composition skills: Self-control strategy training. *Learning Disability Quarterly, 8,* 27–36.

Harris, K. R., & Graham, S. (1992). Self-regulated strategy development: A part of the writing process. In M. Pressley, K. Harris, & J. Guthrie (Eds.), *Promoting academic competence and literacy in school* (pp. 277–309). San Diego: Academic Press.

Harris, K. R., & Graham, S. (1994). Constructivism: Principles, paradigms, and integration. *Journal of Special Education, 28,* 275–289.

Harris, K. R., & Graham, S. (1996). *Making the writing process work: Strategies for composition and self-regulation.* Cambridge, MA: Brookline Books.

Harris, K. R., Graham, S., Reid, R., McElroy, K., & Hamby, R. (1994). Self-monitoring of attention versus self-monitoring of performance: Replication and cross-task comparison studies. *Learning Disability Quarterly, 17,* 121–139.

Hayes, J. (1996). A new framework for understanding cognition and affect in writing. In M. Levy & S. Ransdell (Eds.), *The science of writing: Theories, methods, individual differences, and applications* (pp. 1–28). Mahwah, NJ: Erlbaum.

Hayes, J., & Flower, L. (1986). Writing research and the writer. *American Psychologist, 41,* 1106–1113.

Kazin, A. (1967). *The Paris Review: Writers at work.* New York: Viking.

Kellogg, R. (1996). A model of working memory in writing. In M. Levy & S. Ransdell (Eds.), *The science of writing: Theories, methods, individual differences, and applications* (pp. 57–72). Mahwah, NJ: Erlbaum.

MacArthur, C., Schwartz, S., & Graham, S. (1991). Effects of a reciprocal peer revision strategy in special education classrooms. *Learning Disabilities Research and Practice, 6,* 201–210.

MacArthur, C., Schwartz, S., Graham, S., Molloy, D., & Harris, K. (1996). Integration of strategy instruction into whole language classrooms: A case study. *Learning Disabilities and Practice, 11,* 168–176.

McCutchen, D. (1988). "Functional automaticity" in children's writing: A problem of metacognitive control. *Written Communication, 5,* 306–324.

McCutchen, D. (in press). A capacity theory of writing: Working memory in composition. *Educational Psychology Review.*

Plimpton, G. (Ed.). (1967). *Writers at work: The Paris Review interviews* (3rd series). New York: Viking Press.

Salomon, G., & Globerson, T. (1987). Skill may not be enough: The role of mindfulness in learning and transfer. *International Journal of Educational Research, 11,* 623–637.

Sawyer, R., Graham, S., & Harris, K. R. (1992). Direct teaching, strategy instruction, and strategy instruction with explicit self-regulation: Effects on learning disabled students' compositions and self-efficacy. *Journal of Educational Psychology, 84,* 340–352.

Scardamalia, M., & Bereiter, C. (1986). Written composition. In M. Wittrock (Ed.), *Handbook of research on teaching* (3rd ed., pp. 778–803). New York: Macmillan.

Sexton, M., Harris, K. R., & Graham, S. (in press). Self-regulated strategy development and the writing process: Effects on essay writing and attributions. *Exceptional Children*.

Stoddard, B., & MacArthur, C. (1993). A peer editor strategy: Guiding learning disabled students in response and revision. *Research in the Teaching of English, 27,* 76–103.

Tanhouser, S. (1994). *Function over form: The relative efficacy of self-instructional strategy training alone and with procedural facilitation for adolescents with learning disabilities.* Unpublished doctoral dissertation, Johns Hopkins University, Baltimore, MD.

Tawney, J., & Gast, D. (Eds.). (1984). *Single subject research in special education.* Columbus, OH: Merrill.

Troia, G., Graham, S., & Harris, K.R. (1997). *Teaching students to plan mindfully: Effects on the writing performance and behavior of students with learning disabilities.* Manuscript submitted for publication.

Wong, B. (1994). Instructional parameters promoting transfer of learned strategies in students with learning disabilities. *Learning Disability Quarterly, 17,* 100–119.

Zimmerman, B. (1989). A social cognitive view of self-regulated academic learning. *Journal of Educational Psychology, 81,* 329–339.

Zimmerman, B., & Risemberg, R. (1997). Becoming a proficient writer: A self-regulatory perspective. *Contemporary Educational Psychology, 22,* 73–101.

CHAPTER 3

Transactional Instruction of Comprehension Strategies in the Elementary Grades

Michael Pressley
Pamela Beard El-Dinary
Ruth Wharton-McDonald
Rachel Brown

During our analysis of the nature of language arts instruction throughout the elementary years, we have concerned ourselves with both exceptionally effective elementary instruction and more typical instruction. We have studied classrooms in which comprehension strategies instruction has been a prominent part of the curriculum as well as those in which little comprehension instruction occurs.

The main purpose of this chapter is to describe the nature of effective comprehension strategies instruction. In addition, we offer theoretical analyses and a summary of the empirical support for the type of comprehension instruction we favor. One important source of support for comprehension strategies instruction in the elementary grades comes from research conducted with much older and more mature readers, with this work providing important insights about the nature of the comprehension processing that elementary reading instruction should foster.

THE NATURE OF SKILLED COMPREHENSION

The work at the elementary level that is covered in this chapter has occurred concomitantly with research on the nature of reading by exceptionally effective readers (Pressley & Afflerbach, 1995; Wyatt et al., 1993). The latter research has made clear to us why comprehension strategies instruction makes sense in the elementary curriculum.

Verbal protocol analysis, the main research methodology we have used to study skilled reading, provides a window on consciously controllable comprehension processes. Pressley and Afflerbach (1995) analyzed every verbal protocol of reading that they could find, providing a summary of more than 40 different studies involving a variety of reader types, reading materials, and reader goals. The most striking aspect of these verbal protocol studies is that readers are so driven to construct meaning. Good readers report flexibly interacting with texts as they read, using their prior knowledge to construct interpretations, and relating what they already know to the new ideas in text. Skilled readers often respond passionately to ideas conveyed through text. To use Pressley and Afflerbach's (1995) terms, these readers are "constructively responsive" in their reading.

There are clear indications of constructive responsivity in the verbal protocols: Readers actively search, reflect on, and respond to text in pursuit of main ideas and important details. They overview a text before careful reading of it in order to understand the general type of information covered and where various topics in it are located. There is differential attention to information central to the reader's goals. Readers sometimes jump back and forth during reading, often as part of being consciously inferential. That is, they hold disparate ideas in working memory while searching for related ideas throughout text, trying to find relationships between what was just read, and what came before and will be coming shortly in the text. Good readers keep processing text until they have gotten out of it the information they need. As good readers read, they evaluate the text, including the validity of its claims and its interestingness. After a text has been completed, additional reflection and rereading are common, with good readers monitoring whether they have comprehended a reading.

In short, when good readers read, there is meaning construction and response to meanings constructed throughout the process of reading. Readers often predict what is next in text based on their prior knowledge. Such hypothesis generation continues throughout front-to-back reading of the text. As new ideas are encountered in the text, previous hypotheses are revised. Good readers often are passionate in their responses to text. They can be surprised, laugh, or experience frustration or anxiety during reading.

Another element that is apparent from Pressley and Afflerbach's (1995) review of the verbal protocol literature is that elementary and high school readers are much less active than more mature readers such as adult professionals reading in their domains of expertise. One likely reason for this is that such active comprehension is not taught or encouraged, an insight first offered by Durkin (1978–1979) following extensive observations of elementary-level reading.

Finally, there is evidence in the verbal protocol studies that active comprehension processing affects reading achievement. Correlations between verbal reports of active processing and reading comprehension have been found consistently (e.g., active comprehension processing increases memory of text; Pressley & Afflerbach, 1995, Chap. 2). Based on the verbal protocol data, there seem to be plenty of reasons to teach comprehension strategies to elementary students.

WHAT IS HAPPENING IN ELEMENTARY CLASSROOMS

With others in our research group, we have conducted a number of analyses that are revealing about the nature of comprehension instruction in contemporary elementary classrooms. Several of the lines of research we and our colleagues have pursued are relevant in this context.

Comprehension Instruction in Typical Classrooms

There is very little comprehension strategies instruction going on in elementary classrooms. How do we know? Pressley, Wharton-McDonald, Mistretta-Hampson, and Echevarria (in press) set out to determine in detail the nature of literacy instruction in the fourth and fifth grades. Consistent with Durkin (1978–1979), they observed very little comprehension instruction in the 10 fourth- and fifth-grade classrooms that they studied in upstate New York during the 1995–1996 school year. Each fourth- and fifth-grade teacher that they studied seemed to have a core set of goals and practices that defined his or her classroom. Thus, there were teachers who emphasized reading fine literature and responding to it in many different ways; other aspects of curriculum were defined in relation to students reading long pieces of fiction (i.e., novels) and responding to them (e.g., writing was in response to literature; vocabulary and spelling words were found in novels). There were other teachers who highlighted composition, with much of their instruction driven by students' planning, drafting, and revising of the texts they were writing (e.g., teachers directed students to read particular texts as part of planning to for an essay). One teacher in Pressley et al. (in press) defined his curriculum as a traditional basal-driven curriculum, with basals defining reading, spelling, language arts, science, and social studies instruction.

Regardless of the core emphasis, however, most classrooms studied by Pressley et al. (in press) included (1) reading of trade books, in particular, novels; (2) writing instruction that involved planning, drafting, and revising of compositions, which was supported by procedural facilitators (e.g., sheets reminding students of the parts of a story); (3) connections between reading, writing, and content area coverage (e.g., readings related to a social studies theme that inspired writing of stories related to the theme); (4) skills instruction (i.e., writing mechanics, spelling vocabulary), including use of worksheets and homework; and (5) a variety of pedagogical processes, including class discussions, one-to- one miniconferences, and computer-mediated learning. The point here is, however, that these activities were associated with some teacher-selected core of activities that the teacher defined as his or her approach to literacy instruction.

Teaching of Comprehension Strategies as a Core Fourth- and Fifth-Grade Activity

One possible language arts instruction core is teaching of comprehension strategies. Although no such teachers were observed by Pressley et al. (in press), between 1989 and 1993 Pressley, El-Dinary, Gaskins, et al. (1992) sought out and studied such teachers, identifying activities that seemed to occur in every classroom that had comprehension development as its core. (Notably, consistent with the earlier claim that not much comprehension strategies instruction is occurring, it was challenging to find elementary classrooms in which comprehension instruction was the focus.)

Specifically, Pressley, El-Dinary, Gaskins, et al. (1992) studied school-based, educator-developed comprehension strategies instruction that seemed to be working (i.e., the educators could offer some type of evidence that their instruction was having impact on students, such as pretest–posttest performance differences favoring strategy instructed students compared to conventionally educated students in the same district). The first studies were conducted at Benchmark School (Media, PA), a school dedicated to helping elementary-age children overcome reading problems (Gaskins, Anderson, Pressley, Cunicelli, & Satlow, 1993; Pressley, Gaskins, Cunicelli, et al., 1991; Pressley, Gaskins, Wile, Cunicelli, & Sheridan, 1991). The Benchmark investigations were followed by studies in two Maryland county public school elementary-level programs dedicated to increasing the use of strategies for reading comprehension (Brown & Coy-Ogan, 1993; El-Dinary, Pressley, & Schuder, 1992; Pressley, El-Dinary, Gaskins, et al., 1992; Pressley, El-Dinary, Stein, Marks, & Brown, 1992; Pressley, Schuder, SAIL Faculty and Administration, Bergman, & El-Dinary, 1992).

A variety of qualitative methods were used in this research, including ethnographies, ethnographic interviews, long-term case studies, and analyses of classroom discourse. Although the three programs studied differed in their particulars, a number of conclusions held across programs:

1. Comprehension strategies instruction was long-term, continuing throughout a school year and ideally across school years.
2. The younger the students, the more instructional effort was required

for the students to understand individual strategies and how to coordinate use of strategies.

3. Typically, a few powerful strategies were emphasized, for example, predicting upcoming information in a text, relating text content to prior knowledge, constructing internal mental images of relations described in text, using problem-solving strategies such as rereading and analyzing context clues when meaning was unclear, and summarizing. Interestingly, the strategies taught in comprehension strategies classrooms were aimed at stimulating the processes used by skilled readers (see the previous discussion of Pressley & Afflerbach, 1995).

4. Teachers explained and extensively modeled effective comprehension strategies, with teacher modeling of strategy use continuing long after the original introduction of the strategies, consistent with the outlook on strategy instruction developed by Duffy et al. (1987). Teacher modeling of strategies was not algorithmic, but typically occurred on the run, when an academic task called for it. Such opportunities to model rarely allowed "canned" responses but rather required the teacher to model creative application, modification, and combination of strategies. The teachers also coached students to use strategies on an as-needed basis, providing hints to them about potential strategic choices they might make. There were many minilessons about when it was appropriate to use particular strategies. Throughout instruction, the usefulness of strategies was emphasized, with students reminded frequently about the comprehension gains that accompany strategy use.

5. Students modeled strategy use for one another and explained to one another how they used strategies to process text. This occurred frequently as students dialogued about text, with students reporting the active processing they were using to understand a text being read by a group of students (see especially Gaskins et al., 1993). These dialogues involved students relating text to their prior knowledge, constructing summaries of text meaning, visualizing relations covered in a text, predicting what might transpire in a story, interpreting text, and responding to it (Brown & Coy-Ogan, 1993).

Such instruction came to be known as *transactional strategies instruction*, because it emphasized reader transactions with texts (Rosenblatt, 1978), interpretations constructed by readers thinking about text together (i.e., transacting; e.g., Hutchins, 1991), and teacher's and students' reactions to text affecting each other's individual thinking about text (i.e., interactions were transactional; e.g., Bell, 1968).

In summary, such instruction involved direct explanations and teacher modeling of strategies, followed by guided practice of strategies. Teacher assistance was provided on an as-needed basis as students attempted to use strategies as they read text in groups (i.e., strategy application was "scaf-folded"; Wood, Bruner, & Ross, 1976). Group readings involved flexible, interpretive discussions of texts.

Summary

There is far too little comprehension instruction in American elementary classrooms. Even so, it can be implemented, especially when development of comprehension skills is a focus of the classroom. Our view is that this is a good focus, for the overarching goal of all of reading instruction is the development of readers who can understand what they read.

THEORETICAL ANALYSES OF TRANSACTIONAL STRATEGIES INSTRUCTION AND EMPIRICAL VALIDATION OF THE APPROACH

There has been much scientific reflection on and analysis of transactional strategies instruction. We cover some of the highlights in this section.

General Theoretical Considerations

A main assumption of transactional strategies instruction is that skilled reading is a specific instance of good strategy use and information processing, which involve a number of cognitive components in interaction (Pressley, Borkowski, & Schneider, 1987, 1989): decoding and comprehension procedures, metacognitive knowledge, declarative knowledge, and academic motivation.

Effective reading involves *decoding and comprehension procedures*, which are applied intentionally, consciously, and effortfully at first and eventually are internalized to the point of automatic and relatively effortless application. Before they are applied automatically, however, the effective use of decoding and comprehension procedures depends in part on *metacognitive knowledge* (i.e., knowledge of one's own thinking processes), especially awareness of when and where the known decoding and comprehension procedures apply. Such metacognition develops mostly through extensive experience using the procedures in a variety of contexts, although it can also be affected by explicit instruction about when and where particular strategies are useful (e.g., O'Sullivan & Pressley, 1984).

The use of decoding and comprehension procedures is enabled by *declarative knowledge* (i.e., factual knowledge), from knowledge of words that are so familiar that they are recognized on sight to general knowledge of the world that can be related to ideas presented in a text. Such knowledge also develops, in part, through extensive reading.

The application of decoding and comprehension is effortful and, thus, requires students to possess extensive *academic motivation*. Such motivation depends largely on understanding that success in reading depends largely on effort expended, particularly efforts expended on the processes that skilled readers use (Borkowski, Carr, Rellinger, & Pressley, 1990). Of course, such motivation is a byproduct of past successes in reading. In contrast, when early efforts at reading do not result in success, students can develop beliefs that undermine motivation, for example, that they are too dumb to read well (e.g., Pearl, 1982).

Understandings about Transactional Strategies Instruction Based on Careful Observational Analyses

Comprehension strategies instruction is the centerpiece of language arts instruction in classrooms using the transactional strategies instructional approach (Pressley, El-Dinary, Gaskins, et al., 1992). Typically, students are taught to use a small repertoire of comprehension strategies, to articulate and coordinate the use of these strategies to understand the texts they read. For example, the following are the strategies that might be taught in a transactional strategies classroom:

- Prediction of upcoming content (e.g., after looking at the pictures accompanying the story)
- Visualization (i.e., constructing mental images representing the ideas represented in the text being read)
- Making connections to prior knowledge (e.g., thinking about everything known about Christopher Columbus when Columbus is mentioned in a text)
- Asking oneself questions about the text
- Seeking clarifications when confused (e.g., by rereading)
- Summarization

Transactional strategies instruction is extremely constructivist (Harris & Pressley, 1991; Pressley, Harris, & Marks, 1992), with teacher explanations and modelings of strategies only serving as a beginning point for student construction of knowledge (see Elbers, 1991; Iran-Nejad, 1990; Wittrock, 1990, 1992). Much of teacher modeling of strategies use involves modeling constructive adaptation of strategies. That is, teacher explanations and modeling of strategies in a variety of naturalistically occurring comprehension situations (e.g., a newspaper article being read during current events) invariably require the teacher to model "jerry-rigging" of strategies.

As informative as teacher explanations and modelings can be, they cannot substitute for students learning about strategies through their own efforts. As students practice and adapt strategies, they construct understandings about how and when to use strategies. They come to understand that how much and what they comprehend depends on the cognitive processing they choose to do as they read. They have many opportunities to experience the power of their prior knowledge in facilitating comprehension, constantly attempting to relate what they read to what they know. In short, the teacher's explanations about and modeling of strategies are only the beginning of student knowledge construction processes, with students learning how to be better information processors through their own efforts.

Sometimes student problems in strategy application prompt teacher reexplanations and remodelings of strategies. These can be teacher–student dialogues, with the teacher and student working together to figure out how to apply strategies to a situation. Teacher reexplanations of strategies as students process naturally occurring texts are aimed at helping students "figure out" the situation, rather than simply directing students about how to make correct responses. That is, when teachers reteach comprehension strategies, it additionally encourages student construction of knowledge about comprehension strategies.

Controlled Validations of Transactional Strategies Instruction

There have been three controlled tests of strategies instruction consistent with the transactional strategies instruction approach. Together, they provide evidence of the effectiveness of the approach through the elementary years, extending into middle and high school.

Brown, Pressley, Van Meter, and Schuder (1996)

Brown et al. (1996) conducted a year-long quasi-experimental investigation of the effects of transactional strategies instruction on second-grade children's reading. Five second-grade, previously low-achieving reading groups received transactional strategies instruction. They were matched with second-grade, low-achieving readers taught by teachers who were well regarded as language arts teachers but who were not using a strategies instruction approach.

In the fall of the year, the strategies instruction condition and control participants in the study did not differ on standardized measures of reading comprehension and word attack skills. By the spring, there were clear differences on these measures favoring the transactional strategies instruction classrooms. In addition, there were differences favoring the strategies-instructed students on strategies use measures as well as interpretive measures (i.e., strategies-instructed students made richer and more diverse interpretations of what they read than did controls).

Collins (1991)

Collins (1991) produced improved comprehension in fifth- and sixth-grade students by providing a semester (3 days a week) of comprehension strategies lessons. Her students were taught to predict, seek clarification when uncertain, look for patterns and principles in arguments presented in text, analyze decision making that occurs during text processing, problem solve (including the use of backward reasoning and visualization), summarize, adapt ideas in text (including rearranging parts of ideas in text), and negotiate interpretations of texts in groups. Although the strategies-instructed students did not differ from controls before the intervention with respect to standardized comprehension performance, there was a standard deviation difference of 3 between treated and control conditions on the standardized achievement posttest, a very large effect for the treatment.

Anderson (1992)

Anderson (1992; see also Anderson & Roit, 1993) conducted a 3-month experimental investigation of the effects of transactional strategies instruction on reading disabled students in the 6th through 11th grades. Students were taught comprehension strategies in small groups, with nine groups of transactional strategies students and seven control groups. Although both strategies-instructed and control students made gains on standardized comprehension measures from before to after the study, the gains were greater in the trained group than in the control condition. Anderson (1992) also collected a variety of qualitative data supporting the conclusions that reading for meaning improved in the strategies instruction condition: For example, strategies instruction increased students' willingness to read difficult material and attempt to understand it, collaborate with classmates to discover meanings in text, and react to and elaborate text.

Summary

The transactional strategies instruction model is intended to stimulate good strategy use and information processing in young readers. Teaching is the beginning of a constructivist process as students attempt to understand teacher explanations and modeling and to carry out the strategies being taught.

In classrooms adopting it, the centerpiece of language arts instruction is teaching of comprehension strategies. As in any elementary classroom, however, many other elements of language arts instruction also occur around the teacher-defined core activities. To date, the transactional strategies instruction approach has proven to be effective relative to other language arts instruction, although, at this point there is more evidence of its effectiveness with weaker compared to stronger readers.

PROGRAMMATIC IMPLEMENTATION

In transactional strategies instruction, a few powerful strategies are taught as a package, with students taught explicitly that excellent reading includes choosing to use appropriate strategies as needed during reading. The strategic repertoire typically includes strategies that can be applied before reading (e.g., overviewing, making predictions), during reading (e.g., constructing images representing meaning, asking questions, looking back when confused, relating to prior knowledge), and after reading (e.g., summarizing).

Strategies can be introduced one or a few at a time, so that there is in-depth instruction about and practice of the individual strategies before students attempt to coordinate the entire repertoire of strategies. Once strategies are introduced, there is extensive and diverse practice in use of strategies. Students receive much guidance and feedback as they attempt to apply strategies to text. This often occurs in reading groups, with students reporting on the strategies they are executing as they read. One of the real challenges for the teacher is to diagnose the specific problems experienced by students as they attempt to apply strategies. Thus, it helps if students read aloud as they attempt to apply strategies and think aloud about their strategy choices as they read.

Facile use of strategies across a wide range of tasks and materials is a long-term goal. To meet this goal, strategies teaching and applications of strategies occur across the curriculum, although they are often emphasized more during reading. By practicing use of strategies across the curriculum, it is possible for teachers to provide extensive information to students about when and where to apply the strategies they are learning as well as information about the learning benefits produced by use of strategies. Again, of course, such teacher explanations are the beginning of a constructivist process, with students' understanding about when to apply strategies and when they benefit from strategies application developing as they use strategies across the school day. We emphasize that the effective transactional strategies teacher recognizes that transfer of comprehension strategies to new academic tasks and contents is anything but automatic, but rather requires extensive teaching about when strategies might be applied as well as practice applying strategies across a number of situations.

Teacher explanations and modeling of strategies are most extensive and explicit early in the instruction. After several months, teacher prompting of strategy use (e.g., What strategy might you use here?) is much reduced. The hints occur less often and become more abbreviated as students acquire skill in strategies application.

Although much of the foundational research on comprehension strategies emphasizes memory of information as stated in text (Pressley et al., 1989), in fact, transactional strategies instruction teachers stress much more. Cognitive strategies are interpretational vehicles (i.e., for constructing personally significant understandings). For example, interpretive activities were apparent in the analyses of Benchmark classroom dialogues produced by Gaskins et al. (1993), who studied the strategies instruction lessons of six teachers at Benchmark. The discourse in these classrooms was much different than the discourse in conventional classrooms.

Cazden (e.g., 1988) and Mehan (1979) observed that typical classroom discourse includes many cycles of a teacher asking a question, a student responding, and the teacher evaluating the response (i.e., IRE cycles involving teacher Initiation, student Response, and teacher Evaluation). IRE cycles were not found much in the Benchmark data, however. Instead, 88% of the time, the teachers engaged in interactive dialogues with their students, in what Gaskins et al. (1993) referred to as process-content cycles: The teacher used content as a vehicle to stimulate application and discussion of strategies. When students made comments in discussions, teachers did not attempt to evaluate their responses but rather asked the students to elaborate them— encouraging students to process the content additionally using strategies (e.g., to relate information to prior knowledge if the student had not done so, to self-question). The teachers' goal was to encourage student understanding of content through strategic processing. That is, elementary content coverage was not displaced in favor of strategies instruction; rather, strategies practice occurred as students learned elementary content, presumably helping them to do so.

Consider this example. A teacher might request that a student summarize a passage. Once the summary was offered, the teacher might ask the student to describe any images that came to mind while reading the text or encourage the student to liven up the summary by relating the text content to prior knowledge (e.g., When you visualize how a third-class lever works, where do you see the fulcrum? How is that picture different from what you visualized when the author described first- and second-class levers? Can you tell about an occasion when you have used a third-class lever? How did this simple machine benefit you?).

An extremely important finding in the Gaskins et al. (1993) investigation was the identification of events that occur often in particular lessons:

1. Students are provided instruction about how to carry out the strategies.
2. Students practice strategies, with teacher guidance and assistance provided on an as-needed basis.
3. If there is a particular strategy the teacher wants to emphasize (or introduce), it is mentioned early in the lesson, as is any particular content that is to be emphasized.
4. The teacher often models strategy use and offers anecdotal information about how strategies help them to learn.
5. The teacher offers information about when and where to apply particular strategies.

GOOD STRATEGY USE AND INFORMATION PROCESSING DURING READING: SELF-REFLECTIVE USE OF COMPREHENSION STRATEGIES

The goal of transactional strategies instruction is students who use comprehension strategies intelligently, knowing when to use them and how to adapt them. Such awareness is fostered when students use comprehension strategies in reading groups: Students think aloud as they read and are exposed to other students doing so. There is discussion of why one student thinks visualization makes sense at a particular point, whereas another student is making connections to prior knowledge. Students have many opportunities in such reading groups to reflect on comprehension processes, both their own and those of other students.

Appropriate generalization of strategies often does not occur with short-term strategy instruction (Brown, Bransford, Ferrara, & Campione, 1983). Students in transactional strategies classrooms learn to generalize by practicing use of strategies with many different types of text. Again, as reading proceeds, there are substantial discussions about how students are adapting the strategies they know to new texts and situations so that reflective knowledge of strategies and their application is encouraged additionally.

Students certainly recognize that use of strategies requires effort. As with any skill, however, use of comprehension strategies requires less effort as they are practiced, and, thus, the long-term practice of strategies in groups should go far in motivating students to use strategies. Moreover, the discussions that occur during transactional strategies instruction groups are much more interesting and driven by student concerns than the typical teacher-driven question-and-answer discussion that occurs in most round-robin reading. With input from the teacher about how active reading is mature reading, and the positive reinforcement by the teacher of the students for using strategies, the students have additional reasons for wanting to use the strategies they are learning.

A main message to students during transactional strategies instruction is that they are to take charge of their own reading. Not surprisingly, students in transactional strategies instruction classrooms typically are very strategic even when they are not in reading groups. For example, we have witnessed many partner readings during which students are definitely strategic (i.e., they use the strategies when no teacher is overseeing and reminding them). Moreover, in Brown et al. (1996), the second-grade students in the transactional strategies instruction classrooms clearly were more strategic when reading and thinking aloud on a one-to-one basis with an unfamiliar adult. Not surprisingly, recall of stories by strategies instructed students included many more of the types of inferences that strategy use encourages than did the story recall of students in control classrooms.

In short, the goal of transactional strategies instruction is to develop readers who can adapt the comprehension strategies used by skilled readers and use those strategies adaptively. Although we hope for more data in the future substantiating changes in student cognition as a function of such instruction, there is reason at this juncture to be optimistic that transactional strategies instruction results in reflective, self-regulative readers.

REFERENCES

Anderson, V. (1992). A teacher development project in transactional strategy instruction for teachers of severely reading-disabled adolescents. *Teaching and Teacher Education*, 8, 391–403.

Anderson, V., & Roit, M. (1993). Planning and implementing collaborative strategy instruction for delayed readers in grades 6–10. *Elementary School Journal*, 94, 121–137.

Bell, R. Q. (1968). A reinterpretation of the direction of effects in studies of socialization. *Psychological Review*, 75, 81–95.

Borkowski, J. G., Carr, M., Rellinger, E. A., & Pressley, M. (1990). Self-regulated strategy use: Interdependence of metacognition, attributions, and self-esteem. In B. F. Jones (Ed.), *Dimensions of thinking: Review of research* (pp. 53–92). Hillsdale, NJ: Erlbaum.

Brown, A. L., Bransford, J. D., Ferrara, R. A., & Campione, J. C. (1983). Learning, remembering, and understanding. In J. H. Flavell & E. M. Markman (Eds.), *Handbook of child psychology: Vol. III. Cognitive development* (pp. 77–166). New York: Wiley.

Brown, R., & Coy-Ogan, L. (1993). The evolution of transactional strategies instruction in one teacher's classroom. *Elementary School Journal, 94,* 221–233.

Brown, R., Pressley, M., Van Meter, P., & Schuder, T. (1996). A quasi-experimental validation of transactional strategies instruction with low-achieving second grade readers. *Journal of Educational Psychology, 88,* 18–37.

Cazden, C. B. (1988). *Classroom discourse: The language of teaching and learning.* Portsmouth, NH: Heinemann.

Collins, C. (1991). Reading instruction that increases thinking abilities. *Journal of Reading, 34,* 510–516.

Duffy, G. G., Roehler, L. R., Sivan, E., Rackliffe, G., Book, C., Meloth, M., Vavrus, L. G., Wesselman, R., Putnam, J., & Bassiri, D. (1987). Effects of explaining the reasoning associated with using reading strategies. *Reading Research Quarterly, 22,* 347–368.

Durkin, D. (1978–1979). What classroom observations reveal about reading comprehension instruction. *Reading Research Quarterly, 15,* 481–533.

Elbers, E. (1991). The development of competence and its social context. *Educational Psychology Review, 3,* 73–94.

El-Dinary, P. B., Pressley, M., & Schuder, T. (1992). Becoming a strategies teacher: An observational and interview study of three teachers learning transactional strategies instruction. In C. Kinzer & D. Leu (Eds.), *Forty-first yearbook of the National Reading Conference* (pp. 453–462). Chicago: National Reading Conference.

Gaskins, I. W., Anderson, R. C., Pressley, M., Cunicelli, E. A., & Satlow, E. (1993). Six teachers' dialogue during cognitive process instruction. *Elementary School Journal, 93,* 277–304.

Harris, K. R., & Pressley, M. (1991). The nature of cognitive strategy instruction: Interactive strategy construction. *Exceptional Children, 57,* 392–404.

Hutchins, E. (1991). The social organization of distributed cognition. In L. Resnick, J. M. Levine, & S. D. Teasley (Eds.), *Perspectives on socially shared cognition* (pp. 283–307). Washington, DC: American Psychological Association.

Iran-Nejad, A. (1990). Active and dynamic self-regulation of learning processes. *Review of Educational Research, 60,* 573–602.

Mehan, H. (1979). *Social organization in the classroom.* Cambridge, MA: Harvard University Press.

O'Sullivan, J. T., & Pressley, M. (1984). Completeness of instruction and strategy transfer. *Journal of Experimental Child Psychology, 38,* 275–288.

Pearl, R. (1982). LD children's attributions for success and failure: A replication with a labeled LD sample. *Learning Disability Quarterly, 5,* 173–176.

Pressley, M., & Afflerbach, P. (1995). *Verbal protocols of reading: The nature of constructively responsive reading.* Hillsdale, NJ: Erlbaum.

Pressley, M., Borkowski, J. G., & Schneider, W. (1987). Cognitive strategies: Good strategy users coordinate meta-cognition and knowledge. In R. Vasta & G. Whitehurst (Eds.), *Annals of child development* (Vol. 4, pp. 89–129). Greenwich, CT: JAI Press.

Pressley, M., Borkowski, J. G., & Schneider, W. (1989). Good information processing: What it is and what education can do to promote it. *International Journal of Educational Research, 13,* 866–878.

Pressley, M., El-Dinary, P. B., Gaskins, I., Schuder, T., Bergman, J. L., Almasi, J., & Brown, R. (1992). Beyond direct explanation: Transactional instruction of reading comprehension strategies. *Elementary School Journal, 92,* 511–554.

Pressley, M., El-Dinary, P. B., Stein, S., Marks, M. B., & Brown, R. (1992). Good strategy instruction is motivating and interesting. In A. Renninger, S. Hidi, & A. Krapp (Eds.), *The role of interest in learning and development* (pp. 333–358). Hillsdale, NJ: Erlbaum.

Pressley, M., Gaskins, I. W., Cunicelli, E. A., Bardick, N. J., Schaub-Matt, M., Lee, D. S., & Powell, N. (1991). Strategy instruction at Benchmark School: A faculty interview study. *Learning Disability Quarterly, 14,* 19–48.

Pressley, M., Gaskins, I. W., Wile, D., Cunicelli, E. A., & Sheridan, J. (1991). Teaching literacy strategies across the curriculum: A case study at Benchmark School. In S. McCormick & J. Zutell (Eds.), *Fortieth yearbook of the National Reading Conference* (pp. 219–228). Chicago: National Reading Conference.

Pressley, M., Harris, K. R., & Marks, M. B. (1992). But good strategy instructors are constructivists!! *Educational Psychology Review, 4,* 1–32.

Pressley, M., Schuder, T., SAIL Faculty and Administration, Bergman, J. L., & El-Dinary, P. B. (1992). A researcher–educator collaborative interview study of transactional comprehension strategies instruction. *Journal of Educational Psychology, 84,* 231–246.

Pressley, M., Wharton-McDonald, R., Mistretta-Hampson, J., & Echevarria, M. (in press). Literacy instruction in ten grade-4/-5 classrooms. *Scientific Studies of Reading.*

Rosenblatt, L. M. (1978). *The reader, the text, the poem: The transactional theory of the literary work.* Carbondale: Southern Illinois University Press.

Wittrock, M. C. (1990). Generative processes of comprehension. *Educational Psychologist, 24,* 345–376.

Wittrock, M. C. (1992). Generative learning processes of the brain. *Educational Psychologist, 27,* 531–542.

Wood, S. S., Bruner, J. S., & Ross, G. (1976). The role of tutoring in problem solving. *Journal of Child Psychology and Psychiatry, 17,* 89–100.

Wyatt, D., Pressley, M., El-Dinary, P. B., Stein, S., Evans, P., & Brown, R. (1993). Comprehension strategies, worth and credibility monitoring, and evaluations: Cold and hot cognition when experts read professional articles that are important to them. *Learning and Individual Differences, 5,* 49–72.

CHAPTER 4

Teaching College Students to Be Self-Regulated Learners

Barbara K. Hofer
Shirley L. Yu
Paul R. Pintrich

Self-regulated learning is an important aspect of student academic perform-ance and achievement in classroom settings. There are a number of different models of self-regulated learning (see Schunk & Zimmerman, 1994b), but all have in common the basic assumption that students can actively regulate their cognition, motivation, or behavior and, through these various regula-tory processes, achieve their goals and perform better (Zimmerman, 1989). At the same time, however, there is concern that many students, even college students and adults, do not become self-regulating learners and that we know very little about the naturalistic development of self-regulated learning or about formal interventions to increase self-regulated learning (Schneider & Pressley, 1989; Schunk & Zimmerman, 1994a). Although there is evidence that formal attempts to teach students to be self-regulating learners are somewhat successful (Hattie, Biggs, & Purdie, 1996; Simpson, Hynd, Nist, & Burrell, 1997), there are still many unresolved issues regarding the teaching of cognitive and self-regulatory strategies across the K–12 age range as well as at the postsecondary level.

The purpose of this chapter is to address these issues in the context of a discussion about teaching college students to be self-regulated learners. We believe that some of the issues regarding instructional efforts to improve self-regulated learning are applicable at all levels of education, but some are specific to the college level. We will discuss both the general issues as well as the ones that are particularly relevant to the postsecondary level. Al-though it is unlikely that there will ever be definitive answers to these issues, we hope that our discussion will help to clarify theory, research, and instructional practice in this area. We begin with a brief overview of the general issues involved in teaching students to be self-regulated learners, followed by a description of our conceptual framework and actual implementation of a course for college students. We conclude with some suggestions for future research and practice.

GENERAL ISSUES IN TEACHING COLLEGE STUDENTS TO BE SELF-REGULATED LEARNERS

Although there are many issues regarding the teaching of self-regulated learning, we discuss four general issues in this section including (1) the components and design of an intervention, (2) integrated versus adjunct course design, (3) the issue of transfer, and (4) characteristics of college students.

The Components and Design of an Intervention

The first general issue concerns the target of the intervention in terms of a definition of a self-regulated learner and the potential cognitive, metacognitive, or motivational components that might comprise an intervention. In terms of designing a formal intervention, what is the focus of instruction for the intervention? There are a great many different definitions of self-regulated learning and even more diversity in what interventions have formally tried to teach students (Simpson et al., 1997). For example, Hattie et al. (1996) point out in their meta-analysis of research on the teaching of learning strategies that interventions have varied from very short-term laboratory studies that attempt to train students in one specific strategy (e.g., using a mnemonic; how to underline) to more global, field-based interventions that are spread over several weeks or months and focus on a number of different cognitive, metacognitive, or motivational strategies. These strategies can range from cognitive strategies such as using a mnemonic, to metacognitive strategies such as self-testing, to motivational strategies such as making adaptive attributions. In addition, besides these general learning strategies, research has examined the teaching of very domain-specific strategies (e.g., algorithms for solving quadratic equations) as well as more general thinking, problem-solving, or intellectual skills (e.g., classification, syllogistic reasoning). Simpson et al. (1997) note that programs for college students range from ones that focus on remediation of specific reading deficits and functional reading skills in contrast to more general *learning to learn* courses that target various cognitive and self-regulatory strategies.

There is clearly a great deal of diversity in terms of the focus of different interventions. From an intervention design standpoint then, designers need to consider the *scope* of their program, the *content* of their program, and the *timeframe* for the program. Decisions about these three aspects of a program are interrelated as, for example, the timeframe (short or long term) can constrain the scope of the program. In terms of scope, the issue concerns how many different kinds of strategies the program will focus on over the course of the intervention. Although it is difficult to compare very narrow interventions that focus on just one strategy to more general programs that include a number of different strategies, Hattie et al. (1996) do suggest that what they called unistructural interventions that taught only one specific strategy (often the use of a mnemonic) had the largest effect on student performance. In contrast, more general multistrategy programs had somewhat weaker, but still reasonable effects on performance (Hattie et al., 1996). Studies that taught only one specific strategy were more likely to be experimental studies and have less generalizability to general instructional programs given their narrow range and focus, but they do suggest for any intervention the importance of having clearly defined target strategies. Given the college context, we think that there is a need for multistrategy programs that target a larger range of strategies than just one or two basic strategies, but the analyses of Hattie et al. (1996) suggest a need to place some limits on the scope of any multistrategy program in order to avoid too much dilution of the intervention. In line with this suggestion, Pressley and Woloshyn (1995) note the importance of teaching, modeling, and practicing a few strategies at a time in order for students to learn how to use them most effectively.

In thinking about limitations on the scope of a program, it is important to consider not only how many different types of strategies to teach, but also which ones. The content of a program can vary greatly, ranging from emphasizing general memory and learning strategies to general intellectual and problem-solving skills as well as domain-specific strategies (e.g., strategies specific to mathematics) and motivational strategies (e.g., adaptive attributions). Given that a program cannot teach all of these different strategies within in a limited timeframe, choices have to be made by program designers. Hattie et al. (1996) report that programs with three content thrusts—including (1) memory skills; (2) structural aids or various cognitive and metacognitive strategies for planning, summarizing, elaborating, and organizing material; and (3) adaptive attributions—have good outcomes in their meta-analysis. At the same time, they suggest the need for caution in the generalization of these results given that some of the effect sizes for these three content areas are based on only one or two studies.

From our perspective, however, this emphasis on general cognitive and metacognitive strategies as well as motivational strategies (i.e., adaptive attributions) is in line with our own research on the importance of considering both motivation and cognition in models of self-regulated learning

(Garcia & Pintrich, 1994; Pintrich, 1989; Pintrich & De Groot, 1990; Pintrich & Schrauben, 1992; Wolters, Yu, & Pintrich, 1996). In addition, it parallels other models of self-regulated learning such as the *good strategy user model* of Pressley and his colleagues (e.g., Pressley, Borkowski, & Schneider, 1987, 1989; Pressley, Harris, & Marks, 1992; Pressley & Woloshyn, 1995), social-cognitive models of self-regulated learning (Schunk & Zimmerman, 1994b), and strategic learning models and programs (e.g., Weinstein, 1994a, 1994b; Weinstein & Underwood, 1985). Finally, it coincides with recent reviews of college learning skills programs (e.g., Simpson et al., 1997) regarding the importance of integrating both cognitive and motivational strategies as the focus for an intervention. Accordingly, we would suggest that multistrategy programs that teach more than one or two strategies include a range of cognitive, metacognitive, and motivational strategies in order that students will have both the "skill" and the "will" to use the strategies properly.

The timeframe of an intervention obviously sets constraints on the scope and content of a program. A program of a few weeks or a short-term experimental intervention cannot possibly teach the range of cognitive, metacognitive, or motivational strategies that are important for self-regulated learning. Pressley and Woloshyn (1995) note that cognitive strategy instruction is a complex and time-consuming instructional task and probably cannot be done effectively in a few weeks or months. At the same time, their research has been based mainly in elementary schools and there are important developmental differences between elementary students' and college students' knowledge base, metacognition, and self-regulatory capabilities (Schneider & Pressley, 1989). Elementary students, who are just developing their general metacognitive knowledge about strategies as well as their general self-regulatory capabilities, would likely need more time and practice in the use of cognitive and metacognitive strategies than college students. It seems clear that for younger students strategy instruction programs should involve long-term programs that last longer than a few months.

In contrast, college students have developed some base of knowledge about strategies and some general regulatory strategies that may make it easier for them to benefit from strategy instruction, thereby decreasing the time needed for effective instruction. In this case, shorter-term intervention programs such as semester-long courses may be somewhat helpful (e.g., McKeachie, Pintrich, & Lin, 1985; Pintrich, McKeachie, & Lin, 1987; Simpson et al., 1997; Weinstein & Underwood, 1985). Of course, even many college students may have an impoverished or inaccurate knowledge base about strategies and their cognitive and self-regulatory strategies may be relatively ineffective or inefficient. However, even shorter-term programs can help college students develop their knowledge base and effective use of self-regulatory strategies because these programs can build on the general developmental principle that college students are much more likely to be capable of metacognition and self-regulation than younger students. In this sense, we think that a semester-long course at the college level (approximately 4 months in the United States) can be helpful in developing self-regulated learning in college students.

At the same time, however, there may also be a potential detrimental effect of the more developed knowledge base and strategy use of college students. That is, college students' knowledge base and strategy use may be relatively entrenched in their cognitive and behavioral repertoires through habitual use and relative success in their previous 12–13 years of elementary and secondary schooling. After all, college students have succeeded at some level in their K–12 education and have gone on to college; this may increase their confidence in their knowledge base and self-regulatory capabilities. In this sense, their implicit theory of learning in terms of their knowledge base and use of strategies may be difficult to change, analogous to the difficulties of conceptual change in a content domain (Pintrich, Marx, & Boyle, 1993). Even with the disequilibrium of often receiving lower grades in college in comparison to high school, college students may not believe they need to change their strategies for learning. Following this logic, it may be harder to change college students' knowledge base about strategies and their actual strategy use in comparison to younger students. In fact, in Hattie et al.'s (1996) meta-analysis, they found that college and university students benefited less from learning skills programs than students in K–12 settings. It is not clear from their meta-analysis if these results are due to developmental differences in the students or to characteristics of the interventions at the different age levels, but it does suggest the need to consider time or length of program in relation to the age and experience of the students.

Integrated versus Adjunct Course Design

The time or length of program is related to a second important general issue concerning the design of intervention programs, that is, stand-alone or adjunct course programs versus integrated programs. Adjunct course interventions offer learning strategy instruction as a separate course at the postsecondary level, and at the secondary level the content may be taught as a separate "study skills" course or a separate unit within English or social studies courses. In contrast, integrated programs attempt to embed or infuse strategy instruction throughout the curriculum (e.g., Gaskins & Elliot, 1991). By embedding strategy instruction in the curriculum, integrated programs communicate to students that general cognitive and self-regulatory strategies can be useful in many contexts, not just in a study skills course, increasing the likelihood that students will not just perceive strategies as something to be learned for a study skills course and then forgotten. In addition, by using strategies in many different contexts and across different types of tasks and content areas, integrated programs increase the probability that transfer of strategies will occur (Salomon & Perkins, 1989; Simpson et al., 1997).

Although there is not much research comparing integrated versus adjunct programs directly using experimental or quasi-experimental designs, it seems to us that integrated programs would be the most useful at the elementary and secondary levels. As noted above, there may be developmental differences between younger and older students that make it more productive and easier to adopt an integrated program at the elementary level. However, we also believe that there are very pragmatic reasons why integrated programs may be easier to implement at the elementary level. First, elementary teachers teach all subject areas and spend 4–6 hours per day (for 180 days per year in the United States) with their students, allowing them more time and opportunity to teach not just content knowledge but also general strategies for learning. In addition, there is research to suggest that elementary teachers' beliefs about their role as teachers reflect an emphasis on teaching for learning and development in contrast to secondary school teachers' beliefs that they are mainly responsible for teaching content-specific knowledge and subject areas (Calderhead, 1996). These beliefs may make it easier for elementary teachers to see the value of teaching general strategies and be more likely to attempt to teach them. Given this confluence of time, opportunity, and supportive beliefs about teaching and learning, it seems to us that it would be easier to implement integrated programs at the elementary level.

In contrast, in our experience working with college faculty the vast majority perceive the main instructional goal to be the teaching of discipline-specific content (e.g., chemistry facts, historical trends) and discipline-specific strategies (e.g., algorithms for solving differential equations), not the teaching of general strategies for learning and self-regulation. In fact, we agree with these instructors that this should be their main instructional goal given their expertise in their discipline, their lack of knowledge about self-regulated learning, their lack of expertise on how to teach for it, the general departmental curriculum and expectations, and the limited amount of class time they have with their students (on average about 3–4 hours per week per course in the United States). Given these constraints, it may be more difficult to implement integrated programs at the college level. At the same time, we do believe that there are college students who could benefit from some knowledge about and practice in the use of various learning and regulatory strategies. Accordingly, in our own work we have used an adjunct course format. The decision to use an integrated versus adjunct approach is not a simple one, and designers will have to consider the age level of the students and the contextual constraints operating in the school or college in terms of faculty knowledge, beliefs, skills, and motivation for strategy instruction, as well as departmental and curricular concerns.

The Issue of Transfer

Of course, although it may be easier to implement at the college level, one of the main drawbacks to an adjunct course concerns transfer of learning, which is the third general issue to consider in the design of any intervention program. The issue of transfer is an age-old problem (Cox, 1997; Salomon & Perkins, 1989), and we will not discuss in detail all the issues regarding transfer. However, in terms of an integrated versus adjunct course, an integrated approach may increase the probability of transfer because the students have the opportunity to learn the various strategies in a number of different course contexts, across different content areas, and across different types of academic tasks (Pressley & Woloshyn, 1995; Simpson et al., 1997). In this way, an integrated approach may be promoting transfer through the "low-road" manner (Salomon & Perkins, 1989) by providing practice across different domains and tasks in the hope that students may automatize their use of strategies through this varied practice. This may be especially true for integrated programs at the elementary level, which can provide students with practice across all major content areas in the curriculum (Gaskins & Elliot, 1991). In contrast, an integrated approach at the college level, where instruction in learning strategies is embedded in the context of a regular disciplinary course (e.g., chemistry, history, sociology), still faces the same problem of students learning strategies in one context (e.g., a chemistry course) and having to learn to transfer them to other disciplinary courses (Simpson et al., 1997). The problem of transfer is somewhat different in this case from that of transfer from an adjunct course, where students must transfer from a learning strategies course to all other disciplinary courses, but there are still issues of transfer for integrated programs at the college level.

As Simpson et al. (1997) rightly point out, adjunct courses at the college level must facilitate transfer from the learning of general strategies in a specific learning to learn course to other disciplinary courses. First, they suggest that transfer can be facilitated by providing students with the declarative, procedural, and conditional knowledge about strategy use and how to adapt strategies flexibly to different goals, tasks, content areas, and classroom contexts. In more recent versions of adjunct courses (e.g., McKeachie et al., 1985; Pintrich et al., 1987; Weinstein, 1994a; Weinstein & Underwood, 1985) this is a specific goal of these learning to learn courses, in contrast to older versions of study skills courses that often focused on the rigid application of certain learning or study strategies. Second, Simpson et al. (1997) note that adjunct courses can facilitate transfer by providing students with practice on a variety of different types of academic tasks from different content areas. Finally, in line with the "high road" transfer idea (Salomon & Perkins, 1989), adjunct courses can increase the probability of transfer by encouraging students to be metacognitive and reflective about their strategy use not just in the learning to learn course, but also in other disciplinary courses. Although transfer may be more difficult in adjunct courses than in integrated programs, these three general suggestions can increase the probability of transfer, and the issue of transfer is a concern for all strategy interventions, regardless of format.

Characteristics of College Students

As noted above, there are some important differences between elementary students and college students that can influence the implementation of a strategy intervention program. Of course, in terms of general cognitive development college students and high school students should have better capabilities for metacognition and self-regulation than younger students (Pintrich, 1990; Wigfield, Eccles, & Pintrich, 1996). This does not mean that older students and even adults cannot benefit from strategy instruction (Schneider & Pressley, 1989), but because older students have more of the language, concepts, and experience with and about learning and thinking, it may make the teaching about and discussion of cognition and metacognition easier. At the same time, as noted previously, college students may be more entrenched in their use of certain strategies given their prior experience. Accordingly, although it may be easier to talk about strategies with college students in a strategy instruction program, it may be harder to get them to *change* their actual use of strategies in comparison to younger students, who may not be so committed to the use of certain strategies.

Besides these general developmental differences between younger and older students, there are differences within the college population that can influence the effectiveness of strategy instruction programs. For example, in our work at Michigan we have found that our Learning to Learn course seems to require a reasonable level of basic reading skills (i.e., basic decoding skills, reading comprehension at a secondary level) and that without these basic skills students do not do well in our class in terms of grades (McKeachie et al., 1985). Our course does not focus on these functional reading skills, and for students who are struggling with decoding and basic comprehension problems, strategy instruction that focuses on general learning strategies may not be the most useful for them. As Simpson et al. (1997) note, these underprepared students may need more directed assistance with their reading and writing skills through a variety of programs such as "developmental" courses in reading and writing, tutoring, learning assistance centers, and computer-assisted instruction.

The implication is that even within the college population students have different characteristics that can interact with the strategy instruction program as in any aptitude-treatment interaction design (Corno & Snow, 1986; Snow, Corno, & Jackson, 1996). The types of students that are admitted to the University of Michigan (McKeachie et al., 1985) or the University of Texas (Weinstein & Underwood, 1985) are very different in general aptitude, reading skills, knowledge, and past history of academic success than students who may be seeking academic assistance at a comprehensive university or a community college. For example, students in an early version of the Learning to Learn course at Michigan had a combined average Verbal and Quantitative SAT of 997, below the average 1,100–1,200 SAT for a Michigan undergraduate (McKeachie et al., 1985), but probably about average for most college students. In contrast, students at a community college may have a quite different pattern of aptitude, knowledge, and skills and need somewhat different kinds of interventions. As well, there are certainly many within-group differences among university and community college students. In any event, this variance in college students suggests that there is not one right way, method, or program to help college students become self-regulated learners. The intervention will have to be adapted to the characteristics of the students and the local contextual demands. With this caveat in mind, we now turn to a description of our general conceptual framework for our intervention at the University of Michigan.

CONCEPTUAL FRAMEWORK FOR INTERVENTION TO TEACH SELF-REGULATED LEARNING

Our conceptual framework is based on a general social-cognitive model of motivation and cognition that emphasizes the importance of integrating both motivational and cognitive components of learning (Garcia & Pintrich, 1994; Pintrich, 1989; Pintrich & De Groot, 1990; Pintrich & Garcia, 1991; Pintrich & Schrauben, 1992; Pintrich, Smith, Garcia, & McKeachie, 1993; Pintrich, Wolters & Baxter, in press; Wolters et al., 1996). We have refined our general conceptual model based on both theoretical and empirical considerations since our earlier work on teaching college students to be self-regulating learners (McKeachie et al., 1985; Pintrich et al., 1987). Nevertheless, our focus has been and continues to be on building an integrated model of student academic learning that includes both motivational and cognitive components of learning.

In our current model (Garcia & Pintrich, 1994), we propose that there are two general organizing constructs, (1) knowledge/beliefs and (2) strategies used for regulation, and two general domains, cognitive and motivational. Crossing the domains and constructs results in a simple two-by-two matrix that forms four cells, cognitive knowledge/beliefs, cognitive and metacognitive strategies for regulation, motivational or self-knowledge/ beliefs, and motivational strategies for regulation. These cells are obviously intertwined as students engage in classroom activities, but they can be separated conceptually. The content of these cells serve as the focus of the course at Michigan. For this chapter, we focus on describing the knowledge and use of cognitive strategies together and then turn to self-knowledge and use of motivational strategies.

Knowledge and Use of Cognitive and Regulatory Learning Strategies

These cognitive and regulatory strategies are the various tools and methods that individuals may use to regulate their learning. Students need to have both the declarative knowledge about these strategies (*what* the various strategies are) as well as the procedural knowledge of *how* to use them. Finally, students also should have the conditional knowledge of *when* and *why* to use these various strategies depending on their goals, the academic tasks they confront, and the classroom context (Garcia & Pintrich, 1994; McKeachie et al., 1985; Paris, Lipson, & Wixson, 1983).

Cognitive Learning Strategies

In terms of cognitive learning strategies, we have followed the work of Weinstein and Mayer (1986) and identified *rehearsal, elaboration,* and *organizational* strategies as important cognitive strategies that are related to academic performance in the classroom (McKeachie, et al., 1985; Pintrich, 1989; Pintrich & De Groot, 1990). Regarding the first set of strategies, there are a number of different techniques available that students might use for basic memory tasks including rehearsal, as well as clustering, imagery, and use of mnemonic techniques (see Schneider & Pressley, 1989; Weinstein & Mayer, 1986). Rehearsal strategies involve reciting items to be learned or saying words aloud as one reads a piece of text. Highlighting or underlining text in a rather passive and unreflective manner also can be more like a rehearsal strategy than an elaborative strategy. These rehearsal strategies are assumed to help the student attend to and select important information from lists or texts and keep this information active in working memory. Although we do discuss these types of rehearsal strategies in our course, we suggest that they may have limited utility for the more complex tasks that are often required in college courses. We also discuss various imagery or mnemonic techniques but again note that they may only be relevant to basic memory tasks and that most college courses require more than just memory for information.

In contrast, we spend more time in the course on knowledge and use of various elaborative and organizational strategies. Elaborative strategies include paraphrasing or summarizing the material to be learned, creating analogies, generative note taking (where the student actually reorganizes and connects ideas in their notes in contrast to passive, linear note taking), explaining the ideas in the material to be learned to someone else, and asking and answering questions (Weinstein & Mayer, 1986). The other general type of deeper processing strategy, organizational, includes behaviors such as selecting the main idea from text, outlining the text or material to be learned, and the use of a variety of specific techniques for selecting and organizing the ideas in the material (e.g., sketching a network or map of the important ideas, identifying the prose or expository structures of texts). These strategies usually result in a deeper understanding of the material to be learned in contrast to rehearsal strategies (Weinstein & Mayer, 1986), and we discuss this type of research finding with our students.

Metacognitive and Self-Regulatory Strategies

Besides cognitive strategies, students' metacognitive knowledge and use of metacognitive strategies can have an important influence upon their achievement. There are two general aspects of metacognition, knowledge about cognition and self-regulation of cognition (Brown, Bransford, Ferrara, & Campione, 1983; Flavell, 1979). Some of the theoretical and empirical confusion over the status of metacognition as a psychological construct has been fostered by the confounding of issues of metacognitive knowledge and awareness with metacognitive control and self-regulation (Brown et al., 1983; Garcia & Pintrich, 1994; Paris & Winograd, 1990; Pintrich et al., in press). We consider knowledge about strategy (what kinds of strategies are available to use) and task variables (what aspects of tasks influence performance, i.e., a recall task vs. a recognition task) as part of metacognitive knowledge, but self-knowledge we classify as part of the motivational or self-knowledge cell (discussed below). Metacognitive control or self-regulatory strategies then include the actual strategies that students might use to monitor, control, and regulate their cognition and learning (Garcia & Pintrich, 1994).

Most models of metacognitive control or self-regulatory strategies include three general types of strategies—planning, monitoring, and regulating (cf. Corno, 1986; Zimmerman & Martinez-Pons, 1986)—and our model is no different (see Garcia & Pintrich, 1994; Pintrich, 1989; Pintrich & De Groot, 1990; Pintrich & Garcia, 1991; Pintrich, Smith, et al., 1993). Planning activities that have been investigated in various studies of students' learning include setting goals for studying, skimming a text before reading, generating questions before reading a text, and doing a task analysis of the problem. These activities seem to help learners plan their use of cognitive strategies and also seem to activate or prime relevant aspects of prior knowledge, making the organization and comprehension of the material much easier. Learners that report using these types of planning activities seem to perform better on a variety of academic tasks in comparison to students who do not use these strategies (Brown et al., 1983; McKeachie et al., 1985; Zimmerman, 1989).

Monitoring one's thinking and academic behavior is an essential aspect of self-regulated learning. Weinstein and Mayer (1986) see all metacognitive activities as partly the monitoring of comprehension. Monitoring activities include tracking of attention while reading a text or listening to a lecture, self-testing through the use of questions about the text material to check for understanding, monitoring comprehension of a lecture, and the use of test-taking strategies (e.g., monitoring speed and adjusting to time available) in an exam situation. These various monitoring strategies alert the learner to breakdowns in attention or comprehension that can then be subjected to repair through the use of regulating strategies. This is an important emphasis in our course because if students do not monitor their attention and comprehension, it is unlikely that they will even see the need for regulating or changing their cognition and behavior (Butler & Winne, 1995; Pintrich et al., in press; Winne, 1996). This type of self-reflective practice in learning is important to all models of self-regulated learning. Students must monitor and assess their learning in order to regulate it.

Regulation strategies are closely tied to monitoring strategies. For example, as learners ask themselves questions as they read in order to monitor their comprehension, and then go back and reread a portion of the text, this rereading is a regulatory strategy. Another type of self-regulatory strategy for reading occurs when a student slows the pace of their reading when confronted with more difficult or less familiar text. Of course, reviewing any aspect of course material (e.g., lecture notes, texts, lab material, previous exams and papers, etc.) that one does not remember or understand well while studying for an exam reflects a general self-regulatory strategy. During a test, skipping questions and returning to them later is another strategy that students can use to regulate their behavior during an exam. All these strategies are assumed to improve learning by helping students correct their studying behavior and repair deficits in their understanding. Again, we try to demonstrate for students the utility of using these various self-regulatory strategies by discussing the research in this area as well as presenting class demonstrations and labs on the value and utility of these strategies.

The final aspect in our model of learning and self-regulatory strategies, resource management strategies, concerns strategies that students use to manage their environment such as their time, their study environment, and others including teachers and peers (cf. Corno, 1986; Zimmerman &

Martinez-Pons, 1986). In line with a general adaptive approach to learning, we assume that these resource management strategies help students adapt to their environment as well as change the environment to fit their goals and needs. The resource management strategies that we have focused on in our research include time and study environment and help seeking.

Students' management of their time and the actual place they choose to study are not cognitive or metacognitive strategies that may have a direct influence on eventual learning, but they are general strategies that can help or hinder the students' efforts at completing the academic task (Zimmerman, Greenberg, & Weinstein, 1994). In the same fashion, students who know when, how, and from whom to seek help (see Newman, 1994) should be more likely to be successful than those students who do not seek help appropriately. Again, we find that many college students need assistance in thinking about how to manage their time and seek help. In our course we discuss general issues of time management, but the emphasis is on various ways to organize time, rather than one rigid schedule for work. In terms of help seeking, we discuss the utility of study groups and peer learning, but highlight the importance of managing these groups to keep them focused on academic learning rather than social activities.

Self-Knowledge and Use of Motivational Strategies

In keeping with our general model of integrating motivation and cognition, besides these cognitive strategies, we also discuss the role of motivation in learning. In particular, we highlight the importance of self-knowledge in terms of knowing about strengths and weaknesses as a learner, self-efficacy for various academic tasks and disciplines, as well as general goal orientation to learning, and personal interest and value for academic tasks (Garcia & Pintrich, 1994). In terms of motivational strategies, we discuss the importance of adaptive attributional patterns and of avoiding self-handicapping strategies such as procrastination in order to protect self-worth (Covington, 1992).

In terms of self-knowledge, as part of a general emphasis on monitoring and the importance of knowledge about their strengths and weaknesses as learners, we want students to become aware of their own strategies for learning and motivation and their relative effectiveness. It is through this type of self-knowledge that students may be better able to adjust their learning and make appropriate changes in their use of strategies (Butler & Winne, 1995). For example, for students to know that they basically rely on rehearsal strategies, which may have limited utility for learning, is important self-knowledge. This self-knowledge may motivate them to change their reliance on rehesrsal strategies. In addition, we also highlight the importance of knowing which types of strategies may be better suited to personal goals or preferences. For example, some students may prefer the use of organizational strategies such as concept mapping in their attempts to organize the text material. Other students may not like this type of visual display of information and material and may prefer more text-based (paraphrasing) or outlining strategies. Again, we stress that this type of self-knowledge about preferences combined with knowledge about the relative effectiveness of different strategies can help students to become more flexible and self-regulating learners, rather than students who attempt to apply newly learned strategies rigidly to all tasks and situations. Again, we see this as an important aspect of self-reflective practice in learning.

Besides self-knowledge, we also discuss the role of self-efficacy beliefs and anxiety (or self-doubt) in learning. Self-efficacy beliefs in this context refer to students' judgments of their capabilities to perform academic tasks (Schunk, 1991). We assume that these beliefs are relatively situation specific in line with self-efficacy theory (e.g., Bandura, 1986), but we do discuss these beliefs in terms of some general efficacy beliefs about different domains (e.g., self-efficacy for math) or tasks (e.g., studying for tests), given that we cannot discuss every learning situation or academic task the students will encounter in their academic career. In keeping with our general social-cognitive model we also assume that self-efficacy is not a trait or relatively stable characteristic of the student, but that it can be changed and regulated like other strategies (Schunk, 1994). In this way, we try to communicate to students that they can change their self-efficacy beliefs and that their capabilities are incremental, not entity-like (Dweck & Leggett, 1988). Many students in the course reported that they began college with unrealistically high levels of self-efficacy for their courses, based on high achievement in secondary school, often accomplished with little effort. With repeated poor performance, these students' self-efficacy had decreased, and in enrolling in Learning to Learn these students sought to improve their performance and self-efficacy.

At the same time, however, we stress the importance of having relatively *accurate* perceptions of competence, rather than either extremely low perceptions of efficacy, which are known to be debilitating for learning and performance, or very optimistic and unrealistically high perceptions of efficacy (Pintrich & Schunk, 1996). In terms of our model of self-regulated learning, we think it is important for students to have accurate perceptions of their competence in order to provide appropriate baseline information for judgments of learning. That is, if students are relatively accurate about what they can and cannot do, then they are more likely to be able to use this information to make reasonable changes in their use of learning strategies. In contrast, if students are overly confident about their capabilities to learn, then they may assume that their current learning strategies and study habits are fine and do not need improvement. This emphasis on accurate and realistic self-assessment is in contrast to general programs to boost students' self-esteem or self-worth, which are often not based on students' actual performance. We strongly believe that accurate self-perceptions, coupled with incremental beliefs about the possibility of change, are much more propaedeutic for learning than overoptimistic and general feelings of self-esteem, which can actually be misleading and ultimately detrimental to learning (Pintrich & Schunk, 1996).

As part of this discussion on self-efficacy, we also discuss test anxiety and the kinds of self-doubts and worries that often arise in testing situations. Although we consider test anxiety as a separate construct from self-efficacy, there are usually two subcomponents of test anxiety discussed in the literature, worry and emotionality. The worry component is more cognitive and involves the "self-perturbing ideations" (Bandura, 1986) that arise in testing situations, which can often spiral out of control and disrupt attention and performance (e.g., "Oh, I don't know this one question, I'm going to flunk this test, which means I will flunk the course, and then I'll be kicked out of school."). These worrisome thoughts are related to self-efficacy beliefs, but even students with good efficacy beliefs often become nervous and anxious in a testing situation and can have these disruptive thoughts about themselves and their performance. In our course we try to suggest various test-taking strategies (e.g., working on easier parts of a test first, skipping items and returning to them later if the answer is not forthcoming) that can help students regain control of their thinking and avoid these distracting thoughts (Hill & Wigfield, 1984). In addition, these strategies might be useful for controlling the general negative affect and emotions that can arise in testing situations.

Besides efficacy and anxiety, we also discuss with students their interest in and value for different courses. Interest is assumed to be students' personal interest in the course content, not just their situational interest that is aroused by features of the class or the course content (Hidi, 1990; Schiefele, 1991). Value concerns students' perceptions of the importance and utility of the course content for them, given their goals (Garcia & Pintrich, 1994). We do not assume that all students should develop a personal interest in or high value and utility for all their college courses; rather, we adopt a realistic perspective that suggests that they will have to take some required courses for which their personal interest and value are low. However, we attempt to point out that in these cases the need for self-regulation of their effort and learning may be higher in contrast to those cases where personal interest and value are high (Pintrich & Schrauben, 1992; Sansone, Weir, Harpster, & Morgan, 1992). Again, armed with some self-knowledge of their own interests and values, as well as the relations between interest and value and their learning, we hope that the students will recognize the need for more strategic and self-regulated learning in different courses.

The final aspect of motivational knowledge we discuss is the general distinction between mastery or learning goals, and performance or extrinsic goals. We define these approaches along the lines of goal orientation theory (e.g., Ames, 1992; Dweck & Leggett, 1988; Maehr & Midgley, 1991) where mastery goals define an orientation where the student is focused on learning and mastering the material and seeking self-improvement. In contrast, under an extrinsic orientation, the student is more focused on getting grades for approval from others, seeking rewards, or besting others. There is some work to suggest that there is a need to distinguish between an extrinsic goal orientation concerned with grades and rewards and a relative ability orientation that stresses competing with and besting others (e.g., Pintrich & Garcia, 1991; Wolters et al., 1996).

In general the research suggests that adopting a mastery goal orientation has a positive relation to both motivational and cognitive outcomes as well as overall performance (Ames, 1992; Pintrich & Schunk, 1996). Accordingly, we encourage students to adopt a mastery orientation to their college work. At the same time, however, there is some evidence to suggest that at least for college students adopting an extrinsic goal (at least caring about grades) in the absence of intrinsic goals for learning can be positively related to the use of self-regulated learning strategies and performance (Pintrich & Garcia, 1991). Again, adopting a realistic perspective, we know that grades are a fact of life in college classrooms and that they do have implications for future career options. We do not encourage students to ignore grades, but we try to help them see the role of grades in context and to avoid an overreliance on grades as their "defining" goal for college courses.

Although there are a number of different motivational strategies that students can adopt in the classroom (Garcia & Pintrich, 1994), we focus on the role of attributions in our course. Attributional theory and research (Weiner, 1986) have demonstrated repeatedly the important role that students' attributions for their success and failure play in their future motivation and performance. In particular, it appears that, in the case of failure, attributions to effort or strategy use, rather than innate ability, are especially adaptive (Borkowski, Weyhing, & Carr, 1988; Pintrich & Schunk, 1996; Weiner, 1986). That is, if students attribute their failure to lack of effort or lack of strategies, these attributions are usually perceived as controllable, internal, and unstable, and hence offer the possibility that they can be changed for future tasks. Although we do not do formal attributional retraining (see Foersterling, 1985), we do discuss attributional theory and the general attributional principles that can be used by students to regulate their motivation. We now turn to a discussion of how this conceptual framework is actually implemented at Michigan.

IMPLEMENTATION OF LEARNING TO LEARN INTERVENTION

Description

Learning to Learn is an introductory-level undergraduate course offered through the Department of Psychology at the University of Michigan. It was first taught in the fall semester in 1982. The course fulfills a university distribution requirement for the social sciences, and there are no prerequisites for enrollment.

The goals of this course as presented to students are twofold. The first goal is to teach students basic concepts of cognitive and motivational psychology. We explain to students that they already have a good deal of experience in learning and thinking, but they probably have not thought much about how they go about these processes. An introduction to cognitive psychology can help them understand the mental processes involved in the activities of learning, memory, and problem solving. In addition, by understanding the basic processes of cognition and motivation, we hope that this will help them build their conditional knowledge about when and why to use various strategies.

The second, arguably more important goal is to have students apply these concepts to their own learning at the university. The course aims to increase students' effectiveness as learners by helping them to develop a repertoire of learning and regulatory strategies that will be useful to them in their college courses and beyond. In addition, we hope that students will reflect on their own learning as they attempt to apply the concepts. As the concept of lifelong learning has become increasingly important in education, our rationale is that good teaching involves teaching students how to learn, how to remember and think, and how to motivate themselves as self-regulating and self-reflective learners (Weinstein & Mayer, 1986).

Students

The course is targeted to first- and second-year students who have experienced difficulty in their first semester or year of university coursework, although it is open to anyone who enrolls. Students enroll from all colleges in the university, and the demand for the course has exceeded its enrollment capacity each semester the course has been offered.

Academic advisers counsel some students to register for the course, whereas other students simply select the class on their own. Students who enroll are usually those who are disappointed in their academic performance, want to develop more effective learning skills, and see the need to address this prior to beginning more advanced coursework in their major area of study. Given the self-selecting nature of enrollment, students range from those on academic probation to those who have interpreted their first "B" as an indicator of academic trouble. Among those with genuine difficulty, the reasons are varied: Some lack adequate high school preparation, some are simply overwhelmed by the freedom to manage their own lives and have accorded academic work too low a priority to succeed at it, a few have previously undiagnosed disabilities, and others find that the learning strategies that worked in high school are ineffective in their college classes.

Students in the course often falter in self-regulation on both a micro- and macrolevel. They may be poor at monitoring and assessing their learning as they read, study, work problems, and prepare for tests, and they lack practice in reflecting on and modifying their own learning strategies accordingly. But they also experience problems in self-regulation in a larger sense, as many may have been *other-regulated* by parents or teachers who provided the incentive structures and support that made academic achievement possible in high school, but now find that their ability to self-regulate their own time, effort, and motivation is rather poorly developed. Thus the issue of resource management becomes a focus for many. This range of students in the course and the variety of needs presented provide enormous challenges in course design, pedagogy, and content.

Course Format

The course is 4 semester credit hours, and involves 4 hours of scheduled class time each week, 2 in lecture and 2 in a laboratory/discussion section format. The entire class, comprised of 75–100 students, meets for two 1-hour lectures led by the professor of the course. Principles, concepts, and research findings in cognitive psychology are presented in the lectures. In addition, smaller groups of 20–25 students meet once a week for a laboratory section led by a graduate student instructor. The laboratories provide the link between the concepts presented in lecture and the students' own learning, with demonstrations, group work, and activities designed to enhance application and practice in self-reflective and self-regulated learning.

Course Topics

As has been noted in the previous section, the overarching theme of the course is for students to become self-regulating and self-reflective learners. Accordingly, one of the desired outcomes of the course is for students to take control of their learning by becoming more self-reflective and strategic in their learning processes. The class provides students with exposure to theories of student learning and motivation, a broad array of strategies and the rationale and context for their use, practice in applying these strategies, and opportunities for reflection on this practice. A few of the specific areas of attention and their application are described below as illustrations of course topics.

Information Processing

We teach students about the information-processing model of human memory including the capacity and processes involved in sensory memory, working memory, and long-term memory. We include several demonstrations to highlight how memory is affected by a number of variables, some that enhance retention and some that promote forgetting. We emphasize that meaningfulness of the material particularly affects how well it is learned and remembered. For example, in a short in-class experiment, half of the students are given the topic sentence of a passage that is then read aloud, while the other half has no context for the passage. Afterwards, students are asked to recall as much of the passage as they can, with the results demonstrating how knowing the context of target information aids comprehension and recall. Relatedly, we teach students about the use of concept maps to organize course information. We demonstrate how organizing information into a hierarchical framework facilitates recall. In similar ways, students learn the value of elaboration and organizational strategies and of connecting new material to prior knowledge.

Note Taking

In one in-class activity, pairs of students examine the notes they have taken in two of their classes, both Learning to Learn and their *target course*, a course selected by each student in which they specifically apply and reflect on the strategies and principles from Learning to Learn. The students discuss similarities and differences in the type of note taking represented, as well as the rationale for the different styles. Students then rewrite a portion of their notes so that the material will be better organized and ready for use in studying for an exam. We emphasize to the students that the point is not that they should spend their time rewriting all of their lecture notes, but that they should practice better note-taking technique so that it will become more automatized, and they can elaborate on their notes while studying. Students are also given practice in the Cornell note-taking system (Pauk, 1993), using a two-column note method for the further elaboration of ideas after class.

Test Taking and Preparation

We routinely have students generate possible exam questions, and both the writing and the answering of other students' questions are used as a means of review before exams. We provide a practice multiple-choice exam that consists of nonsense phrases, which helps make the structure of the activity more transparent, and use this to discuss test-taking strategies. Similarly, we provide opportunities for improving skills on essay tests. Students respond in writing to an essay question pertinent to the Learning to Learn course, and then are given a set of anonymous answers to read, evaluate, and rank. They then identify characteristics that distinguish better responses from the others. In small groups students compare their rankings, critically examine the responses, and consider how even the best answer in their selection might be improved. The class then discusses a range of issues in writing effective essay responses, such as addressing all parts of the question, understanding the difference between analysis and reporting, omitting irrelevant filler information, and so forth. Students then rewrite their essays, and both versions are submitted for feedback by the graduate student instructors.

Goal Setting

In order to help students break larger goals into more manageable ones, we have them identify several of their goals, from distal to more proximal goals. For example, we ask them to identify two goals they have for each of the following: life, college, semester, course, next week, and today. We encourage students to focus on what they could be doing now in order to work toward their larger goals, and to attribute their successes and failures along the way to their own effort or strategies. We want students to view their performance outcomes as internal and controllable, and to see that taking a course such as Learning to Learn represents one way they are taking steps to reach their goals.

Time Management

During one 2-day period during the course, all students are expected to keep a log of their daily activities. Using a grid with hour-long blocks, students indicate when they are engaged in various activities: sleeping, attending class, studying, socializing, watching television, eating, and so forth. Students bring these logs to the laboratory and share them with partners; following what they have learned in lecture about time management, students serve as consultants to one another, assessing current patterns of time use and strategizing alternatives. The outcome of this activity is for each individual to develop a tentative, flexible guide for their weekly study, with the knowledge that the relative attention paid to a particular class would shift depending on course requirements throughout the term, such as exams and paper assignments. This activity enables students to reflect on current time use practices, to assess their effectiveness, to develop better regulatory strategies, and to regain a sense of personal control over their own schedule, with tools for future monitoring and revision.

Additional course topics (cooperative learning, motivational strategies, etc.) are treated in similar fashion, with the lecture and textbook providing theoretical frameworks for the self-reflective activities that take place in the laboratory section and in homework assignments. Where possible, topics are revisited to provide for continued monitoring and reflection on practice. For example, student note-taking practices are addressed again later in the term to assess the effectiveness of techniques learned in class, and class examinations are used as a continuing vehicle for reflection on study strategies. Discussions of motivational strategies are included throughout the class, beginning on the first day with administration of the self-scoring version of the Motivated Strategies for Learning Questionnaire (MSLQ; Pintrich, Smith, et al., 1993), with the key concepts illuminated further in lectures and then illustrated in student role plays later in the course.

Course Materials and Requirements

Textbooks

There have been two textbooks used in the course. The primary text is a cognitive psychology textbook (Matlin, 1994), which presents theories and research on the cognitive processes in learning. In general, we have found that a cognitive psychology textbook is often difficult for students who have not had introductory psychology, although the applied nature of the course does make the material more explicable to these students than it might be otherwise. We supplement this textbook with a practical study skills book (Pauk, 1993). Although this book is easy for students to read and provides specific suggestions that students find useful, it is generally atheoretical in presentation. The course is in need of a textbook that presents principles of cognitive psychology along with practical learning strategies and applications based on theory. The ideal textbook would introduce the theoretical concepts to those with little or no background in psychology.

Examinations

Student understanding of material in the textbooks, lectures, and labs is usually tested with two short quizzes, two midterm examinations, and a final examination in the course. These assessments are comprised of multiple-choice, short answer, and essay questions and involve increasing difficulty and demands. Lab sessions include attention to cognitive strategies and metacognitive processes applicable to test taking, and demonstrations of the effectiveness and value of various study strategies. Throughout the course the length and difficulty of the assessments increases progressively, presumably becoming more challenging for students. Grades on these assessments as well as other course requirements are not competitive or "curved." Accordingly, students are encouraged to learn from their classmates and to help them learn as well.

Research Project

Students work in groups of three to five to develop, conduct, and write up an empirical research project during the course of the semester. Students also present their completed research to their laboratory sections in short oral reports. There are three main goals for the research project. The first is to give students hands-on experience in the way psychologists conduct research. The research projects are focused on learning and studying issues, so the projects generate data that help students see the relative advantages and disadvantages of different ways of learning, thereby increasing their conditional knowledge. The second goal is to have students elaborate and apply ideas from the course in planning their own project. The third goal is to give students practice in learning cooperatively with other students in a situation where attention is given to group process and to the skills necessary for effective groupwork.

Topics for the research projects focus on some aspect of learning and generally take the form of small experiments, surveys, or observational studies. For example, in one particular study, students compared rehearsal strategies to elaborative strategies for their relative effectiveness. In another project, an observational study, students compared the number of distractions and off-task behavior that students engaged in while studying at several different libraries on campus. The projects students choose generally provide opportunities for students to reflect both on their own learning practices in light of existing research as well as on their skills in conducting collaborative research. Each research group conducts a midterm assessment of their effectiveness as a team, providing opportunities for midcourse corrections in group process, under the guidance of the instructors when needed.

Journal

Students keep an academic journal throughout the semester. Each week, students are provided with several guiding questions that prompt them to reflect on the readings, lecture, and lab and to integrate this course material with their own experience as a learner. Examples of guiding questions include the following: "Reflect on your test-taking preparation for this week's test. Describe how you studied for the exam. Based on how you did on the exam, and your reading of the text, identify how strategies you used worked or did not work for you, and describe those you might want to use in the future";

and "Under what conditions (or situations) has stress or anxiety impaired your efficiency? What can you do to reduce detrimental effects of stress or anxiety in these situations?" Students are also encouraged to write about any insights they may have about themselves as learners, such as changes they have made in their learning strategies or processes during a particular week. These assignments are designed to encourage habits of self-reflective practice in learning.

A primary focus of the journal is for students to report on their learning and motivation in their target course. While we anticipate that many of the strategies students acquire will benefit their learning in all of their courses, we also want students to identify a course where they will quite deliberately apply new strategies and report on their own progress in doing so. Students are expected to describe in their journals the specific strategies they utilize in their target course and the effects this has on their studying and performance.

The journal serves as a form of conversation between the student and the graduate student instructor. Several times during the semester, students turn in their journal entries, and the instructors provide written comments. In addition, each time before a set of entries is submitted, students trade their journals with another student in the class in order to give comments, reactions, suggestions, and support, and so that students may learn from each other's experiences. The journal was designed to encourage students' metacognitive thinking and self-regulation and to enhance their practice as self-reflective learners.

FUTURE DIRECTIONS FOR RESEARCH AND PRACTICE

At various points in the teaching of the Learning to Learn course we have conducted research about the effect of this intervention on the motivation and cognition of students enrolled in the course (e.g., Hofer, Yu, & Pintrich, 1997; McKeachie et al., 1985). This research has helped us refine both our conceptual model and our teaching of the course. The earlier research showed that the course had some influence on students' grade point average (GPA) and decreased the level of test anxiety and increased efficacy (McKeachie et al., 1985). More recently, when we assessed a fuller range of motivational and cognitive variables (Hofer et al., 1997), we found that students increased in their mastery orientation to learning, self-efficacy, and value and interest for the course, and decreased in test anxiety. In addition, they increased in their self-reported strategy use. More importantly, correlational analyses have shown that for students in the course, their motivational beliefs (mastery goals, efficacy, and interest and value) were positively correlated with their use of cognitive and self-regulatory strategies (Hofer et al., 1997). This is in line with our model regarding the importance of both motivational and cognitive components in self-regulated learning.

In general, in terms of the four main issues raised earlier in this chapter, our work suggests that an intervention that targets a range of cognitive and motivational components can have some utility for college students. Of course, most of our research conducted to date only concerns students' performance in a learning to learn course, and further research is needed on how these students fare in other courses in terms of transfer. However, our earlier work (McKeachie et al., 1985) and Weinstein's work (e.g., Weinstein & Underwood, 1985) suggest that there is some payoff in terms of overall GPA and performance in college. It does seem clear, however, from our results here and our previous correlational findings (e.g., Pintrich & Schrauben, 1992; Wolters et al., 1996) as well as others' (e.g., Borkowski, Carr, Rellinger, & Pressley, 1990; Pressley & Woloshyn, 1995) that motivational components are an important component and can help to facilitate students' use of various cognitive and self-regulatory strategies. Accordingly, we think that motivational issues should be addressed in any intervention designed to teach cognitive and self-regulatory strategies.

The second issue we raised concerned the use of an integrated versus adjunct course design. Our work has used only an adjunct course design, so we cannot offer empirical evidence in favor of one or the other. However, we think this issue may be more related to contextual constraints that operate in schools, regardless of the empirical evidence. We think there is utility to an adjunct approach, especially at the college level, where it is very unlikely that college faculty will be able to teach general learning and self-regulatory strategies in their discipline-specific courses. At the same time, there is clearly a need for adjunct interventions that focus on general strategies for at least some college students, if not all. However, there is still a need for research on how best to design adjunct courses in terms of the tasks and instructional strategies used in these courses. Simpson et al. (1997) suggest the need to design interventions around the types of tasks that different courses and disciplines use. This type of *contextualization* of the general strategy instruction should be useful for college students and help them in their efforts to transfer the strategies. However, there is a clear need for research on a taxonomy of different tasks in different disciplines and the types of strategies and knowledge they may require (Burrell, Tao, Simpson, & Mendez-Berrueta, 1997; Pintrich, 1994).

In terms of transfer, there are still many unanswered questions that arise in a discussion of teaching college students self-regulatory strategies. We do have evidence that there is some transfer of the general strategies, at least in terms of some small changes in GPA (e.g., McKeachie et al., 1985). However, we still have little information about the process of transfer, that is, how students think about using these strategies they learned in an adjunct course in other classes. This type of information is not easily obtainable with general self-report measures or global measures such as GPA or retention rates. There is a clear need for more process-oriented studies, which will probably involve more qualitative and ethnographic observations and interviews of students as they are enrolled in a learning to learn course as well as when they leave it. This type of research would involve in-depth analysis of students as they attempt to use the strategies (or not use them) in different courses. In addition, longitudinal research that follows these students over time would be helpful to examine the developmental trajectory of students' self-regulation over their college career and to inspect the *cognitive residue* of any strategy interventions in college.

Finally, most of the strategy intervention work at the college level has focused on the *main effects* of these interventions and not examined the potential for interactions with different types of students. Of course, there is work on learning styles of college students and how they might interact with course characteristics, but we think the assumption of strong trait models and personal learning styles are not the most useful in this area. In contrast, we assume that the different cognitive and motivational beliefs and strategies that students bring with them to college courses are not traits and are amenable to change. However, there has not been much research on how these different entry beliefs and strategies may constrain or facilitate the learning of self-regulatory strategies.

For example, in the area of epistemological beliefs (see Hofer & Pintrich, 1997), Schommer (1993) has shown that certain types of beliefs about knowledge seem to constrain the use of deeper processing strategies. Accordingly, it may be that it is not just that college students do not know about strategies and how and when to use them, but that they have other beliefs that actually limit their use of strategies. If this is the case, then it suggests that interventions might also have to target these beliefs as part of the intervention. The same type of analysis could be offered in terms of students' general goals for college and their goal orientation for learning. That is, students that adopt certain types of goals may be predisposed to use only certain types of strategies (Pintrich & Garcia, 1991; Pintrich & Schrauben, 1992). There is little work on how these different beliefs and goals might interact with the characteristics of a strategy intervention and more research on these types of aptitude–treatment interactions is needed in research on strategy instruction with college students.

In conclusion, it seems clear that we are making progress in this area as our conceptual models, research, and instructional programs become more sophisticated and effective. However, there are still many important theoretical and empirical issues to be resolved in future research. In addition, there is a need for more explicit sharing of our pedagogical content knowledge about how we go about teaching college students, or any students for that matter, to become self-regulating learners. We hope this discussion of one approach to the teaching of self-regulated learning at the college level is helpful in sparking a discussion of the different methods, strategies, and curricula that can be used to facilitate self-regulated learning in the classroom.

ACKNOWLEDGMENTS

We thank the editors of this volume, Dale Schunk and Barry Zimmerman, for helpful comments on an earlier draft. More importantly, we thank our colleague at the University of Michigan, Bill McKeachie, for all his insight, knowledge, and help in our work in this area. As the orginator and developer of the Learning to Learn course at the University of Michigan, Bill made all our work on this chapter possible.

REFERENCES

Ames, C. (1992). Classrooms: Goals, structures, and student motivation. *Journal of Educational Psychology, 84,* 261–271.

Bandura, A. (1986). *Social foundations of thought and action: A social cognitive theory.* Englewood Cliffs, NJ: Prentice-Hall.

Borkowski, J. G., Carr, M., Rellinger, E., & Pressley, M. (1990). Self-regulated cognition: Interdependence of metacognition, attributions, and self-esteem. In B. F. Jones & L. Idol (Eds.), *Dimensions of thinking and cognitive instruction* (pp. 53–92). Hillsdale, NJ: Erlbaum.

Borkowski, J. G., Weyhing, R., & Carr, M. (1988). Effects of attributional retraining on strategy-based reading comprehension of learning-disabled students. *Journal of Educational Psychology, 80,* 46–53.

Brown, A. L., Bransford, J. D., Ferrara, R. A., & Campione, J. C. (1983). Learning, remembering, and understanding. In J. H. Flavell & E. M. Markman (Eds.), *Handbook of child psychology: Cognitive development* (Vol. 3, pp. 77–166). New York: Wiley.

Burrell, K., Tao, L., Simpson, M., & Mendez-Berrueta, H. (1997). How do we know what we are preparing our students for?: A reality check of one university's academic literacy demands. *Research and Teaching in Developmental Education, 13,* 55–70.

Butler, D., & Winne, P. (1995). Feedback and self-regulated learning: A theoretical synthesis. *Review of Educational Research, 65,* 245–281.

Calderhead, J. (1996). Teachers: Beliefs and knowledge. In D. Berliner & R. Calfee (Eds.), *Handbook of educational psychology* (pp. 709–725). New York: Macmillan.

Corno, L. (1986). The metacognitive control components of self-regulated learning. *Contemporary Educational Psychology, 11,* 333–346.

Corno, L., & Snow, R. (1986). Adapting teaching to individual differences among learners. In M. Wittrock (Ed.), *Handbook of research on teaching and learning* (pp. 605–629). New York: Macmillan.

Covington, M.V. (1992). *Making the grade: A self-worth perspective on motivation and school reform.* New York: Cambridge University Press.

Cox, B. (1997). The rediscovery of the active learner in adaptive contexts: A developmental-historical analysis of transfer of training. *Educational Psychologist, 32,* 41–55.

Dweck, C. S., & Leggett, E. L. (1988). A social-cognitive approach to motivation and personality. *Psychological Review, 95,* 256–273.

Flavell, J. H. (1979). Metacognition and cognitive monitoring: A new area of cognitive-developmental inquiry. *American Psychologist, 34,* 906–911.

Foersterling, F. (1985). Attributional retraining: A review. *Psychological Bulletin, 98,* 495–512.

Garcia, T., & Pintrich, P. R. (1994). Regulating motivation and cognition in the classroom: The role of self-schemas and self-regulatory strategies. In D. H. Schunk & B. J. Zimmerman (Eds.), *Self-regulation of learning and performance: Issues and educational applications* (pp. 127–153). Hillsdale, NJ: Erlbaum.

Gaskins, I., & Elliot, T. (1991). *Implementing cognitive strategy training across the school: The Benchmark manual for teachers.* Cambridge, MA: Brookline Books.

Hattie, J., Biggs, J., & Purdie, N. (1996). Effects of learning skills interventions on student learning: A meta-analysis. *Review of Educational Research, 66,* 99–136.

Hidi, S. (1990). Interest and its contribution as a mental resource for learning. *Review of Educational Research, 60,* 549–571.

Hill, K., & Wigfield, A. (1984). Test anxiety: A major educational problem and what can be done about it. *Elementary School Journal, 85,* 105–126.

Hofer, B., & Pintrich, P. (1997). The development of epistemological theories: Beliefs about knowledge and knowing and their relation to learning. *Review of Educational Research, 67,* 88–140.

Hofer, B., Yu, S., & Pintrich, P. R. (1997, August). *Facilitating college students motivation and self-regulated learning.* Paper presented in a symposium on "Learning strategies: Conceptual and methodological issues" at the European Association for Research on Learning and Instruction, Athens, Greece.

Maehr, M., & Midgley, C. (1991). Enhancing student motivation: A schoolwide approach. *Educational Psychologist, 26,* 399–427.

Matlin, M. (1994). *Cognition.* New York: Holt, Rinehart & Winston.

McKeachie, W. J., Pintrich, P. R., & Lin, Y. G. (1985). Teaching learning strategies. *Educational Psychologist, 20,* 153–160.

Newman, R. S. (1994). Adaptive help-seeking: A strategy of self-regulating learning. In D. H. Schunk & B. J. Zimmerman (Eds.), *Self-regulation of learning and performance: Issues and educational applications* (pp. 283–301). Hillsdale, NJ: Erlbaum.

Paris, S. G., Lipson, M. Y., & Wixson, K. K. (1983). Becoming a strategic reader. *Contemporary Educational Psychology, 8,* 293–316.

Paris, S. G., & Winograd, P. (1990). How metacognition can promote academic learning and instruction. In B. F. Jones & L. Idol (Eds.), *Dimensions of thinking and cognitive instruction* (pp. 15–51). Hillsdale, NJ: Erlbaum.

Pauk, W. (1993). *How to study in college.* Boston: Houghton-Mifflin.

Pintrich, P. R. (1989). The dynamic interplay of student motivation and cognition in the college classroom. In C. Ames & M. L. Maehr (Eds.), *Advances in motivation and achievement: Motivation-enhancing environments* (Vol. 6, pp. 117–160). Greenwich, CT: JAI Press.

Pintrich, P. R. (1990). Implications of psychological research on student learning and college teaching for teacher education. In W. Houston (Ed.), *Handbook of research on teacher education* (pp. 826–857). New York: Macmillan.

Pintrich, P. R. (1994). Continuities and discontinuities: Future directions for research in educational psychology. *Educational Psychologist, 29,* 137–148.

Pintrich, P. R., & De Groot, E. V. (1990). Motivational and self-regulated learning components of classroom academic performance. *Journal of Educational Psychology, 82,* 33–40.

Pintrich, P. R., & Garcia, T. (1991). Student goal orientation and self-regulation in the college classroom. In M. L. Maehr & P. R. Pintrich (Eds.), *Advances in motivation and achievement: Goals and self-regulatory processes* (Vol. 7, pp. 371–402). Greenwich, CT: JAI Press.

Pintrich, P. R., Marx, R., & Boyle, R. (1993). Beyond cold conceptual change: The role of motivational beliefs and classroom contextual factors in the process of conceptual change. *Review of Educational Research, 63,* 167–199.

Pintrich, P. R., McKeachie, W. J., & Lin, Y. G. (1987). Teaching a course in learning to learn. *Teaching of Psychology, 14,* 81–86.

Pintrich, P. R., & Schrauben, B. (1992). Students' motivational beliefs and their cognitive engagement in classroom tasks. In D. Schunk & J. Meece (Eds.), *Student perceptions in the classroom: Causes and consequences* (pp. 149–183). Hillsdale, NJ: Erlbaum.

Pintrich, P. R., & Schunk, D. H. (1996). *Motivation in education: Theory, research and applications.* Englewood Cliffs, NJ: Merrill Prentice-Hall.

Pintrich, P. R., Smith, D. A. F., Garcia, T., & McKeachie, W. J. (1993). Predictive validity and reliability of the Motivated Strategies for Learning Questionnaire (MSLQ). *Educational and Psychological Measurement, 53,* 801–813.

Pintrich, P. R., Wolters, C., & Baxter, G. (in press). Assessing metacognition and self-regulated learning. In G. Schraw (Ed.), *Issues in the measurement of metacognition.* Lincoln, NE: University of Nebraska Press.

Pressley, M., Borkowski, J., & Schneider, W. (1987). Cognitive strategies: Good strategy users coordinate metacognition and knowledge. In R. Vasta & G. Whitehurst (Eds.), *Annals of child development* (Vol. 5, pp. 89–129). Greenwich, CT: JAI Press.

Pressley, M., Borkowski, J., & Schneider, W. (1989). Good information processing: What it is and what education can do to promote it. *International Journal of Educational Research, 13,* 857–867.

Pressley, M., Harris, K., & Marks, M. (1992). But good strategy instructors are constructivists! *Educational Psychology Review, 4,* 3–31.

Pressley, M., & Woloshyn, V. (1995). *Cognitive strategy instruction that really improves children's academic performance.* Cambridge, MA: Brookline Books.

Salomon, G., & Perkins, D. (1989). Rocky roads to transfer: Rethinking mechanisms of a neglected phenomenon. *Educational Psychologist, 24,* 113–142.

Sansone, C., Weir, C., Harpster, L., & Morgan, C. (1992). Once a boring task, always a boring task? The role of interest as a self-regulatory mechanism. *Journal of Personality and Social Psychology, 63,* 379–390.

Schiefele, U. (1991). Interest, learning, and motivation. *Educational Psychologist, 26,* 299–323.

Schneider, W., & Pressley, M. (1989). *Memory development between 2 and 20.* New York: Springer-Verlag.

Schommer, M. (1993). Epistemological development and academic performance among secondary students. *Journal of Educational Psychology, 85*(3), 406–411.

Schunk, D. H. (1991). Self-efficacy and academic motivation. *Educational Psychologist, 26,* 207–231.

Schunk, D. H. (1994). Self-regulation of self-efficacy and attributions in academic settings. In D. H. Schunk & B. J. Zimmerman (Eds.), *Self-regulation of learning and performance: Issues and educational applications* (pp. 75–99). Hillsdale, NJ: Erlbaum.

Schunk, D. H., & Zimmerman, B. J. (1994a). Self-regulation in education: Retrospect and prospect. In D. H. Schunk & B. J. Zimmerman (Eds.), *Self-regulation of learning and performance: Issues and educational applications* (pp. 305–314). Hillsdale, NJ: Erlbaum.

Schunk, D. H., & Zimmerman, B. J. (1994b). *Self-regulation of learning and performance: Issues and educational applications.* Hillsdale, NJ: Erlbaum.

Simpson, M., Hynd, C., Nist, S., & Burrell, K. (1997). College academic assistance programs and practices. *Educational Psychology Review, 9*, 39–87.

Snow, R., Corno, L., & Jackson, D. (1996). Individual differences in affective and conative functions. In D. Berliner & R. Calfee (Eds.), *Handbook of educational psychology* (pp. 243–310). New York: Macmillan.

Weiner, B. (1986). *An attributional theory of motivation and emotion.* New York: Springer-Verlag.

Weinstein, C. E. (1994a). Strategic learning/strategic teaching: Flip sides of a coin. In P. R. Pintrich, D. R. Brown, & C. E. Weinstein (Eds.), *Student motivation, cognition, and learning* (pp. 257–273). Hillsdale, NJ: Erlbaum.

Weinstein, C. E. (1994b). Students at risk for academic failure: Learning to learn classes. In K. W. Prichard & R. M. Sawyer (Eds.), *Handbook of college teaching: Theory and applications* (pp. 375–385). Westport, CT: Greenwood Press.

Weinstein, C. E., & Mayer, R. (1986). The teaching of learning strategies. In M. Wittrock (Ed.), *Handbook of research on teaching and learning* (pp. 315–327). New York: Macmillan.

Weinstein, C. E., & Underwood, V. L. (1985) Learning strategies: The how of learning. In J. Segal, S. Chipman, & R. Glaser (Eds.), *Thinking and learning skills: Relating instruction to research* (Vol 1, pp. 241–258). Hillsdale, NJ: Erlbaum.

Wigfield, A., Eccles, J., & Pintrich, P. R. (1996). Development between the ages of 11 and 25. In D. Berliner & R. Calfee (Eds.), *Handbook of educational psychology* (pp. 148–185). New York: Macmillan.

Winne, P. (1996). A metacognitive view of individual differences in self-regulated learning. *Learning and Individual Differences, 8*, 327–353.

Wolters, C., Yu, S., & Pintrich, P. R. (1996). The relation between goal orientation and students' motivational beliefs and self-regulated learning. *Learning and Individual Differences, 8*, 211–238.

Zimmerman, B. J. (1989). A social cognitive view of self-regulated academic learning. *Journal of Educational Psychology, 81*, 329–339.

Zimmerman, B. J., Greenberg, D., & Weinstein, C. E. (1994). Self-regulating academic study time: A strategy approach. In D. H. Schunk & B. J. Zimmerman (Eds.), *Self-regulation of learning and performance: Issues and educational applications* (pp. 181–199). Hillsdale, NJ: Erlbaum.

Zimmerman, B. J., & Martinez-Pons, M. (1986). Development of a structured interview for assessing student use of self-regulated learning strategies. *American Educational Research Journal, 23*, 614–628.

CHAPTER 5

Teaching Self-Monitoring Skills in Statistics

William Y. Lan

Self-monitoring, a subprocess of self-regulation that consists of giving "delib-erate attention to some aspects of one's behavior" (Schunk, 1996, p. 342), has attracted the attention of self-regulated learning researchers in recent decades. Self-monitoring has been shown to be an influential factor in students' learning: Researchers have found that by involving students in self-monitoring, they can improve students' academic performance (Malone & Mastropieri, 1992; McCurdy & Shapiro, 1992), achievement (Sagotsky, Patterson, & Lepper, 1978; Schunk, 1983), time on task (DiGangi, Maag, & Rutherford, 1991; Harris, 1986; Morrow, Burke, & Buel, 1985), classroom behavior (Lloyd, Bateman, Landrum, & Hallahan, 1989; Maag, Rutherford, & DiGangi, 1992), and problem-solving ability (Delclos & Harrington, 1991).

Thus, it is not surprising that among the multiple facets of self-regulated learning researchers have paid the most attention to self-monitoring. When discussing subprocesses of self-regulated learning, psychologists from various theoretical perspectives have agreed that self-monitoring is the most impor-tant subprocess because of its initiative function in self-regulation. For example, Pressley and Ghatala (1990) depicted a self-monitoring process as one in which learners evaluate the effectiveness of a particular learning strategy by using such criteria as (1) how the strategy helps them make progress toward a goal and (2) how much expenditure of time and effort the strategy requires. Applying these two criteria enables the learners to deter-mine whether the strategy should be continued or abandoned in favor of another strategy. Self-monitoring, therefore, is "an executive process, acti-vating and deactivating other processes, as a function of on-line evaluation of thought processes and products as they occur" (Pressley & Ghatala, 1990, p. 19). As pointed out by Zimmerman (1989a) when reviewing theoretical models of self-regulation, such a self-oriented feedback loop during learning described by Pressley and Ghatala is a common feature among models proposed by researchers from operant, phenomenological, social-cognitive, and volitional backgrounds.

If self-monitoring functions as the key subprocess underlying self-regulation, we will expect to see effects of self-monitoring on all elements of self-regulation. According to social-cognitive theory (Zimmerman, 1989b), self-regulation is composed of three components: a specified self-regulated learning strategy, perception of self-efficacy, and commitment to a goal. When a self-regulated learning strategy is chosen and used to regulate learning behavior, the learning environment, and covert cognitive processes in a learning situation, the selection of the strategy must be based on results of self-monitoring regarding the effectiveness of a currently used strategy and other alternatives (Thoresen & Mahoney, 1974; Zimmerman, 1989b). A learner's perception of self-efficacy also relies on the learner's self-monitoring of progress in learning and self-judgment of his or her own ability on a task (Diener & Dweck, 1978; Kuhl, 1985; Pearl, Bryan, & Herzog, 1983). Commitment to a goal cannot be held without awareness of the goal and of self-regulated learning strategies, such as self-consequence or volitional effort, which in turn determine the learner's task persistence (Zimmerman & Ringle, 1981). It seems that self-monitoring, when applied to a learning situation, initiates a self-reflective practice that makes the learner carefully reflect on all aspects of the learning process, including characteristics of the learner and the learning environment. This self-reflective practice may be the reason that self-regulated learners behaviorally, motivationally, and metacognitively differentiate themselves from learners who either are not or are less involved in the self-regulated learning process and the reason that self-regulation facilitates learning (Zimmerman, 1990). As one of the researchers who have been interested in effects of self-monitoring on students' learning, I present in this chapter findings of studies I conducted with students in a college statistics course and show how self-monitoring has affected various aspects of college students' learning.

A CLASSROOM STUDY OF SELF-MONITORING AND STUDENT LEARNING

An Introductory Statistics Course for Graduate Students

The course in which I used self-monitoring as an intervention was a graduate level introductory statistics course offered in a college of education at a major state university. The class met twice a week for 15 or 16 weeks in regular semesters or $1\frac{1}{2}$ hours daily for 6 weeks in summer semesters. The course covered the major content of descriptive statistics, including frequency distributions, measures of central tendency and dispersion, normal distribution and standard scores, correlation, and regression, and some inferential statistics, including probability, binomial distribution, sign test, Z test, t tests for different research designs, and one-way analysis of variance. As a required course for most graduate programs in the college of education and some other colleges in the university, the course was offered every semester (four times yearly) and was taken primarily by graduate students in the colleges of education and of human sciences; occasional students from a school of nursing and from an interdisciplinary graduate program also took this course. Although there were more students who were teachers in local elementary and secondary schools taking the course during summer sessions than regular semesters, student composition in the regular and summer semesters was comparable in terms of age, gender, and college they were from.

As an instructor in the statistics course, I found that many students thought statistics was one of the most difficult subjects in their graduate study. Consequently, they entered the course with high anxiety and low expectation, as illustrated by such comments as "I had my last math course 20 years ago"; "Don't try to teach me statistics, I cannot work with numbers"; and "This is the last course I need for my degree; I just want to survive it." More disturbingly, I found that when we progressed from relatively easy to more difficult content of the course, students were losing their sense of what they were doing in the class. For example, when we started the chapter on regression, where students needed to conduct cumbersome calculations to find the intercept or slope for a regression equation, some students lost the purpose of the calculation. Although the textbook and the instructor both stressed that a final product of a regression analysis was a regression equation that would be used for prediction, students might stop after finding only one of the two parameters of the regression equation and think they had already finished the problem. Some students found values for both intercept and slope but failed put them into an equation and wondered how to solve a sequential problem of prediction. In the unit on correlation, some students knew that the range of correlation coefficients was between -1 and $+1$ but still handed in assignments with unreasonable values of coefficients such as 32.06. Some students felt confident in their learning of inferential statistics before tests, saying inferential statistics was easier than descriptive statistics because the former was based on logical thinking rather than tedious calculations as was the latter. But their performance on the tests covering inferential statistics was worse than that on tests covering descriptive statistics. Apparently, students manifested deficits in self-monitoring when learning tasks in the statistics course became increasingly difficult for them.

Analyzing the reasons for students' self-monitoring deficits in this class, I decided that the deficits were primarily caused by cognitive factors. I believed that it was the challenging learning tasks and students' state-oriented thinking (worry, anxiety, and frustration) (Kuhl, 1985) that used up the students' information-processing capacity and prevented them from self-monitoring their own learning. If this was the case, an external cue triggering a self-monitoring process was needed to help students to engage in self-monitoring when studying statistics. Previous research already showed that an auditory cue helped children with learning disabilities to focus their attention on an arithmetic computation task (Heins, Lloyd, & Hallahan, 1986).

A Self-Monitoring Intervention

Manipulation

The self-monitoring cue used in the statistics class was a protocol that was designed to direct students' attention to their learning activities and understanding of the learning materials. A total of 75 basic concepts derived from a textbook (Pagano, 1994) used in the statistics course were listed in the left column of the protocol. Accompanying each concept on the protocol was a row of boxes in which students recorded the amount of time and frequency of reading the textbook, completing required assignments, voluntarily participating in discussion with classmates after class, receiving tutoring, and engaging in other activities needed to master the concept. The last box in the row was used for students to rate their self-efficacy in solving problems related to the concept on a 10-point scale, with 1 representing low self-efficacy and 10 representing high self-efficacy. This self-monitoring protocol was used by students in a self-monitoring condition in the study. Figure 5.1 shows a sample section of the self-monitoring protocol.

I questioned whether exposing students to the list of 75 statistical concepts might influence their learning by helping them organize and review the course content so that the amount of exposure to the course content itself, rather than the self-monitoring process, would be responsible for any observed effect. To control for the confounding variable of exposure to course content, I designed an instructor-monitoring protocol for an alternative treatment condition. The instructor-monitoring protocol contained the same 75 statistical concepts, but it directed students to monitor the instructor's teaching activities, rather than their own learning activities. Accompanying each concept in the instructor-monitoring protocol was a row of boxes in which students evaluated the instructor's pace of instruction, sufficiency of examples, number of assignments, and time allowed for students' questions on a 10-point scale. A value of 1 in the scale indicated an inadequate amount of instruction (faster instructional pace, fewer examples and assignments, and less time for students' questioning than students needed), and a value of 10 indicated an excessive amount of instruction (slower instructional pace, more examples and assignments, and more time for students' questioning

Your I.D. Number _____		Time and Exposure					
Chapter	Knowledge Elements	Text Time & Exposure	Assign. Time & Exposure	Discussion Time & Exposure	Tutoring Time & Exposure	Total Time & Exposure	Self-Efficacy of the Element
1	Observational vs. Experimental Studies	A ☐	☐	☐	☐	☐	C
1	Independent vs. Dependent Variables	☐	☐	☐	☐	☐	

FIGURE 5.1. Sample section of the self-monitoring protocol. In the box with the letter A, students recorded the amount of time in minutes that they spent using various techniques to understand the concept. In the box with the letter B, students recorded the number of times they exposed themselves to the concept. In the box with the letter C, students filled in a number from 1 to 10 to indicate their self-efficacy to solve problems regarding the concept, with 1 signifying low confidence and 10 signifying high confidence.

than they needed). This instructor-monitoring protocol was used by students in an instructor-monitoring condition in the study.

Psychologists contend that regularity and proximity are two important characteristics of effective self-monitoring (Bandura, 1986; Shapiro, 1984). By *regularity*, they mean that learners continuously, rather than intermittently, monitor their own learning behavior. By *proximity*, they mean that a behavior is self-monitored close to the time of its occurrence, rather than a long time afterward. When I piloted the two protocols in the statistics class, I found that students used the protocols neither as regularly nor as proximately as I expected. Some of students did not use the protocols that they had received at the beginning of the semester at all until the end of the semester when I collected the protocols from them. Then they filled out the protocols with any numbers they could think of right before protocols were handed in. This indicated that simply providing students with an external cue (the protocol) would not engage them in the self-monitoring process. To ensure that students used the protocols regularly and proximately, I encouraged students to record their protocols every time they studied for the statistics course. I also prepared two copies of the protocol (Copy A and Copy B) for each student. Students received Copy A of either the self-monitoring or the instructor-monitoring protocol on the first day of the class, and at the next class meeting, they exchanged the Copy A for Copy B. I checked the copies after each class to make sure that students followed the directions to fill out the protocols. The procedure of recording and exchanging protocols continued throughout the semester. My frequent reviewing of protocols indicated that students completed the protocols correctly.

In addition to the treatment and the alternative treatment conditions, there was a control condition where students took the course without any experimental treatment.

Procedure

To recruit students to participate in the study in the statistics class, I offered 10 bonus points (5% of the total course grade) for their participation. With very few exceptions, all students enrolled in the class volunteered. Because there were only 20–25 students enrolled in the course each semester, I had to conduct the study over 4 successive semesters to accumulate a sufficient number of subjects. Ideally, I should have randomly assigned students into the self-monitoring, instructor-monitoring, and control conditions within the same semester. However, I realized that by doing this, students in the control condition would earn the bonus points without doing anything. I was afraid that this situation would cause resentment among students in the other two conditions, who would be asked to engage in extensive monitoring work. To avoid this problem, I decided that students enrolled in the first three semesters would be participants in the treatment and alternative treatment condition, and students in the fourth semester would be participants in the control condition.

Students enrolled in the first three semesters were informed of the opportunity of participating in a study to earn bonus points during the first class meeting of the semester. After signing consent forms, students were randomly assigned to the self-monitoring and instructor-monitoring conditions and were given either the self-monitoring protocol or the instructor-monitoring protocol. Students were also informed that because more than one research project was being conducted in this class, their protocol might be different from that of their classmates.

The two protocols were designed to direct students to monitor either their own learning activities or the instructor's teaching activities. Whether the protocols manipulated students' attention as expected became crucial for the success of the study. Written comments collected from students using different protocols verified that the manipulation was successful. Students using the self-monitoring protocol tended to perceive the protocol as a way to obtain information about their learning (e.g., "Good tool to evaluate myself in understanding the materials; also helps identify areas that I need to clarify"; "The protocol helped me realize what I didn't understand and how I could study to learn it more effectively."), whereas students using the instructor-monitoring protocol tended to perceive the protocol as a way to improve classroom instruction (e.g., "This is a very good way to evaluate teaching a class"; "The protocol shows you care very much about your teaching effectiveness.").

Data Collection

Following Zimmerman's (1990) postulation that self-regulated learners behaviorally, motivationally, and metacognitively differentiate themselves from
learners who are not or are less involved in the self-regulation process, I
designed various instruments to collect data regarding behavioral, motivational, and metacognitive differences of students in the three experimental
conditions. There were three instruments measuring behavioral variables,
including course examinations, use of self-regulated learning strategies, and
mastery learning and challenge seeking; two instruments measuring motivational variables of perceived control over learning and intrinsic motivation
toward statistics; and two instruments measuring metacognitive variables of
accuracy of self-judgment and knowledge structure. In addition to these
instruments, a mathematics achievement test was designed to measure
students' mathematics achievement prior to the treatment.

I used four course examinations in a semester to evaluate students'
learning in the statistics class. Each examination was composed of 40
multiple-choice problems chosen from a test-item bank associated with the
textbook used for the class covering about three to four chapters of the
textbook. These tests were designed to measure students' understanding of
statistical concepts and ability to perform statistical calculations. Statistics
formulas needed for each test were provided to students on sheets attached
to the test booklets, and calculators were allowed during the tests. After
several years of modification, the examinations yielded reliable measurement
of students' learning. During the period of the four semesters when the study
was conducted, the Kuder–Richardson-20 reliability coefficients for the
examinations varied between .73 and .86. The four examinations produced
four test scores and an average of test scores, with a possible range between
0 to 40. I regarded these course examination scores as an ultimate dependent
variable in the study. If self-monitoring manipulated in this study could not
increase students' learning as measured by the examinations, any other
changes in behavior, motivation, or metacognition would be less meaningful.
Although in a similar study I conducted previously (Lan, Bradley, & Parr,
1993), I had already shown that self-monitoring improved students' test
performance in the course examinations, I wanted to replicate the findings
of the enhancing effects of self-monitoring on students' learning.

As discussed before, self-regulation researchers regard self-monitoring as
an initial and sometimes the sole subprocess of self-regulation, so it is
reasonable to expect that students who are involved in self-monitoring are
also likely to use other self-regulated learning strategies. To examine this
prediction, I measured the students' use of self-regulated learning strategies
in the statistics course. The instrument measuring the variable of using
self-regulated learning strategies contained 13 strategies identified by Zim-

merman and Martinez-Pons (1986): self-evaluation, organizing instructional materials, goal setting and planning, seeking information, keeping records and monitoring, environmental structuring, self-consequences, rehearsal and memorization, seeking assistance from peers, seeking assistance from teachers, reviewing the textbook, reviewing the notes, and reviewing the previous tests and assignments in preparation for a test. One strategy on Zimmerman and Martinez-Pons's list, seeking assistance from parents, was not included in my instrument because all students in my study were adults. For each strategy listed in the instrument, I provided a sample of behaviors that exemplified the strategy. For example, "checking one's own homework assignments" for the strategy of self-evaluation, "making outlines of course materials" for organizing instructional materials, "planning time and sequences of learning activities" for goal setting and planning, and "making a list of errors in homework" for keeping records and monitoring. Students were asked to indicate on a 5-point scale the frequency of using these strategies when studying statistics: never (1), rare (2), sometimes (3), often (4), and always (5).

To check the construct validity of the instrument measuring the use of self-regulated learning strategies, correlation coefficients between the frequencies of using the strategies and the average of students' performance in the course examinations were calculated. Six out of 13 strategies—self-evaluation, seeking information, rehearsal and memorization, seeking peers' assistance, reviewing the textbook in preparation for a test, and reviewing previous tests in preparation for a test—were related significantly to students' performance in examinations. With the exception of the strategy of seeking peers' assistance, the strategies correlated positively with academic performance.

Achievement motivation theorists suggest that self-regulated learners are likely to be learning-goal-oriented people who exhibit an interest in mastery learning and a preference for challenging tasks (Elliot & Dweck, 1988; Meese, 1991; Nicholls, 1984). I provided students with opportunities for mastery learning and challenge seeking in the statistics class to investigate the effects of self-monitoring on these variables. Students, after receiving feedback from the instructor, were allowed to resubmit their homework as many times as they wanted to gain all credits for the assignment. Also, I provided students with five sets of mastery problems for the first five chapters of the course if they felt the problems in the textbook were not challenging enough. (Nobody asked for more challenging problems after the first five chapters.) Students could hand in their work on the mastery problems to get feedback from the instructor; however, their performance on the mastery problems did not affect their course grade. The number of students in each condition who resubmitted homework or did mastery problems was recorded as a measure of mastery-learning and challenge-seeking behavior.

It has been well documented in correlational research that self-regulated learners are self-efficacious and intrinsically motivated (Pintrich & De Groot, 1990; Zimmerman & Martinez-Pons, 1988, 1990). I hoped to show that self-monitoring influenced the motivational variables of perceived control over learning and intrinsic motivation toward statistics in this experimental study. The instrument that measured perceived control over learning included six statements such as "I know what I am doing when studying for this course." The instrument measuring intrinsic motivation toward statistics included six statements such as "I would like to take more statistics classes, even if I am not required to do so." Students responded to the two instruments on 6-point Likert scales to indicate the extent to which they agreed or disagreed with the statements. Low scores on the measurements indicated low levels of perceived control and intrinsic motivation, and high scores indicated high levels of perceived control and intrinsic motivation. Unfortunately, the Cronbach alpha reliability coefficients for the two instruments were relatively low: .52 for the perceived control scale and .60 for the intrinsic motivation scale.

Two variables were measured in the study to examine the effects of self-monitoring on metacognition. First, a variable of accuracy of self-judgment was developed by comparing students' confidence level in their correct answers and incorrect answers for the test items among students in the three conditions. In front of each test item was a space where students were asked to write in a number between 1 to 10 to indicate their confidence of their answers to the problem, a value of 1 representing low confidence and a value of 10 representing high confidence. Students' answers to the problems in the four examinations were sorted into correct and incorrect clusters and means of the confidence ratings for correct and incorrect answers were computed separately. It was expected that students in the self-monitoring condition would manifest more accurate self-judgment than those in the instructor-monitoring and control conditions; accordingly, their confidence level on correct answers should be higher and their confidence level on the incorrect answers should be lower than those of the other two groups.

Researchers have also shown that self-monitoring is positively related to self-awareness (Zimmerman & Martinez-Pons, 1988). Based on that relationship, I expected that self-monitoring would help students to be aware of the structure or organization of the statistical knowledge they learned in the course; therefore, the students in the self-monitoring condition should show a better knowledge structure than those in the instructor-monitoring and control conditions. The variable of knowledge structure was measured by 12 questions attached to the four course examinations. In each question, several related or unrelated statistics concepts were listed, and students were asked to delete an unrelated concept and organize the related concepts in an outline format, and then indicate the headings of the outline. For example, I listed four concepts of *correlation coefficient, variability of a distribution, characteristics of a distribution,* and *standard deviation* in a question measuring knowledge structure. An appropriate answer to this question would be to delete the concept of correlation coefficient, then organize the concepts of characteristics of a distribution, variability of a distribution, and standard deviation as the first, second, and third level of headings of an outline. Although sometimes there might be more than one reasonable way to organize the concepts, I tried to minimize the arbitrariness of answers by asking students to reproduce the outlines that had been used in the textbook, course syllabus, and class instruction. The instrument measuring knowledge structure was composed of 12 such questions and ranged between 0 and 12. A high score indicated a good knowledge structure, and a low score indicated a poor knowledge structure.

The mathematics achievement test was composed of 22 multiple-choice problems, varying in difficulty from elementary mathematics to college algebra. The students were required to answer all questions on the test. The reliability coefficient of the test was .86. The test was administered at the beginning of each semester to check the equivalence of prior mathematics achievement of students among the three conditions. Results showed that there was no significant difference in prior mathematics achievement and further ensured comparability of students in the three experimental conditions.

The four course examinations, each accompanied by the measures of self-judgment accuracy and knowledge structure, were administered during the semester at intervals of 3 or 4 weeks. The scales measuring use of self-regulated learning strategies, perceived control over learning, and intrinsic motivation toward statistics were administered at the end of the semesters. I recorded frequencies of students who resubmitted homework or did mastery problems throughout the semesters as measurements of mastery learning and challenge-seeking behaviors.

Results of the Intervention

Results of Quantitative Analysis

During a period of four successive semesters, I collected data from 73 graduate students. After 4 students were excluded from the sample due to incomplete responses, the sample was composed of 69 students: 23 in the self-monitoring condition, 21 in the instructor-monitoring condition, and 25 in the control condition. Among the 69 students were 38 females and 31 males. Data analyses were conducted to test the predictions on behavioral, motivational, and metacognitive differences of the students across the three conditions.

As predicted, students in the self-monitoring condition outperformed their counterparts in the instructor-monitoring and control conditions on the course examinations. The mean of the average examination scores for students in the self-monitoring condition was 34.95, which was higher than that of the instructor-monitoring condition (mean = 32.71) and the control condition (mean = 32.53). Further analysis indicated that the difference between the self-monitoring and instructor-monitoring conditions was significant, and the difference between the self-monitoring and the control conditions barely failed to achieve the significant level of .05. The mean of the average examination scores in the self-monitoring condition was 0.59 standard deviation higher than that of the instructor-monitoring condition and 0.66 standard deviation higher than that of the control condition. The effect size of self-monitoring on learning, as evaluated by Cohen's (1977) standard, was between medium and large.

Among the 13 self-regulated learning strategies examined, I found significant differences in 5 strategies: self-evaluation, environmental structuring, rehearsal and memorization, seeking assistance from peers, and reviewing tests and assignments in preparation for a test. Except for the strategy of seeking assistance from peers, where the students in the instructor-monitoring condition used the strategy more frequently than did students in the self-monitoring and control conditions, students in the self-monitoring condition used the other four strategies more frequently than students in either the instructor-monitoring or the control condition. The findings suggest that when students are involved in the self-monitoring process, they increase the frequency with which they use other self-regulated learning strategies, such as self-evaluation, environmental structuring, rehearsal and memorization, and reviewing previous tests and assignments preparing for tests. This can be regarded as evidence that self-monitoring starts a learners' self-reflective practice that causes them to reflect on various aspects of a learning process being currently executed, including the social and physical learning environment, cognitive strategies employed, sources of useful information and assistance, and progress toward a learning goal.

The mastery-seeking behaviors measured by frequencies of resubmitting homework assignments and doing mastery problems did not show significant group differences. Almost every student taking the statistics course resubmitted homework assignments for full homework credit. However, only 4 of 25 students in the self-monitoring condition and 1 in each of the instructor-monitoring and control conditions did some mastery problems. Although the difference was in the predicted direction, it was not significant. One explanation for this finding is that students' interest in their course grade was so intense that it overpowered the effects of self-monitoring. When homework assignments were rewarded with grade points, everyone across the experimental conditions resubmitted homework. Inasmuch as the mastery problems were not related to grades, not many students were interested in doing them.

With regard to the effects of self-monitoring on students' motivation in the statistics course, no significant group difference was found in either perceived control over learning or intrinsic motivation toward statistics. The lack of treatment effect on motivation can be explained by particular characteristics of the course. As mentioned earlier, many students took the course with high anxiety and low expectation. As the instructor of the course, I tried several things to change their negative attitudes toward statistics. For example, I slowed the instruction pace at the beginning of the course to ease anxiety, provided students with ample opportunities for individualized interaction between them and me in and after classes, and applied the policy of allowing them to resubmit homework for full credit. These instructional practices created a generally positive attitude among students enrolled in the course. Many students said that the policy of resubmitting homework was their favorite class policy because the policy gave them at least 20% control over the course grade that they could ensure by their effort. Their positive attitudes were also reflected in the fact that all group means on the two motivational variables of perceived control over learning and intrinsic motivation toward statistics fell above the midpoint of the 6-point scales, ranging from 3.71 to 4.67. These positive attitudes among students might have prevented the self-monitoring intervention from further boosting students' motivation. Of course, the relatively low reliability of the two measurements might also account for the lack of treatment effects on motivation.

The prediction that students in the self-monitoring condition would manifest more accurate metacognitive ability of self-judgment than those in the non-self-monitoring conditions was not supported by the data. Generally, all students manifested an accurate self-judgment ability. Their confidence levels on correct answers, with values above 8.00 on a 10-point scale, were significantly higher than those on their incorrect answers, with values about 6.50 on the scale. No group difference was found in students' accuracy of self-judgment.

Another prediction pertaining the effects of self-monitoring on the metacognitive variable of knowledge structure was supported in the study. Students in the self-monitoring condition developed a better organized knowledge structure than did students in the other two experimental conditions. Out of 12 questions measuring knowledge structure, students in the self-monitoring condition answered an average of 7.68 questions correctly, compared with the means of 5.89 and 6.63 for the students in the instructor-monitoring and control conditions, respectively. Further analysis indicated that only the difference between the self-monitoring and the instructor-monitoring conditions was significant.

As a summary, the quantitative analysis of the results indicates that self-monitoring enhanced students' performance in course examinations and use of self-regulated learning strategies. It also helped students to organize knowledge they learned in the course. Table 5.1 summarizes the findings.

Results of Qualitative Analysis

I also collected students' comments on using the protocols in the statistics course in written evaluation forms at the end of semesters. The written comments helped me to understand how self-monitoring brought self-reflective practice into the students' learning.

Many students in the self-monitoring condition appreciated the protocol because it made them reflect on their learning outcomes in the class and

TABLE 5.1. Summary of Effects of Self-Monitoring on Behavioral, Motivational, and Metacognitive Variables

Variables	Comparison[a]
Behavior	
Course examination	S > I , S > C
Using self-regulated learning strategies	
Self-evaluation	S > I
Organizing instructional materials	S = I = C
Goal setting and planning	S = I = C
Seeking information	S = I = C
Keeping records and monitoring	S = I = C
Environmental structuring	S > I, S > C
Self-consequences	S = I = C
Rehearsal and memorization	S > C
Seeking assistance from peers	I > S, I > C
Seeking assistance from teachers	S = I = C
Reviewing textbook for tests	S = I = C
Reviewing notes for tests	S = I = C
Reviewing tests/assignments for tests	S > C
Mastery seeking	S = I = C
Motivation	
Perceived control over learning	S = I = C
Intrinsic motivation toward statistics	S = I = C
Metacognition	
Accuracy of self-judgment	S = I = C
Knowledge structure	S > I

[a]S, self-monitoring condition; I, instructor-monitoring condition; C, control condition.

helped them to diagnose their weak knowledge areas. Comments of this kind included the following: "Good tool to evaluate myself in understanding the materials; also helps identify areas that I need to clarify"; "The protocols helped me realize what I didn't understand and how I could study to learn it more efficiently."

Students' self-reflection can also be seen from their awareness of the progress of instruction and learning in the course. In contrast with what I usually observed in the statistics class where students passively followed the instructor's lecture, students in the self-monitoring condition, as their written comments indicated, actively monitored content and pace of instruction and tried to match their learning to the progress of instruction and focus on content emphasized in instruction. Comments of this type included the following: "The protocol helps me to observe instructional content constantly in class"; "I felt it was a good way for me to keep tabs on the information learned or taught in class"; "When I studied the textbook, I was pretty confident about what I had studied. However, when I worked with the protocol, some new words were listed. I had to go back to take one more look. That was helpful"; "The protocol helps to exemplify the important aspects of each chapter."

The self-monitoring protocol also helped students to manage their studying time efficiently. Students wrote in such comments as the following: "It helped me to manage my studying time, and it helped me to determine when I felt comfortable with the material because I could rate my understanding while studying"; "The protocol helped me to realize how much time I should be spending on preparations of the course." It seems that with the self-monitoring protocol students were carefully allocating their precious studying time to reach the maximum of expenditure–outcome efficiency.

Still other students said the protocol decreased their anxiety toward the class and increased their interest or motivation. A sample comment would be the following: "I have a 'calculation-phobia' but I am pleased to see that it is self-imposed (to a certain extent). I'll avoid stat classes in the future, but at least I won't think negatively of this class." One student expressed a feeling that he was "pushed" to spend extra time studying for this course. It is possible that the self-monitoring process increased students' expenditure of time and effort in the course as a result of self-reflection.

Students' written comments echoed psychologists' postulation that self-monitoring makes learners self-reflective (Corno, 1986; Mace & Kratochwill, 1988; Shapiro, 1984). The comments were also consistent with findings reported in the quantitative analysis of the study, that self-monitoring increased the use of other self-regulated learning strategies. A self-monitored learner, therefore, can be depicted as one who constantly reflects on a learning process, including the learner, the learner's behavior, the learning environment, and outcomes of learning, then adjusts these components of learning appropriately to optimize the learning process.

Nevertheless, some students thought that the protocol contained too many details and sometimes became a distraction to their learning. All the positive and negative comments were very useful for me when I tried to apply the findings of the study in the statistics course later.

EDUCATIONAL APPLICATIONS OF THE STUDY

The study discussed in this chapter offers a number of suggestions for teachers who want to improve students' learning and learning strategies by enhancing their self-monitoring. One direct product of the study is a sheet titled, "Have You Spent Enough Time Studying for the Statistics Class?", which I have inserted in the course syllabus for all students enrolled in the statistics course since the completion of the study. In the sheet, I list the 75 basic statistics concepts that were used in the two protocols. Considering students' complaints about the tediousness of using the protocols, instead of using a row of boxes to record time and frequency of students' learning activities, I list beside each concept an amount of time that an average student taking this course needs to spend to learn the concept. This average learning time was calculated based on data from the 47 students who had used the self-monitoring protocols in two studies (Lan, 1996; Lan et al., 1993). A note at the top of the sheet informs students that the average learning time (in minutes) included the time students spend in attending classes, doing homework, participating in discussions with classmates, and searching for tutorial assistance if needed. It is also stated in the instructions that the chart is intended to give students an idea of how much time they should spend on these concepts. There is another column rating self-efficacy, which allows students to check their understanding of the concepts (see Figure 5.2). Students enrolled in the course felt positive about this novel part of their syllabus. They said that the sheet not only helped them to plan their studying time,

Chap.	Concept	Minutes Spent	Self-Efficacy	Chap.	Concept	Minutes Spent	Self-Efficacy
1	Experimental and Correlational Research	25		1	Independent and Dependent Variable	39	
1	Sample and Population	25		1	Statistic and Parameter	20	

FIGURE 5.2. Sample section of the sheet "Have You Spent Enough Time to Study for the Statistics Class?"

but also caused them to spend more time studying than they would have spent otherwise. Some students wished that a similar chart or information would be provided in other classes they took.

The study also suggested that instructors implement instruction on self-regulated learning strategies into their teaching as an instructional component to increase students' learning. Traditional instruction emphasizes conveying the content or knowledge to students but expects learning skills or strategies, including self-regulated learning strategies, to be automatically developed by students with their increase in learning experiences. My data showed that even graduate students, the most experienced veterans in education, need assistance to be involved effectively in self-regulation. If we plan and design instruction that teaches knowledge content as well as learning skills and cognitive strategies, we should have a better chance to help our students to become lifelong learners, because they will be equipped with strategies of self-monitoring, self-reflection, self-motivation, and self-instruction when they leave school. They will not have to rely on external sources of motivation, instruction, and evaluation to initiate and maintain their learning processes. Although an increasing number of researchers and educators have realized the need for teaching learning skills and strategies and have developed courses that teach learning strategies explicitly (Ellis, Sabornie, & Marshall, 1989; McKeachie, Pintrich, & Lin, 1985; Pintrich, McKeachie, & Lin, 1987; Stahl, Brozo, Smith, & Henk, 1991; Wood, Fler, & Willoughby, 1992), instruction in learning skills and strategies is still a random occurrence in schools and has not become a part of curriculum objectives. Furthermore, the current practice of instruction in learning skills and strategies is primarily focused on college students. If we are convinced by research evidence that self-regulated learning strategies are beneficial and teachable to students, we should systematically implement instruction in self-regulated learning strategies at all levels of education and start the instruction as early as possible in students' learning experience.

Among various self-regulated learning strategies, self-monitoring seems to be a good breakthrough point for instruction in learning strategies. As discussed earlier, theorists with different theoretical perspectives all agree on the importance of self-monitoring to a self-regulation process. The effects of self-monitoring on students' behavior, motivation, and metacognition demonstrated in this and other studies also support the idea that self-monitoring is a component in a self-regulated learning process that brings about self-reflective practice on part of learners. If the ultimate goal of education is to produce self-reflective learners, the importance of self-monitoring cannot be overemphasized.

For instructors who are going to use self-monitoring to help students' learning, there are several lessons that can be learned from the study reported herein. For students who do not use much self-monitoring, introducing a self-monitoring process into their learning conflicts with their old way of learning; therefore, using self-monitoring may be unpleasant or even annoying to them at beginning. We cannot expect students to self-monitor simply because external assistance is delivered, such as the self-monitoring protocol used in this study or an auditory cue, as used by Heins et al. (1986). As observed in piloting this study, students provided with the protocol did not use it regularly during the semester, and some did not use it at all. From a motivational point of view, students are likely to maintain self-monitoring only when they experience the beneficial effects of self-monitoring. Sometimes, instructors need to force the initial experience of self-monitoring to happen. Several students in my study who initially worried that working with the protocol would detract from their studying time later enjoyed using the protocol because they found that the protocol helped them to study and understand statistics.

Providing students with opportunities to practice self-monitoring strategies is also crucial to whether the students will use the strategies in current and future learning tasks. Self-regulated learning strategies will be used and transferred only when they do not compete sharply with other cognitive activities for learners' cognitive capacity, and this is especially true for moderately difficult and difficult learning tasks (Schunk, 1996; Winne, 1995). There is not much we can do to reduce the difficulty of a learning task as learning continually progresses, so the only way to reduce the competition for cognitive capacity between learning activities and self-regulation strategies is to make the execution of self-regulated strategies automatic through repetition or practice.

Finally, researchers and educators should pay close attention to self-regulated learning strategies students have already developed and employed in their learning. Some of the self-regulated learning strategies developed by students are very creative and efficient and should be shared with other students through instruction in the strategies. This valuable source of information has been ignored by most self-regulated learning researchers. For example, it is apparent from the literature that in most self-monitoring studies it was the researchers who operationally defined the variable of self-monitoring then either measured or manipulated the variable accordingly. As pointed out by Winne (1995), one problem of the self-regulated learning strategies invented by researchers is that the strategies are usually novel to students. Sometimes, the novelty of the strategies makes it difficult for students to see the relevance of the strategies to their learning and makes the learning and transfer of the strategies less possible. Future research is warranted to discover the self-regulated learning strategies students are using in their real learning situations, and this information will be helpful in research and instruction in self-regulated learning.

REFERENCES

Bandura, A. (1986). *Social foundations of thought and action: A social cognitive theory.* Englewood Cliffs, NJ: Prentice-Hall.

Cohen, J. (1977). *Statistical power analysis for the behavioral sciences.* New York: Academic Press.

Corno, L. (1986). The metacognitive control components of self-regulated learning. *Contemporary Educational Psychology, 11,* 333–346.

Delclos, V. R., & Harrington, C. (1991). Effects of strategy monitoring and proactive instruction on children's problem-solving performance. *Journal of Educational Psychology, 83,* 35–42.

Diener, C. I., & Dweck, C. S. (1978). An analysis of learned helplessness: Continuous changes in performance, strategy, and achievement cognitions following failure. *Journal of Personality and Social Psychology, 36,* 451–462.

DiGangi, S. A., Maag, J. W., & Rutherford, R. B. (1991). Self-graphing of on-task behavior: Enhancing the reactive effects of self-monitoring on on-task behavior and academic performance. *Learning Disability Quarterly, 14,* 221–230.

Elliot, E., & Dweck, C. (1988). Goals: An approach to motivation and achievement. *Journal of Personality and Social Psychology, 54,* 5–12.

Ellis, E. S., Sabornie, E. J., & Marshall, K. J. (1989). Teaching learning strategies to learning disabled students in postsecondary settings. *Academic Therapy, 24,* 491–501.

Harris, K. R. (1986). Self-monitoring of attentional behavior versus self-monitoring of productivity: Effects on on-task behavior and academic response rate among learning disabled children. *Journal of Applied Behavior Modification, 10,* 235–254.

Heins, E. D., Lloyd, J. W., & Hallahan, D. P. (1986). Cued and noncued self-recording of attention to task. *Behavior Modification, 10,* 235–254.

Kuhl, J. (1985). Volitional aspects of achievement motivation and learned helplessness: Self-regulatory processes and action versus state orientation. In J. Kuhl & J. Beckman (Eds.), *Action control* (pp. 101–128). New York: Springer.

Lan, W. Y. (1996). The effects of self-monitoring on students' course performance, use of learning strategies, attitude, self-judgment ability, and knowledge representation. *Journal of Experimental Education, 64,* 101–115.

Lan, W. Y., Bradley, L., & Parr, G. (1993). The effects of a self-monitoring process on college students' learning in an introductory statistics course. *Journal of Experimental Education, 62,* 26–40.

Lloyd, J. W., Bateman, D. F., Landrum, T. J., & Hallahan, D. P. (1989). Self-recording of attention versus productivity. *Journal of Applied Behavior Analysis, 22,* 315–323.

Maag, J. W., Rutherford, R. B., & DiGangi, S. A. (1992). Effects of self-monitoring and contingent reinforcement on on-task behavior and academic productivity of learning disabled students: A social validation study. *Psychology in the Schools, 29,* 157–172.

Mace, F. C., & Kratochwill, T. R. (1988). Self-monitoring: Application and issues. In J. Witt, S. Elliott, & F. Gresham (Eds.), *Handbook of behavioral therapy in education* (pp. 489–502). New York: Pergamon Press.

Malone, L. D., & Mastropieri, M. A. (1992). Reading comprehension instruction:

Summarization and self-monitoring training for students' with learning disabilities. *Exceptional Children, 58,* 270–279.

McCurdy, B. L., & Shapiro, E. S. (1992). A comparison of teacher-, peer-, and self-monitoring with curriculum-based measurement in reading among students with learning disabilities. *Journal of Special Education, 26,* 162–180.

McKeachie, W. J., Pintrich, P. R., & Lin, Y. G. (1985). Teaching learning strategies. *Educational Psychologist, 20,* 153–160.

Meese, J. (1991). The classroom context and children's motivational goals. In M. Maehr & P. Pintrich (Eds.), *Advances in achievement motivation research* (pp. 261–285). Greenwich, CT: JAI Press.

Morrow, L. W., Burke, J. G., & Buel, B. J. (1985). Effects of a self-recording procedure on the attending to task behavior and academic productivity of adolescents with multiple handicaps. *Mental Retardation, 23,* 137–141.

Nicholls, J. G. (1984). Achievement motivation: Conceptions of ability, subjective experience, task choice, and performance. *Psychological Review, 91,* 328–346.

Pagano, R. P. (1994). *Understanding statistics in the behavioral sciences.* St. Paul, MN: West.

Pearl, R., Bryan, T., & Herzog, A. (1983). Learning disabled children's strategy analyses under high and low success conditions. *Learning Disability Quarterly, 6,* 67–74.

Pintrich, P. R., & De Groot, E. V. (1990). Motivational and self-regulated learning components of classroom academic performance. *Journal of Educational Psychology, 82,* 33–40.

Pintrich, P. R., McKeachie, W. J., & Lin, Y. G. (1987). Teaching a course in learning to learn. *Teaching of Psychology, 14,* 81–86.

Pressley, M., & Ghatala, E. S. (1990). Self-regulated learning: Monitoring learning from text. *Educational Psychologist, 25,* 19–33.

Sagotsky, G., Patterson, C. J., & Lepper, M. R. (1978). Training children's self-control: A field experiment in self-monitoring and goal setting in the classroom. *Journal of Experimental Child Psychology, 25,* 242–253.

Schunk, D. H. (1983). Progress of self-monitoring: Effects on children's self-efficacy and achievement. *Journal of Experimental Education, 51,* 89–93.

Schunk, D. H. (1996). *Learning theories: An educational perspective.* New York: Merrill/Macmillan.

Shapiro, E. S. (1984). Self-monitoring procedures. In T. H. Ollendick & M. Hersen (Eds.), *Child behavior assessment: Principles and procedures* (pp. 148–165). New York: Pergamon Press.

Stahl, N. A., Brozo, W. G., Smith, B. D., & Henk, W. A. (1991). Effects of teaching generative vocabulary strategies in the college developmental reading program. *Journal of Research and Development in Education, 24,* 24–32.

Thoresen, C. E., & Mahoney, M. J. (1974). *Behavioral self-control.* New York: Holt, Rinehart & Winston.

Winne, P. H. (1995). Inherent details in self-regulated learning. *Educational Psychologist, 30,* 173–187.

Wood, E., Fler, C., & Willoughby, T. (1992). Elaborative interrogation applied to small and large group contexts. *Applied Cognitive Psychology, 6,* 361–366.

Zimmerman, B. J. (1989a). Models of self-regulated learning and academic achievement. In B. J. Zimmerman & D. H. Schunk (Eds.), *Self-regulated learning and academic achievement: Theory, research, and practice* (pp. 1–26). New York: Springer-Verlag.

Zimmerman, B. J. (1989b). A social cognitive view of self-regulated academic learning. *Journal of Educational Psychology, 81*, 329–339.

Zimmerman, B. J. (1990). Self-regulated learning and academic achievement: An overview. *Educational Psychologist, 25*, 3–17.

Zimmerman, B. J., & Martinez-Pons, M. (1986). Development of a structured interview for assessing student use of self-regulated learning strategies. *American Educational Research Journal, 23*, 614–628.

Zimmerman, B. J., & Martinez-Pons, M. (1988). Construct validation of a strategy model of student self-regulated learning. *Journal of Educational Psychology, 80*, 284–290.

Zimmerman, B. J., & Martinez-Pons, M. (1990). Student differences in self-regulated learning: Relating grade, sex, and giftedness to self-efficacy and strategy use. *Journal of Educational Psychology, 82*, 51–59.

Zimmerman, B. J., & Ringle, J. (1981). Effects of model persistence and statements of confidence on children's efficacy and problem solving, *Journal of Educational Psychology, 73*, 485–493.

CHAPTER 6

Computing Technologies as Sites for Developing Self-Regulated Learning

Philip H. Winne
Denise B. Stockley

Governments, school boards, teachers, parents, and almost everyone concerned about education is clamoring for students to have access to computing technologies for everyday classroom activities. Although there rarely are enough computers and peripheral devices to allow every student access on demand, even modestly equipped schools can usually inventory an array of resources such as modems, printers, scanners, word processors, e-mail and Internet browsers, graphic applications, spreadsheets, databases, CD-ROMs, and games (which developers claim are educational). In fact, most paper-based resources and tools for recording and manipulating information found in today's classrooms could, with sufficient will, funding, and in-service support, be replaced by computing technologies. At first blush, it seems that almost all learning might thus be enticingly and usefully enhanced.

Amidst a flurry of promises and policy making, students are busy exploring and using computing technologies. Like conventional tools students use to learn, they will need to be taught how to use computing technologies. For instance, learning to form cursive letters now must be supplemented with keyboarding and mousing skills. The topics are sufficiently complex and valued that most jurisdictions now include computer literacy or some variant as a core goal of education. Because hardware and software are evolving exponentially, everything, especially students' and teachers' knowledge and skills, is insatiably in need of upgrading.

PROMISES ABOUT COMPUTING
TECHNOLOGIES AND LEARNING

There is much debate about roles for computing technologies in education (e.g., for "early" views, see Papert, 1980; Schank, 1984). A limiting feature of these dialogues is that educational research is just beginning to develop a broad and reliable database of results from lab and field experiments. In reviewing research on technological supports for writing, Herman (1994) concluded that *"one cannot separate the effects of technology from the quality of the instruction and curriculum in which it is embedded"* (p. 151, emphasis in original). We (Winne, 1993) concur with Herman, and with Hativa and Lesgold (1996): "Little is known about instructional design issues that affect students' learning with technology. Almost all technological (particularly computer) applications have been designed on the basis of theories developed for nontechnological setting [sic] as well as on the educational philosophies and beliefs of the designers themselves. Case studies show that this basis is not good enough" (p. 167).

Self-regulation is inherent when learning is guided by goals of any sort (Winne, 1995, 1996a). Some forms of self-regulated learning are theorized to help students learn more of what they study, develop and sustain positive motivation, and practice and extend skills for learning. Prior work (Schunk & Zimmerman, 1994; Zimmerman & Schunk, 1989) reveals a variety of complexly interacting factors that affect students' development and use of tactics that comprise academically effective forms of self-regulated learning. The number and complexity of these factors multiplies when students themselves try to bootstrap more productive forms of self-regulated learning (Winne, 1997).

Interventions designed to guide students toward academically effective forms of self-regulated learning must acknowledge that "relatively little is currently known about the development or acquisition of self-regulation and what can be done to facilitate its development" (Weinstein, 1996, p. 272). Nonetheless, current methods have approximately the same efficacy as research-validated principles for teaching other topics (e.g., see Pressley, 1995). The fruits of such instruction, however, will not be quickly harvested. If developing expertise in self-regulated learning is like developing expertise in other domains (Ericsson, Krampe, & Tesch-Römer, 1993), developing expertise in self-regulated learning will require approximately 85% of the 12,000 hours allocated to students' first 12 years of school. In light of this time frame, our and others' claims about the potential of computing technologies to revolutionize schools quickly, empower learners today, and achieve goals society sets for education should be moderate. We make one claim without reservation, however: No single educational tool, no matter what its powers, can redress the spectrum of social and institutional issues that teachers and learners face in schools.

What Is to Come

Despite these caveats, we are optimistic that today's and the near future's computing technologies, appropriately coupled with other educational innovations, can increase the efficacy, efficiency, and extent of students' self-regulated learning. We shun technological opportunism (Salomon & Perkins, 1996) whereby "a whole instructional wardrobe of theory and practice becomes tailored to fit a new and shiny button" (p. 112). Instead, we favor a theory- and research-based approach to designing computing technologies for supporting learning (Winne, 1992). To this end, we review select theory and research to illustrate how extant or imminent educational technologies might guide students toward developing more academically effective forms of self-regulated learning. Rather than superficially cover a large volume of topics relevant to designing such adaptive learning systems, we focus on four issues that arise from the model of self-regulated learning that we present next.

SELF-REGULATED LEARNING

Self-regulated learning is a dualistic construct with properties of an aptitude (Snow, 1996) and an event (Winne, 1997; Winne & Hadwin, 1997). Viewed as an aptitude, self-regulated learning describes a state of the student's cognition that predicts the cognition and motivation that will be involved when the student addresses future instructional activities. To date, self-regulated learning as an aptitude has been measured by students' reflections on past activities in responses to questionnaires or comments gathered with a stimulated recall protocol. Like other aptitudes, self-regulated learning varies within individuals over time, within individuals across tasks, and across individuals (Pintrich, Wolters, & Baxter, in press).

A few studies have investigated self-regulated learning as it is applied during engagement with instructional activities, using indicators observed during classroom activities (e.g., students' utterances; Perry, 1997) or by counting traces that students deposit in archival work (e.g., notes that students made while planning a report; Howard-Rose & Winne, 1993). Some of this work describes self-regulated learning using two-term, IF–THEN events. Few researchers have examined self-regulated learning as larger, temporally patterned cognitive operations that students apply over the course of one or a series of instructional activities (cf. Butler, Chapter 8; Biemiller, Shany, Inglis, & Meichenbaum, Chapter 10; and Graham, Harris, & Troia, Chapter 2, this volume). Two facts accounting for this lacuna are that efficient tools have been just recently developed to track such data and that quantitative methods for examining sequences and complex patterns of cognitive events are only now being created (see Guzdial et al., 1996; Winne, Gupta, & Nesbit, 1994).

Winne and Hadwin's (1997) 3 + 1 phase model characterizes self-regulated learning as an event involving three necessary phases and an optional fourth phase: perceiving the task, setting goals, enacting tactics to approach goals, and, optionally, adapting tactics. Each phase transforms or constructs information, thereby creating the potential for metacognitive monitoring and control (Winne, 1996a). Figure 6.1, which we describe in the following descriptions of each phase, models locations and types of information involved in self-regulated learning as an event and probable flows of information across (1) locations in the learner's cognitive system and (2) interfacing with the environment. Although this model may imply that self-regulated learning unfolds in sequence from phase 1 to 2 and so on, this is probably not so. Once self-regulated learning is underway, it is recursive and weakly sequenced. Recursive means that the information generated in a

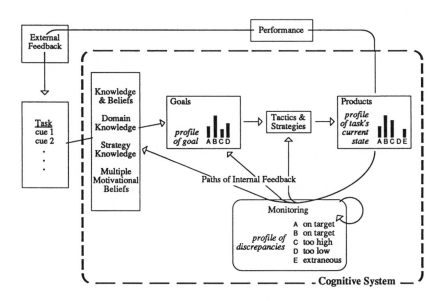

FIGURE 6.1. A model of self-regulated learning showing the profile of a goal, the current state of a task's products, and a profile of discrepancies that monitoring creates. Reprinted with permission from "A metacognitive view of individual differences in self-regulated learning" by P. H. Winne, 1996, *Learning and Individual Differences*, 8, p. 331. Copyright 1996 by JAI Press, Inc.

given phase of self-regulated learning may feed into that same phase again when monitoring operations identify that a standard is not met. Weakly sequenced means that although self-regulated learning begins with phase 1 (perceiving the task), once information is generated in any phase, the event may jump phases or recurse to the same phase.

Phase 1: Perceiving the Task

In every self-regulated learning event, the learner generates a perception about the instructional activity, a perception that may be updated as the task unfolds. These perceptions are complex, multifaceted, and personal blends of information attended to in the environment coupled with memories about tasks (Butler & Winne, 1995; Winne, 1997). One facet of these perceptions is understandings and inferences about the domain of the task (e.g., a science project or a composition in argument form). A second facet reflects memories about attributes such as interest and efficacy in this domain. A third facet involves memories of tactics that might be enacted to address the task.

Hypothetically, learners always generate at least two perceptions about an activity. A *default* perception characterizes how the activity will unfold if a particular tactic is not engaged. This perception is complemented by another that describes how the activity will unfold if a particular tactic is applied in it. For example, consider a student searching for information on the World Wide Web. The student understands that taking notes about information found on Web pages not only supports work on a larger project, but also creates a record of the search tactic itself. That record can provide data for self-regulating search tactics. However, nothing forces the student to take notes. This option is matched by a default perception of how the activity unfolds if note taking is bypassed in general or at a particular Web page. Thus, even when there is just one tactic to use, the student can exercise choice or agency. If the student knows different forms of note taking—for example, just copying the Web page's title, copying the title plus drawing a concept map of information displayed on the page, copying the title plus developing a propositional summary of the page's information—options for expressing agency expand in proportion to perceptions about the activity's development if alternative tactics are applied in it.

Phase 2: Setting Goals

Choosing between a default activity and an *active* alternative, or selecting one activity from multiple alternatives, is something the learner always can do unless the environment prevents it (e.g., if a computer is not equipped with note-taking software). Having these options empowers the learner to exercise agency, which is realized when he or she decides which of the alternatives will be enacted. This act of deciding among alternatives is the second phase of self-regulated learning. The product of this decision making creates a goal that the student has elected to pursue (Winne, 1997) by a particular tactic(s). If memory automatically provides (McKoon & Ratcliff, 1992) or is searched to identify a tactic(s) or strategy(ies) for taking notes, the learner has inherently coupled a plan to that goal. As Figure 6.1 depicts, we model a goal as a multifaceted profile of information (Butler & Winne, 1995). Each criterion or standard in the profile—represented by the letters A, B, C, and D in Figure 6.1—is a basis against which the student can monitor engagement with the activity by comparing the profile of a product's features to the goal's criteria. Beginning to enact tactics and strategies that approach the goal is the point of transition into phase 3 of a self-regulated learning event.

Phase 3: Enacting Tactics

Tactics are bundles of memories that we model in two main parts: conditional knowledge (IFs) characterize a tactic's appropriateness; cognitive operations (THENs) transform and construct information. Conditional knowledge is more than *cold* propositions about whether certain cognitive operations can achieve a goal. Blended into conditional knowledge are at least two other kinds of propositions. One is epistemological beliefs (Schommer, 1994), for example, whether knowledge in a domain is certain versus probabilistic, or how much effort is needed to complete tasks like this. The other is a collage of *hot* motivational beliefs that stimulate affect—efficacy expectations, outcome expectations, incentives associated with products a tactic constructs, and attributions (Pintrich, Marx, & Boyle, 1993; Winne, 1995, 1997; Winne & Marx, 1989).

When tactics developed as part of phases 1 and 2 are enacted, phase 3 of a self-regulated learning event is initiated. Tactics copy information to or construct information in working memory. Paralleling our multifaceted model of goals, we also model the information produced by tactics as a multifaceted profile (Figure 6.1). If the learner monitors the profile of a tactic's product in relation to a goal profile, internal feedback is generated. If a product is translated into behavior, external feedback also may be available if the computer, a peer, or a teacher reacts to the student's behavior.

Phase 4: Adapting Tactics for Self-Regulated Learning

In the midst of any of the preceding phrases or when students quit an activity, they may initiate an optional phase to edit knowledge, beliefs, and actions that comprise tactics and strategies (Winne & Hadwin, 1997). Editing typically involves a process of mindful abstraction (Salomon & Perkins,

1989) that modifies or creates new metalevel models of activities as well as means for engaging in them. Three kinds of changes to metalevel models are proposed (after Rumelhart & Norman, 1978). First, propositions representing conditional knowledge (IFs) may be added to (or subtracted from) cognitive tactics and strategies, or steps may be added to (or subtracted from) actions (THENs) that assemble, translate, and rehearse information. Accretion specializes the student's understanding about when a tactic or strategy is appropriate to or augments what the student does. Reduction generalizes (transfers) actions to other sets of conditions or curtails what the student does. Second, the student may adjust weights or thresholds that govern how propositions of conditional knowledge are used in decision making (see Butler & Winne, 1995). This tunes the process of decision making for a better fit with the same conditions as before. Third, the student may rearrange links between conditional knowledge and actions, creating new tactics or restructuring strategies that arrange tactics.

Monitoring: A Pivot for Self-Regulated Learning

In each phase of self-regulated learning, metacognitive monitoring is central (Butler & Winne, 1995; Winne, 1996a, 1996b). Like all cognitive operations, monitoring produces information. In this case, the product is a list of matches and mismatches between the student's standards (schema) and a representation in working memory of the product(s) of a phase of self-regulated learning. For example, in phase 1, generating a perception of the activity involves monitoring input from the environment relative to prototypes for tasks. In phase 3, monitoring compares products that tactics create to goals from phase 2.

The list of matches and mismatches that monitoring creates can be fed back into the process to update any or all of (1) the student's perception of the activity, (2) the goal chosen on the basis of perception about the activity, and (3) tactics and strategies enacted to approach the goal. Within the limits of cognitive resources (working memory capacity, knowledge/beliefs) and external constraints (e.g., time available, reference materials), the student can exercise metacognitive control to make midcourse adaptations in the unfolding event. For example, in phase 1, the student may seek further information about the activity, such as standards by which success will be judged. In phase 3, tactics can be toggled on and off (Winne & Hadwin, 1997).

Four Targets for Technological Support in Aid of Developing Self-Regulated Learning

Winne and Hadwin's (1997) 3 + 1 phase model of self-regulated learning and Figure 6.1 (1) imply how educational technologies can invite students to explore new forms of self-regulated learning and (2) target topics where adaptive computing systems might help students toggle and edit knowledge on which self-regulated learning is based (see also Pressley, 1995). In point form, these topics are as follows:

1. Factors that influence how students perceive activities have potential to affect self-regulated learning because the perception of an activity generates an *activity space* (akin to a problem space) within which a student's engagement will unfold.

2. Factors that affect how students select goals can influence how students regulate learning because the profile of a goal's features defines standards used in metacognitive monitoring. External feedback that arises as the student interacts with the computing system has potential to influence self-regulated learning by providing new standards or by tuning standards in the profile of a goal (Butler & Winne, 1995; Winne, 1989).

3. Variables that affect how students enact tactics and strategies within a learning activity have potential to affect self-regulated learning because differences in these enactments may lead to differences in products that tactics and strategies create. In particular, conditions that affect whether and how students monitor products they create relative to goals have potential to influence self-regulated learning because metacognitive monitoring and the internal feedback it generates are pivotal in self-regulated learning.

4. Features that support a student in editing—accreting, tuning, and restructuring—knowledge and tactics that power self-regulated learning as an event affect immediate performance. If edits are preserved in long-term memory, self-regulated learning as an aptitude is reshaped and has potential to support transfer.

Shortly, we present four sections that discuss how computing technologies might support students within each phase in the 3 + 1 phase model of self-regulated learning. For each phase, we lay a theoretical foundation that identifies critical issues to address in designing an adaptive learning system that can support that phase of the development of self-regulated learning. We remind you of our view that theory should shape instructional designs in which technology is used, a stance in direct contrast to technological opportunism. Using this theoretical base, we then sketch a scene in which a student is studying. By studying, we mean an activity in which the student sets out to investigate information with a goal to learn at least some of it (see Winne & Hadwin, 1997). In each scene, we assume the student is using a high-end notebook computer and has access to common peripheral media (CD-ROM, DVD, PCMCIA cards, graphics tablets, Internet access technologies such as Netscape™ 3.0). The system we envision is equipped with software tools that are available now or whose development will be completed within a year (e.g., STUDY v. 3.2, a system used to design tools that students can use as they study; Field & Winne, 1997). We annotate each scene to explain how the system scaffolds (i.e., supports and sensitively withdraws support for) the development of academically effective forms of self-regulated learning.

GUIDING PHASE 1:
PERCEPTIONS ABOUT EFFORT AND TASKS

A Model of Effort

As a learner engages with an instructional activity, self-regulated learning manages cognitive tactics primarily by toggling them on and off as the learner strives to reach goals. Some tactics are automated to an extent that the learner need neither deliberate about toggling them nor attend to "running" them after they are toggled on. An accomplished reader, for instance, implicitly draws inferences to generate comprehension, becoming deliberate about tactics for making inferences only when the text is inconsiderate relative to the reader's knowledge or incoherent relative to its macrostructure (McKoon & Ratcliff, 1992). For most learners in most situations, however, regulating most cognitive tactics requires effort.

What is effort? Eisenberger (1992) describes effort as "a fundamental response-produced experience" (p. 261). Winne (1997) hypothesizes that an experience of effort reflects three factors: (1) the number of separable steps in a tactic, (2) the time it takes to identify and enact those steps, and (3) the probability that the tactic creates a product that meets standards for the task. Automated tactics have a profile across these three factors that has levels of steps = 1, time = trivial, and probability = 1. Hence, using an automated tactic generates a perception of minimal effort, if there is any perception of effort at all. Other tactics that we perceive as effortful have a profile across these three factors in which the factors of steps and time are at levels greater than 1 and the probability factor is less than 1. According to this model, effort's factors also can be integrated so that the experience can be characterized by an overall level of effort. Thus, two different tactics can have profiles of effort that differ in overall level as well as the pattern of levels of effort's factors.

For example, we can reconcile bank statements with our checkbook using just a few automated tactics. Each tactic builds on automated arithmetic rules (literally so when we use a calculator), takes just a few seconds, and the product of each tactic is highly predictable. We do not perceive this task as calling for much effort. Although most of the tactics we use to fill in our annual income tax forms are the same as for reconciling a bank statement, tax filing requires several additional tactics that each require several separate steps, span minutes or longer, and have unpredictable outcomes (at least for us). The effort of doing income taxes is perceived quite differently.

Memory records the effort required to enact a tactic. This information is one element of conditional knowledge (IFs) that the learner uses when deciding whether to toggle a tactic and forms an important part of the student's perception of an activity in phase 1 of self-regulated learning. When a tactic is enacted, it is "the substance of effort, *how* effort is applied" (Winne, 1995, p. 176).

Supporting Learned Industriousness within Self-Regulated Learning

Like the kind of practice that achieves expertise in other areas, deliberate practice for approaching expertise in self-regulated learning "requires effort and is not enjoyable. Individuals are motivated to practice because practice improves performance" (Ericsson et al., 1993, p. 368) rather than just to spend effort practicing or to demonstrate competence to others. Deliberate practice is a hallmark of motivationally positive task involvement and a mastery goal orientation (see Ames, 1992). To sustain this kind of industriousness when learning how to regulate learning, better students need to perceive incentives for applying effort-bearing tactics, along with receiving feedback about the results of that effort.

As does Eisenberger (1992), we believe people learn to be industrious, that is, to hold a belief that challenging tasks should be approached with effort. Under this view, an interesting question arises: Can industriousness transfer? This is not a question about whether a particular tactic is maintained and transfers, but rather about whether learners will choose to toggle on effortful tactics when facing a challenging task in any domain.

Eisenberger (1992) reviewed a sizable body of research on this question. He concluded that effort can transfer from one task to others because it "is exquisitely sensitive to secondary reward effects" (p. 261). That is, when effortful tactics are applied, the experience involves more than just practicing a tactic. In accord with our model of conditional knowledge as a bundle of information that integrates motivational and epistemological propositions, deliberate practice also enhances the incentive for applying effortful tactics to difficult tasks. A study by Eisenberger, Masterson, and McDermitt (1982) demonstrates such transfer of effort after deliberate practice. In the first part of an experimental session, one group of undergraduates was assigned three types of problems: addition, anagrams, and finding differences between pairs of cartoon pictures. Three other groups were set only one problem type each. Half the students in each of the four groups were given problems that did not require much effort (e.g., anagrams known to require 3–5 seconds to solve) and half were given problems that called for high effort (e.g., anagrams normed at 25–30 seconds for solution). In the second half of the experimental session, all the students wrote an essay about a controversial topic.

Effort applied in writing essays was measured by length and by quality. We interpret both to indicate the extent to which students used effortful writing tactics. Students who first worked on all three types of difficult problems wrote the longest and highest quality essays. According to Eisenberger's (1992) notion of learned industriousness and our model of conditional knowledge, students who experienced varied and difficult problems were primed to believe that effort was appropriate to the composition task. It was perceived with positive incentive and was expressed by applying writing tactics that produced longer and better essays. Students posed all three types of easy problems in the first half of the session wrote the shortest and lowest quality essays. Their experience was that relatively automated, noneffortful tactics were appropriate for tasks. The other groups scored in between these extremes on length and quality. Our model would suggest their conditional knowledge was not clear about how much effort to transfer to the essay task.

This backdrop suggests that two interesting results should follow if an adaptive learning system is to guide a student to use effort-demanding tactics in learning activities. First, each time a tactic is practiced and the student receives or generates feedback about its utility, that tactic is nudged a little closer toward automaticity, the state in which, after considerable practice, it will not require self-regulation. Second, research on the transfer of beliefs about effort, what Eisenberger (1992) terms *learned industriousness*, suggests the student will tune that element of conditional knowledge that addresses the effort apparently called for by a task: When tasks are challenging, those tasks are better approached with effort, and effort is realized by applying tactics that entail effort.

Systems designed to implement this principle might also help learners overcome two other hurdles to developing more effective forms of self-regulated learning, the *production deficiency* and the *utilization deficiency* (e.g., see Miller & Seier, 1994). A production deficiency occurs when a learner knows a potentially useful tactic but that tactic remains inert. The tactic is not toggled on because it is not searched for. A utilization deficiency arises when the learner toggles on a tactic that will ultimately work effectively but, because that tactic has not been practiced enough to convert it from a list of separate declarative propositions (steps) to a smoothly running procedure, performance suffers slightly. Learning systems already adopting this approach are Salomon, Globerson, and Guterman's (1989) reading partner and Zellermayer, Salomon, Globerson, and Givon's (1991) writing partner.

Scene

For simplicity, we will call the student in this scene Paul. The computing system here and in subsequent scenes is STUDY, a software tool for designing adaptive instructional tools and providing computer-supported instruction (Field & Winne, 1997).

Paul is a ninth-grade student who has been using STUDY since school started 10 weeks ago. He is now quite proficient with its features, including a stock notebook that STUDY supplies. He has also become a World Wide Web addict, often searching (idiomatically called *surfing*) it for information to use in class assignments. The STUDY notebook is a window with four regions or fields that are used to enter and record textual information. The fields are labeled Key Terms, Source, URL (Universal Resource Location), and Analysis. The notebook also is equipped with menus that Paul can pop up over text that he selects. Options on those menus "do things" to the text that is selected. Over the past weeks, Paul has developed two tactics that he uses while surfing for useful information. One finds information within a Web page; another organizes information he borrows from Web pages so that he can find it. Call these tactics *searching* and *indexing*, respectively.

Paul is presently working on a project that investigates what his city government might do about a major bridge that is expected to become unsafe in 3–5 years. With his partner, Tia, he wanted to surf the Web for information about what is involved in building bridges such as costs, plans to pay for projects of this magnitude, and environmental issues; and alternatives to bridges such as tunnels and ferry systems. To get started, Paul and Tia brainstormed, with help from their teacher, a list of key topics to address in their report. They entered those terms into the notebook's field called Key Terms.

Now, Paul is ready to begin a surfing safari. When using his searching tactic, Paul uses key terms to locate regions of a Web page that might provide information to use for Tia's and his report. In searching, Paul clicks on one of the items in the Key Terms list, say, "bond issue." STUDY pops up a menu over the selection and Paul chooses one of its options, "Copy this key term." Then, he moves over to his Web browser window. STUDY had automatically pasted that key term into the browser's find tool. Paul now uses the browser's find tool to scan the Web page for successive instances of "bond issue."

Paul studies each instance that is found. Sometimes, he decides to copy some of the material into his notebook's Source field. STUDY also inserts the key term that was the topic of the search at the beginning of this text. Thus, each source note lists the key term Paul used to locate the information ("bond issue" in this case) followed by the block of text he copied from the Web page. STUDY distinguishes the key term that indexes the text by coloring it red. In the notebook's URL field, STUDY automatically records the Web address for information Paul copies so that he can easily return to it if he wants. After a Web page has been entirely searched using "bond issue" as a key term, Paul repeats the job for the next key term in his list, say, "cost overrun." Searching is an automated tactic for Paul that he has used with bound encyclopedias since the third grade.

Paul's indexing tactic is more effortful because he is not very practiced in inventing his own system for indexing information. After he copies material into the Source field, he begins to analyze it more thoroughly. First, he scans it for any other key terms from the list of Key Terms. Paul has discovered that almost every block of source information mentions another key term that he and Tia should discuss in their report. For example, many entries about bond issues also discuss alternative methods for financing, such as bridge tolls. Paul can easily add the index "bridge tolls" to "bond issue," which is currently the single index for this source material. Paul moves over the Key Terms list and selects "bridge tolls," and STUDY pops up a menu. One option on the menu is "Index Source using this." Paul chooses this option and STUDY adds the key term "bridge tolls" after the first index, "bond issue." Now, this source is indexed by two items.

As Paul continues analyzing this source information, he discovers a new idea that seems important: "referendum." He decides to index the source by this term, too. He selects this word in the block of source text and STUDY pops up a menu on which Paul selects "Index Source using this." Now, the source has three indexes: bond issue, bridge tolls, and referendum.

As Paul applies his indexing tactic, he builds a database of sources that can be searched by multiple indexes. He has to monitor whether source material is worth indexing with key terms other than the one used to search the Web page, and whether sources suggest useful new indexes. We infer that Paul's indexing tactic is more effortful than his searching tactic. It entails more monitoring and, because Paul is learning how to develop his own index terms, the tactic's utility is less predictable. In other words, Paul is more industrious when indexing than when searching.

So far, Paul has not added any new items into the Key Terms list. To do that, all he has to do is type new terms such as "referendum" into that list, exactly as he did after the brainstorming session that created the original list of key terms.

The models of effort and of learned industriousness described earlier suggest how STUDY can guide Paul to change his searching tactic, that is, to regulate his approach to this task. First, the model of learned industriousness suggests that Paul is primed to apply more effort to searching. Why? Adding new indexes is effortful because Paul has not yet automated procedures for this work and the utility of new indexes is not assured. The same applies to adding new items to Key Terms that he uses when searching. In this sense, both tactics share the feature of effort observed in Eisenberger et al.'s (1982) study. He could apply this effort by adding terms to the Key Terms list, perhaps just by borrowing from new indexes he is adding to entries in the Source field.

STUDY affords this transfer but it is up to Paul to realize that creating new indexes during note taking might also enhance his searching tactic. STUDY can also be more instructional. For example, it can count the number of times Paul creates a new index across all the sources he copies from Web pages. When the count reaches some arbitrary threshold, say 8, and STUDY has recorded that Paul has not yet added a new item to the Key Terms list, it might intervene with a message when Paul creates a new index: "Can you make learning better by applying this same idea to something else you do?" It is still up to Paul to figure out what to do. Even more explicitly, STUDY might remind Paul that the Key Terms list can be edited and ask if he thinks that might enhance his work (after King, 1992).

The intent of this instructional design for STUDY's notebook is to accomplish two objectives. First, it affords opportunities for Paul to monitor metacognitively his perceptions of studying activities, specifically, about where and how he applies effort. Because effort is an inherent perception, monitoring effort may not be deliberate in the sense that Paul realizes he monitors how much effort he applies. The model of learned industriousness does not require deliberate monitoring, though it nonetheless predicts that when effort is increased the odds increase that Paul will generalize an effortful tactic to tasks he perceives as requiring more effort. If he does that, he is engaging in self-regulated learning. Second, if Paul does transfer the notion of augmenting Key Terms in the same way he augments indexes for source material, he is practicing procedures for making an indexed database of information. As this component of learning becomes automated, cognitive resources are freed to allow Paul to allocate resources to other aspects of learning.

GUIDING PHASE 2: HELPING LEARNERS RESHAPE GOALS

As we noted earlier, metacognitive monitoring is the pivot on which self-regulated learning turns. In self-regulated learning, learners use goals as standards against which they monitor both the conditions of tasks at the outset and the successive updates to the task they create as cognitive tactics are applied to search out, assemble, and translate information. When meta-cognitive monitoring identifies that updates are diverging or discrepant from goals, self-regulating learners exercise metacognitive control to toggle tactics off and on. This model suggests two ways to support the development of self-regulated learning that toggles tactics: Help the learner change conditional knowledge used to judge when specific tactics are suitable, and help the learner change goals in terms of which activities are monitored.

Goal Setting to Guide Selection of Tactics

We hold that learners are goal-directed agents (Winne, 1995, 1997). Different goals will often lead learners to use different tactics. (Exceptions will occur when a particular tactic effectively serves multiple goals.) According to Schunk (1996), properties of goals affect achievement: "Goals that incorporate specific performance standards, are close at hand, and are moderately difficult are more likely to enhance performance than goals that are general, extend into the distant future, or are perceived as overly easy or difficult" (p. 360). This accords with the theoretical account presented earlier about the value of tasks where effort, realized by applying tactics, contributes to engagement and points to the value of goals that have specific properties.

A study by Morgan (1985) suggests learners may not set goals that have all these properties. In a two-semester educational psychology course, a quarter of the students studied without any intervention. Three other groups were trained at the outset of the course to set goals for studying, specify criteria for judging whether the goal(s) had been achieved, and record at the end of each study session how well they met goal(s) they had set. One group set a single, overall performance goal for each study session (e.g., "I'll understand these theories of learning."). Another group defined a small number of relatively proximal subgoals for segments of the material they studied. These were instructional objectives that identified the conditions, products, and standards to achieve (e.g., "Without the book, I'll compare and contrast positive reinforcement and negative reinforcement using the book's two dimensions for behavioral consequences."). The third group set a goal for the time they would study (e.g., "I'll study for 45 minutes."). In each of the four groups, a random half were required to submit their notes every 2 weeks. Analyses of these materials confirmed that students participated in the interventions as intended.

On measures of achievement and interest in the course, students who set more specific proximal subgoals outscored all other groups. Among students who set precise, proximal goals, there were no differences in achievement as a function of whether they were monitored for compliance with the goal-setting procedure. But students who had to hand in notes every other week were more interested in course content than peers who set similarly precise, proximal goals but were not monitored. This suggests that neither learning nor motivation is undermined if an external agent examines students' goals.

Students who set goals that provided a criterion for monitoring study time did study longer than peers in other groups, but they realized no gains in interest or achievement for that extra effort. Under the assumption that effort is given substance by using study tactics, whatever adjustments these students made to studying tactics were relatively less effective in the absence of precise, proximal goals that described content to be learned.

In a very different context, Schunk (1996) studied how well fourth graders learned addition and subtraction of fractions when their teacher set either learning goals or performance goals at the beginning of each of six study sessions. Learning goals describe "trying to learn how to solve problems" as the primary standard for monitoring tactics' effectiveness; performance goals focus on "trying to solve problems" as the prime criterion for monitoring (p. 367). In the first experiment, at the end of each study session, half the students in each goal group self-evaluated their skills by using parallel examples of problems like those they had been studying. In the second experiment, self-evaluation was explicitly required only after the sixth and last study session.

Results differed across Schunk's (1996) two experiments. When the experimental condition required students to self-evaluate at the end of each study session, there were no differences between students who were set learning versus performance goals on postexperiment self-efficacy, task orientation, and achievement. In the second experiment, where explicit requirements for self-evaluation were delayed until all six study sessions were over, students for whom the teacher set learning goals expressed higher self-efficacy, more task orientation, and learned more than students who were set performance goals.

Schunk's (1996) studies indicate that young students differentially self-regulate depending on the topic of goals, learning versus performance, but this difference can be erased if monitoring is more frequent. The 3 + 1 phase model of self-regulated learning suggests students who adopt performance goals and who frequently monitor success have standards for adapting studying tactics that are productive.

Although we must proceed cautiously because of significant differences in the topics studied, length of study, and developmental level of participants, when combining Morgan's (1985) and Schunk's (1996) findings, it seems learners either lack skills for setting useful goals or do not use skills they may have. Left to their own devices, goals they set do not appear to provide precise, proximal standards for monitoring the effects of study tactics. If learners use proxies for studying tactics, such as time spent, they also do not seem able to bootstrap regulation of tactics.

These studies on the effects of different kinds of goals indicate that goals students set in phase 2 of the 3 + 1 phase model of self-regulated learning are key variables that affect engagement. Thus, adaptive learning systems should be designed to help students set goals that enhance studying. Morgan's (1985) study suggests that helping students frame goals with more precise and proximal standards can enhance the quality of metacognitive monitoring in the midst of studying. Schunk's (1996) studies indicate that guiding students to monitor products of their work more frequently in relation to well-framed goals creates explicit occasions to self-regulate. Importantly, this latter intervention appears to be helpful independently of whether students' adopt learning or performance goals.

Scene

Andie is just about to start reading the essay her teacher assigned for language arts. She opens her laptop and launches STUDY to begin. Before STUDY opens the file with the essay Andie will read, it first presents a window that has five columns labeled as follows: Conditions, Operations, Products, Evaluations, Feedback. Under Conditions are listed three options: Class Notes, Title and Headings, and Nate (her partner in language arts). In the operations are listed the following: Scan, Jot First Thoughts, Predict, Read Through. Products has these options: New Vocabulary, Theme, Questions in Margins, Summary. Evaluations specifies the following: Me, Outside Sources. Standards includes these options: My Call, Teacher's List, Nate Gets It. Beneath each column is a button labeled, New.

All these options are Andie's own terms for how she sets goals. She created them by clicking New and typing something in a column. Now, she is using her labels by selecting one or more options in each column. She chooses Class Notes, Title and Headings; Scan; Jot First Thoughts; Theme; Me; My Call. Next, she clicks a button opposite one of several descriptors of difficulty—hard, moderate, easy—then clicks a button labeled, Set it. She decided this task was easy.

Andie has just set a proximal, specific, and, by her standards, easy goal for the task she will use to start studying. To her, it means, "I'll review, but not too deeply, my notes from class and look over the title and headings in the essay. Then, I'll write some impressions about what the theme of this essay might be and evaluate as best I can on my own whether I'm on track." Before Andie begins studying per se, she sets a few more goals. STUDY records all her selections.

Andie opens her STUDY notebook and finds today's notes. Then, she opens the file containing the assigned essay and starts to scan through it. When she reaches the end, she scrolls back to the beginning of the essay and starts to read. STUDY was observing in the background. It recorded that nothing further was done to examine notes in the notebook. No scrolling was recorded, nor was the Find tool used to locate some particular information. At no point in the first pass through the essay nor before she scrolled back to the beginning did Andie enter information in the notebook. As well, the index term Theme was not applied to any information in the notebook (in the way that Paul indexed information in the prior scene). STUDY starts a timer set at a maximum of 1.5 minutes. Based on prior sessions, STUDY "knows" this is an average interval for Andie to read 100 words. During this interval, Andie enters nothing in the notebook.

STUDY computes that the goal Andie set has not been satisfied. It interrupts Andie with a message: "Hi, Andie. Did you forget to work on Goal #1?" STUDY then opens the window Andie used to set her goal for this study session and changes Andie's selections in each column from black text to red, showing Andie exactly what she set as her goal. After 10 seconds, STUDY displays a second message: "By the way, did you mean to set an easy goal this time? Remember we've talked about how moderately difficult goals are better?" In the message window are several buttons below the label Options. One is labeled, Oops! If Andie clicks this button, STUDY begins again to record whether Andie satisfies her goal. A second is labeled, Help. If Andie clicks it, STUDY displays some information about how moderately difficult goals create the best situations for generating self-evaluations about how well domain information is being learned. The third button is labeled, Skip It. If Andie clicks it, STUDY quits watching the indicators that signal Andie is acting in accord with her goal.

At the end of the session, Andie tells STUDY she is done. STUDY displays a final message: "Andie, how well do you think you met your goals?" STUDY offers Andie the option to fill in a form to help Andie record information about how well her goals correlate with her achievement.

In this scene, STUDY guides Andie to set goals and helps her monitor whether she actually studies in accord with those goals. When Andie forgets goals or studies in a way contrary to goals she set, STUDY reminds her of the goal but does not dictate what she must do. Over many study sessions, Andie has opportunities to practice framing goals that "work for her." By scaffolding occasions to examine how learning correlates with goal setting, STUDY guides Andie toward regulating the goals she sets as well as regulating her coordination of tactics for approaching those goals. Thus, STUDY serves two ends: It leads Andie toward setting the kinds of goals that Morgan's (1985) and Schunk's (1996) research suggest will help her learn more while simultaneously providing tools to invite Andie to tune and restructure tactics for learning in relation to their effectiveness in reaching those goals.

GUIDING PHASE 3: SUPPORTING TACTICS THAT CONSTRUCT SCHEMAS

Goal-Free Problems

Like many theorists (see Austin & Vancouver, 1996), we assume students are agents. Agents purposefully channel their engagement in learning activities, events that we model theoretically as setting goals and choosing tactics for working toward those goals. There is abundant evidence (e.g., McKoon & Ratcliff, 1992) that tactics can be automated to the extent that invoking and applying them is not deliberate, not part of everyday awareness. In this same sense, goal setting need not call for deliberate cognition in circumstances where cognitive processes that generate perceptions of activities are automatic. Indeed, a hallmark of self-regulated learning is the capability to interfere with automated goal setting and memory's automated process of spreading activation that activates tactics for approaching goals (Anderson, 1991).

Whether purposefully or inadvertently, many curriculum designers appear to have taught learners to perceive problem-solving activities as typically well served by a tactic called *means–ends analysis*. Briefly, a means–ends tactic involves comparing the initial conditions of a task against the goal set for that task, then searching for a tactic that will transform either the goal or the initial conditions to be a bit more like one another. Metaphorically, the distance between the task's initial conditions and its goal is reduced by this transformation to update conditions or formulate a subgoal. Once a first reduction in this discrepancy has been achieved, the tactic is repeated, analyzing or breaking down the overall problem. In each iteration, if appropriate tactics are selected, the discrepancy between updated conditions and successively constructed subgoals is reduced further. If means–ends analysis is successful, after enough iterations a series of subgoals is generated along with a tactic for achieving each subgoal given success on the preceding subgoal. Metaphorically, again, a path has been developed for moving from the starting point to the goal. Voila! The problem is solved.

Although means–ends analysis can be very effective, it has two drawbacks (Sweller, 1989). First, it is very demanding of working memory's limited resources. All the intermediate stages have to be recorded, and, at the point when the discrepancy has been fully reduced, products must be threaded together to accomplish the task. Learning systems (as well as paper notebooks) provide an obvious remedy for this. Students can record each of those middle stages. Anecdotal evidence that students must regularly be reminded to show their work, draft compositions, and so forth suggests that such self-regulation is not as prevalent as it might be.

The second drawback to means–ends analysis is that it focuses the learner's attention on step-by-step transitions. When students view problems this way, the larger schema that describes the task may go unnoticed. Because such schemas are keys that experts use to understand tasks in their domains of expertise, means–ends analysis can delay a novice's progress toward expertise. The novice cannot see the forest (schemas) for the trees (individual steps in solving problems).

One method for avoiding both drawbacks is to avoid means–ends analysis. How? When solving multistep problems, one available option is to change the goal. Rather than seek the answer to a focused question (e.g., "Find angle *D* in the figure."), replace this goal with a radically different one. Identify everything about the situation that can be solved for, then solve for whichever of these goals is easiest. This solution will increase information about the problem that will often make a goal on the reduced list of unknowns easier to reach. Solve for the easiest goal on this list, and iterate this method until all the goals on the initial list have been solved.

This approach transforms a single-goal problem into a *goal-free* problem (Sweller, 1989). Students engaging with a goal-free problem inherently work forward from current conditions. As they add successive solutions to the problem space, they increase the number and richness of givens that can scaffold problem solving. As they explore for intersections between current knowledge and successively updated "initial" conditions, they are developing information for a schema for the problem. And, because each iteration is a self-contained step that uses whichever problem-solving technique is easiest for the student, the drain on working memory's resources is minimized. This frees cognitive resources for the student to reflect on the overall structure of information about the problem, that is, to "see" its schema.

Research shows that freeing problems of singular goals can help students acquire schemas for solving problems (Sweller, 1989). Learning systems can mimic these interventions to help students develop self-regulated learning that changes goal structures by inviting students to transform goal-specific problems into goal-free problems. By providing students with a list of problem-solving tactics used in the past, the system also could help them avoid difficulties that arise when tactics remain inert. Furthermore, if the system provides a tool for the student to keep track of how well and under what conditions each problem-solving tactic works, it could scaffold the development of schemas that underlie genuine understanding. This is conditional knowledge students need in order to become more adept at selecting useful tactics in the first place and toggling tactics when needed. An added bonus of a goal-free approach is that more problem-solving tactics are practiced than when single-goal problems are addressed. Practicing tactics helps to automate them.

Scene

TJ (Theodore Jonathan's preferred moniker) is beginning to work on his essay, "The History of the Tuba." STUDY provides a problem-solving tool called SOLVER, which he has found useful for writing compositions in English class, as well as for science labs and computing science projects. TJ's teacher explained how to use SOLVER, and TJ and his peers have had several months to work with it. TJ has found that it works both as a technique for recording what he finds works in these various assignments, and as a scaffold for work on particular assignments.

STUDY's SOLVER is a window with three panels: Tasks, Methods (tactics in our terminology of this chapter), and Ratings. In the Tasks panel, TJ has been keeping track of different kinds of tasks he is assigned. Initially, Tasks simply listed the names of his subjects: English, math, and so forth. As he worked with SOLVER notes, however, he edited that list to characterize tasks less in terms of subject areas and more in terms of kinds of tasks: essays, experiments, drawing data (by which TJ means making graphic and tabular representations), and so forth. TJ uses a glossary, developed by his teacher and sent to TJ on the classroom local area network to add to TJ's folder containing STUDY, to help him determine what kinds of tasks he works on in his different subjects. STUDY invites him to characterize tasks just before he quits working each day, suggesting he scroll through the glossary to search for any descriptions that fit.

In the Method panel in SOLVER, TJ can write shorthand labels for tactics he uses in a task. The contents of this panel change depending on which task TJ clicks in the Tasks panel. TJ just clicked "essay," so SOLVER is displaying a list of methods TJ recorded earlier in the year when writing essays. Currently, the list includes background, break up, encyclopedia, get started, main points, opposites, quote, thesaurus. Some of these are entirely TJ's own invention. Others he copied from friends who sent them as e-mail, and a few were "suggestions" from his teacher.

When TJ clicks on an entry in the Methods panel, STUDY opens a new window that displays TJ's description of that tactic. For instance, when TJ clicks on "break up," the window describes this tactic: "Look at the idea you just wrote and see if you can find something it depends on, or something that is a part of it. When you find one, ask yourself if it should go in the essay." Clicking on "encyclopedia" displays this description: "If you have an idea, look it up the name of it in the encyclopedia because there is always a lot of stuff there that links to the idea you had." SOLVER is designed so that each of these windows also has a second field, labeled See Also. . . . There TJ can record another tactic that relates to the one described in the main entry. For example, TJ has noted that "encyclopedia" also works well with "break up." Clicking on an entry in See Also . . . opens the description of that tactic.

TJ starts with the tactic "get started." Its description is: "Take the assignment the teacher gave you and make a list of everything you can think of about it." His prior entries in See Also . . . remind him to check his "thesaurus" tactic and his "encyclopedia" tactic. He begins to collect information for his essay about tubas, using STUDY's simple word processor to develop his text. Occasionally, when he switches out of the word processor to SOLVER notes, STUDY displays a stock message: "Hey, TJ! How's it going?

Just wanted to ask if you're remembering to think about organizing all of your work so it makes sense to someone else." The message window has two buttons that close it: Later and Yeah. If TJ clicks Later, STUDY increases the value of the parameter for displaying this message from every third time by two (i.e., making it every fifth time). Yeah changes the value of this parameter to zero, but sets up a condition whereby STUDY displays a similar message when TJ quits using the word processor.

In the third panel of SOLVER, Rating TJ can record how valuable a tactic is for each task. It includes two rating scales and a text field for notes. One rating scale is TJ's judgment about effort the tactic requires. The second is a rating of the tactic's general usefulness. In the free-entry text area, TJ has written notes about the tactic. One says, "The encyclopedia is too interesting, so make sure you don't get sucked into just looking around for neat stuff. Set STUDY's timer for 10 minutes when you start taking notes from wherever you find the first thing."

SOLVER helps TJ structure tasks while inviting him to choose goals he pursues for each task. By serving as external storage for tactics and by providing a record about how tasks and tactics coordinate, TJ can engage in goal-free problem solving, freeing cognitive resources to allow him to explore the schemas for problem-based tasks. By practicing tactics, those he creates as well as those contributed by peers and the teacher, he also has the opportunity to consolidate conditional knowledge of the kind that supports the forward-search problem-solving characteristic of expertise.

GUIDING PHASE 4: ADAPTING APPROACHES TO LEARNING

If goal-directed learners are inherently self-regulating (Winne, 1995), it follows that students inherently work to edit tactics that are objects of regulation. Our casual conversations with students across the age spectrum suggest this inference is plausible. They readily describe studying tactics they have developed on their own and adaptations made to their studying tactics, as well as tactics suggested by peers or teachers (Winne & Marx, 1982).

Regardless of how often students edit studying tactics, wide individual differences in the effectiveness of students' studying prove that some editing produces suboptimal or mistaken change. Several reasons might explain this, such as a production deficiency or young students' limited memory for steps they take in activities (see Winne, 1997). Another plausible barrier to editing tactics effectively may be that students hold misconceptions about how effective particular studying tactics are.

Pressley and Afflerbach (1995) surveyed studies that investigated tactics that active readers use while reading. After reading through a text a first time, one often-used tactic is self-questioning or self-testing over the content just read. This is a common and often recommended studying tactic. It can contribute positively to learning and problem solving, though students across the developmental spectrum typically need support to use self-questioning effectively or to use it at all. For instance, elementary students instructed to generate self-testing questions while studying will comply. But, the questions they produce are not as effective as those generated by peers who use a set of question stems that cue particular kinds of questions to create (King, 1991).

Mature students may not generate instructionally effective self-testing questions without several practice sessions that enhance and explicitly cue them to use this tactic. In another study by King (1992), one group of undergraduates participated in several training sessions where they learned to use a set of question stems to generate self-testing questions. These students and another group that had no special preparation then listened to a lecture, took notes, and were given an opportunity to review their notes just before taking a test. King confirmed that students who were trained actually generated and answered questions during the review period. In the group that did not receive training on self-generating questions, fewer than 10% of students applied any observable studying tactics, such as underlining or adding to notes, during the review period. On both an immediate achievement test and a retention test administered a week later, students trained and observed to generate self-testing questions scored higher than their peers who took and studied notes "their own way."

Whether self-generated, posed by a teacher, or presented by a system such as STUDY, questions invite a student to search memory for answers. When searches of memory are thorough (deep) and yield information, both the content retrieved and the search process are rehearsed. It is well known that rehearsal strongly increases the likelihood that retrieval can be repeated successfully. Interestingly, although feedback enhances learning under certain conditions (Kluger & DeNisi, 1996), feedback is not a necessary ingredient in learning (Foos & Fisher, 1988; Glover, 1989). Simply searching memory and retrieving information can increase learning, a phenomenon termed the *testing effect*. Another research finding is that separating studying activities, such as searches of memory, into several sessions is much more effective than massing studying into one continuous session (Dempster, 1989). This robust finding is termed the *spacing effect*.

Glover (1989) performed an elegant series of experiments that investigated the joint impact of the testing effect and the spacing effect. A first pair of studies involved one sample of undergraduates and a second sample of seventh graders. Students in both samples read an age-appropriate text and were told they would be given a free recall test about the material. One group of students at each age was asked to return to take the free recall test 2 days later; 2 days after that, a total 4 days after studying the passage, this group and the other group of students took the free recall test. Even though students who took the "practice" test after 2 days did not receive any feedback on it, they remembered substantially more (approximately twice as much) on the second free recall test as peers who took only one free recall test 4 days after studying the text. This established that even a very general question—"What can you remember about the passage?"—yields a testing effect.

In the next experiment, one group of undergraduates in a control group studied a text and took a free recall test 4 days later. A second group experienced massed testing. They studied the text, immediately took a free recall test, and then repeated the free recall test 4 days later. A third group experienced spaced testing. They studied the text, took a free recall test 2 days later, then took another free recall test 2 days after that, 4 days after their studying session. The amount of information recalled by students in the control and massed testing groups was practically identical and only one-third that recalled by students in the spaced testing group.

In another experiment in this series, Glover (1989) found that deeper searches of memory enhance the effect. Undergraduates were divided into four groups. A control group studied a text and took a free recall test 4 days later. Three other groups studied the text, took an intervening test 2 days later, then took a free recall test 2 days after that, a total of 4 days after the study session. The intervening test differed for each of these three groups in a sequence that required increasingly deeper searches of memory. One group was asked to recognize whether each of a dozen sentences was or was not drawn from the text. The second group took a cued recall (fill-in-the-blank) test. The third group took a free recall test. Overall, Glover's studies convincingly demonstrate that the mere opportunity to "practice retrieving" information enhances learning *provided* that the opportunity is delayed or spaced relative to the initial study session. In addition, the more challenging the search task, the stronger the effect.

These findings from research on self-generating questions, the testing effect, and the spacing effect suggest items students might edit in questioning tactics they use to study. First, if they do not already self-generate questions about the material they study, they should be guided to do so regularly. This accretes a tactic to their current collection of studying methods. The testing effect indicates that students should try to answer their questions, which we assume they probably do anyway if they generate questions in the first place. But the spacing effect implies they should delay searching memory for those answers for a few days, tuning the tactic by changing the occasion for answering those questions. Finally, because the most effective questions require deep searches of memory, students should be guided to generate more questions that require deep search. Depending on a student's knowledge, this may tune a current tactic or it may constitute a larger-scale restructuring of perceptions of and tactics for studying.

Scene

In her first-year course on engineering design problems, Pam's professor wrote his own text and installed it in STUDY. STUDY's package for the course includes a notebook with a variety of features designed to help Pam study more effectively. Pam is reading the first chapter in one of STUDY's windows. As usual, she's underlining some of its information. Occasionally, she moves over to the notebook window to type a brief entry. STUDY automatically links each entry to the section of text Pam is viewing (unless Pam indicates otherwise by checking a box described below). In a prior self-contained tutorial about the notebook, STUDY suggested that Pam classify each entry she makes in the notebook to facilitate reviewing the material. The notebook displays a set of checkboxes for this purpose, each of which STUDY explained in the tutorial. The first four checkboxes are labeled as follows: Clarification (where Pam elaborates the chapter's information in her own words), Link to Another Note (for cross-referencing information Pam has entered elsewhere in the notebook), Link to Other Text (for cross-referencing this note to information at a spot in the chapter other than the one to which the present entry is indexed), and Question (a self-generated question that might be on a test or that Pam wants to ask the professor).

In the first three study sessions, STUDY records that Pam does not classify any of her notebook entries as questions. So, at the beginning of the next session, STUDY interrupts Pam using its computer-generated voice:

> Hi, Pam! Am I right that you're not posing *any* questions about what you read? Do you know that making up your own questions is a good way to study, even if you think you understand everything? If you'd like me to suggest some basic types of questions to pose, click the button Show Me. Otherwise, just click OK, and I'll open up the chapter where you left off last time.

Pam realizes that STUDY is right about the absence of questions in her notes, and she is curious. She clicks Show Me. STUDY opens a window of question stems that the professor adapted from STUDY's stock set (based on King, 1991, 1992). STUDY offers these guidelines:

> Not every bit of material should be the target of a question. Some cues for generating a question are when the chapter first introduces main ideas, identifies a rule or principle, or signals that bits of information relate to one another, as in "Recall that . . . " or "In comparison to. . . . "
>   Here is a list of stems you might use or adapt

```
when you generate your own questions. Leave this
window open if you want to refer to it. I'll save
your typing and paste a stem directly into your
notebook if you double-click it.
    Do you want me to remind you every so often to
generate questions? If you do, click the Remind Me
button. Otherwise, just click OK.
```

Most of the question stems are pitched to address higher-order relations that will involve Pam in deep searches of memory. Pam judges that she is busy enough coping with the text's information, so she clicks Remind Me. STUDY activates a procedure to remind Pam to generate questions if she makes three notes in a row in which she does not double-click a question stem or check the box that classifies the note as a question. STUDY activates a second procedure to intervene again three study sessions later.

Over the next three study sessions, STUDY records that Pam poses questions at a rate of one for approximately every fourth note. STUDY intervenes again in the next study session, opening the window of question stems and another window with this message:

```
Happy Monday, Pam! Glad to see your generating
questions. Since you've mostly not double-clicked on
stems I suggested, I hope you're focusing on stems
like those I've colored red. (STUDY changes text for
specific stems from black to red.) Research suggests
that posing more questions of the red kinds has
stronger effects on learning.
```

STUDY continues:

```
I'd like to suggest something else about this
studying tactic. Questions are made for answering,
right? Well, odd as it may seem, you shouldn't try
to answer your questions right away. What I suggest
is that you enter questions whenever you want but
don't answer them right away. Instead, return to
your questions when you begin your next study
session. Believe it or not, this approach might
double what you remember!
```

Pam decides to follow STUDY's guideline. STUDY will index the questions Pam generates in each study session and, at the beginning of the next study session, display them one by one for Pam to enter answers. As the semester progresses, Pam takes over from STUDY all these functions. She does not bother to have STUDY display the window of question stems or automatically start a studying session with the questions she posed last time. Instead, she uses a feature in her notebook herself that does the same thing. By the end of the term, Pam is surfing through questions generated in several prior study sessions rather than just the most recent one. We interpret that she has significantly restructured tactics for reviewing material.

CONCLUSIONS

We hold that, because students are goal-directed agents, they intrinsically develop techniques for managing tactics that bring about learning (Winne, 1995). We used the phrase "forms of self-regulated learning" to acknowledge explicitly that there are different approaches to regulating tactics for learning and to invite the inference that different forms of self-regulated learning may have differential effectiveness. Ipso facto, guiding students toward forms of self-regulated learning that are more useful is an important issue to address in education.

Weinstein (1996) and we (Winne & Hadwin, 1997; Winne, 1995, 1996a, 1997) agree that the field's present models of self-regulated learning and the development of self-regulated learning are works in progress. Hence, we adopt a tentative stance about the effectiveness of current principles for instructing more effective forms of self-regulated learning, regardless of whether such principles are acted on by people or by computer surrogates. As the chapters of this volume attest, however, substantial efforts in researching self-regulated learning are beginning to pay noticeable dividends to designing instruction that teaches students about academically effective forms of self-regulated learning. Appropriately configured, computing technologies can be efficient vehicles for this instruction. Today's technologies provide more than this, however. We now are able to structure systems students can use to design their own instructional activities. These designs for self-instruction are clear evidence of self-regulated learning.

Computing technologies also offer researchers powerful tools for studying self-regulated learning because adaptive systems can "work with" students in the midst of self-regulated instructional activities. As replacements for the researcher's intrusive methods for gathering data, technological tools can meticulously and reliably observe, tirelessly and unerringly sift, and usefully assemble and coordinate massive volumes of data that characterize a student's (1) achievements and (2) the studying tactics the student uses to forge those accomplishments. Because a computer can be a student's companion in almost any instructional setting, the need to sample is eliminated. Such depth and breadth of data about self-regulated learning as an event will allow the field to model self-regulated learning at multiple levels of resolution and extension (Howard-Rose & Winne, 1993). We predict this will significantly enhance foundations for designing powerful instruction.

The scenes we presented illustrate how today's computing technologies might support students as they bootstrap forms of self-regulated learning. It is worth explicitly stating the obvious, however, that these hypotheses need empirical study. It is also the case that present computing technologies can not do anything more than a sensitive and effective teacher or peer can do. In fact, computing technologies are capable of much less. This is not to say, however, that computing technologies only offer slight advantages. Because these technologies can interact adaptively with students when teachers or peers are unavailable, they can provide students with significantly more feedback than would otherwise be on hand. If information is power, such feedback offers the potential to empower students further in learning and in becoming better at learning.

The keys that unlock the instructional power of computer technologies will be forged in the crucible of basic research followed by tests of those findings in field experiments. This is why we opted for descriptions of computer-supported tools that were first grounded in research-based models. As noted earlier, we hope that neither educators nor researchers will be seduced by technological opportunism wherein new technologies, rather than understandings about learning and instruction, drive educational change. Technological advances afford educational innovation, but we argue they must be perceived as roads for transporting productive change rather than as engines of it. To the extent that educational technologies help students develop knowledge, skills, motivation, and academically effective forms of self-regulated learning, students should begin using these tools as early as possible. Educators and other sectors, particularly governments and publishers, should strive to make technological systems available. And researchers should take advantage of such technological tools to enhance research (Guzdial et al., 1996; Winne, 1992), on which rational use of these technologies depends.

ACKNOWLEDGMENTS

Support for this work was provided by a grant to Philip H. Winne from the Social Sciences and Humanities Research Council of Canada (No. 410-95-1046). We thank Allyson Hadwin for valuable comments on drafts of this chapter.

REFERENCES

Ames, C. (1992). Classroom goals, structures, and student motivation. *Journal of Educational Psychology, 84,* 261–271.

Anderson, J. R. (1991). The adaptive nature of human categorization. *Psychological Review, 98,* 409–429.

Austin, J. T., & Vancouver, J. B. (1996). Goal constructs in psychology: Structure, process, and content. *Psychological Bulletin, 120*, 338–375.

Butler, D. L., & Winne, P. H. (1995). Feedback and self-regulated learning: A theoretical synthesis. *Review of Educational Research, 65*, 245–281.

Dempster, F. N. (1989). Spacing effects and their implications for theory and practice. *Educational Psychology Review, 1*, 309–330.

Eisenberger, R. (1992). Learned industriousness. *Psychological Review, 99*, 248–267.

Eisenberger, R., Masterson, F. A., & McDermitt, M. (1982). Effects of task variety on generalized effort. *Journal of Educational Psychology, 74*, 499–506.

Ericsson, K. A., Krampe, R. T., & Tesch-Römer, C. (1993). The role of deliberate practice in the acquisition of expert performance. *Psychological Review, 100*, 363–406.

Field, D., & Winne, P. H. (1997). *STUDY: An environment for authoring and presenting adaptive learning tutorials* (Version 3.2) [Computer program]. Simon Fraser University, Burnaby, BC.

Foos, P. W., & Fisher, R. P. (1988). Using tests as learning opportunities. *Journal of Educational Psychology, 80*, 179–183.

Glover, J. A. (1989). The testing phenomenon: Not gone but nearly forgotten. *Journal of Educational Psychology, 81*, 392–399.

Guzdial, M., Berger, C., Jones, T., Horney, M., Anderson-Inman, L., Winne, P. H., & Nesbit, J. C. (1996). *Analyzing student use of educational software with event recordings.* Manuscript submitted for publication.

Hativa, N., & Lesgold, A. (1996). Situational effects in classroom technology implementations: Unfulfilled expectations and unexpected outcomes. In S. Kerr (Ed.), *Ninety-fifth yearbook of the National Society for the Study of Education: Part II. Technology and the future of schooling* (pp. 131–171). Chicago: University of Chicago Press.

Herman, J. L. (1994). Evaluating the effects of technology in school reform. In B. Means (Ed.), *Technology and educational reform* (pp. 133–167). San Francisco: Jossey-Bass.

Howard-Rose, D., & Winne, P. H. (1993). Measuring component and sets of cognitive processes in self-regulated learning. *Journal of Educational Psychology, 85*, 591–604.

King, A. (1991). Effects of training in strategic questioning on children's problem-solving performance. *Journal of Educational Psychology, 83*, 307–317.

King, A. (1992). Comparison of self-questioning, summarizing, and notetaking-review as strategies for learning from lectures. *American Educational Research Journal, 29*, 303–323.

Kluger, A. N., & DeNisi, A. (1996). The effects of feedback interventions on performance: A historical review, a meta-analysis, and a preliminary feedback intervention theory. *Psychological Bulletin, 119*, 254–284.

McKoon, G., & Ratcliff, R. (1992). Inference during reading. *Psychological Review, 99*, 440–466.

Miller, P. H., & Seier, W. L. (1994). Strategy utilization deficiencies in children: When, where, and why. In H. W. Reese (Ed.), *Advances in child development and behavior* (Vol. 25, pp. 107–156). San Diego: Academic Press.

Morgan, M. (1985). Self-monitoring of attained subgoals in private study. *Journal of Educational Psychology, 77*, 623–630.

Papert, S. (1980). *Mindstorms: Children, computers, and powerful ideas.* New York: Basic Books.

Perry, N. E. (1997). *Young children's self-regulated learning and contexts that support it.* Manuscript submitted for publication.

Pintrich, P. R., Marx, R. W., & Boyle, R. A. (1993). Beyond cold conceptual change: The role of motivational beliefs and classroom contextual factors in the process of conceptual change. *Review of Educational Research, 63,* 167–199.

Pintrich, P. R., Wolters, C. A., & Baxter, G. P. (in press). Assessing metacognition and self-regulated learning. In G. Schraw (Ed.), *Issues in the measurement of metacognition.* Lincoln, NE: Buros/University of Nebraska Press.

Pressley, M. (1995). More about the development of self-regulation: Complex, long-term, and thoroughly social. *Educational Psychologist, 31,* 207–212.

Pressley, M., & Afflerbach, P. (1995). *Verbal protocols of reading: The nature of constructively responsive reading.* Hillsdale, NJ: Erlbaum.

Rumelhart, D. E., & Norman, D. A. (1978). Accretion, tuning, and restructuring: Three modes of learning. In J. W. Cotton & R. Klatzky (Eds.), *Semantic factors in cognition* (pp. 37–53). Hillsdale, NJ: Erlbaum.

Salomon, G., Globerson, T., & Guterman, E. (1989). The computer as a zone of proximal development: Internalizing reading-related metacognitions from a reading partner. *Journal of Educational Psychology, 81,* 620–672.

Salomon, G., & Perkins, D. N. (1989). Rocky roads to transfer: Rethinking mechanisms of a neglected phenomenon. *Educational Psychologist, 24,* 113–142.

Salomon, G., & Perkins, D. (1996). Learning in Wonderland: What do computers really offer education? In S. Kerr (Ed.), *Ninety-fifth yearbook of the National Society for the Study of Education: Part II. Technology and the future of schooling* (pp. 111–130). Chicago: University of Chicago.

Schommer, M. (1994). Synthesizing epistemological belief research: Tentative understandings and provocative conclusions. *Educational Psychology Review, 6,* 293–319.

Schank, R. (1984). *The cognitive computer.* Reading, MA: Addison-Wesley.

Schunk, D. H. (1996). Goal and self-evaluative influences during children's cognitive skill learning. *American Educational Research Journal, 33,* 359–382.

Schunk, D. H., & Zimmerman, B. J. (Eds.). (1994). *Self-regulation of learning and performance: Issues and applications.* Hillsdale, NJ: Erlbaum.

Snow, R. E. (1996). Self-regulation as meta-conation? *Learning and Individual Differences, 8,* 216–267.

Sweller, J. (1989). Cognitive technology: Some procedures for facilitating learning and problem solving in mathematics and science. *Journal of Educational Psychology, 81,* 457–466.

Weinstein, C. E. (1996). Self-regulation: A commentary on directions for future research. *Learning and Individual Differences, 8,* 269–274.

Winne, P. H. (1989). Theories of instruction and of intelligence for designing artificially intelligent tutoring systems. *Educational Psychologist, 24,* 229–259.

Winne, P. H. (1992). State-of-the-art instructional computing systems that afford instruction and bootstrap research. In M. Jones & P. H. Winne (Eds.), *Foundations and frontiers of adaptive learning environments* (pp. 349–380). Berlin: Springer-Verlag.

Winne, P. H. (1993). A landscape of issues in evaluating adaptive learning systems. *Journal of Artificial Intelligence in Education, 4,* 309–332.

Winne, P. H. (1995). Inherent details in self-regulated learning. *Educational Psychologist, 30,* 173–187.

Winne, P. H. (1996a). A metacognitive view of individual differences in self-regulated learning. *Learning and Individual Differences*, 8, 327–353.

Winne, P. H. (1996b, June). *Children's decision making skills and the development of self-regulated learning.* Paper presented at the meeting of the Canadian Association for Educational Psychology, St. Catharines, Ontario.

Winne, P. H. (1997). Experimenting to bootstrap self-regulated learning. *Journal of Educational Psychology*, 89, 397–410.

Winne, P. H., Gupta, L., & Nesbit, J. C. (1994). Exploring individual differences in studying strategies using graph theoretic statistics. *Alberta Journal of Educational Research*, 40, 177–193.

Winne, P. H., & Hadwin, A. F. (1997). Studying as self-regulated learning. In D. J. Hacker, J. Dunlosky, & A. C. Graesser (Eds.), *Metacognition in educational theory and practice* (pp. 279–306). Hillsdale, NJ: Erlbaum.

Winne, P. H., & Marx, R. W. (1982). Students' and teachers' views of thinking processes for classroom learning. *Elementary School Journal*, 82, 493–518.

Winne, P. H., & Marx, R. W. (1989). A cognitive processing analysis of motivation within classroom tasks. In C. Ames & R. Ames (Eds.), *Research on motivation in education* (Vol. 3, pp. 223–257). Orlando, FL: Academic Press.

Zellermayer, M., Salomon, G., Globerson, T., & Givon, T. (1991). Enhancing writing-related metacognitions through a computerized writing partner. *American Educational Research Journal*, 28, 373–391.

Zimmerman, B. J., & Schunk, D. H. (Eds.). (1989). *Self-regulated learning and academic achievement: Theory, research, and practice.* New York: Springer-Verlag.

CHAPTER 7

Teaching Elementary Students to Self-Regulate Practice of Mathematical Skills with Modeling

Dale H. Schunk

Much has been written on the poor mathematical achievement of American schoolchildren, especially in relation to that of students in other nations (Steen, 1987; Stevenson, Chen, & Lee, 1993; Stigler, Lee, & Stevenson, 1987; Uttal, Lummis, & Stevenson, 1988). Differences in mathematical achievement between Americans and students from European and East Asian countries begin to appear in first grade and widen successively throughout the formal schooling years (Geary, 1996). These differences do not appear to be biological in origin; rather, they emerge with the onset of schooling and are most pronounced in domains heavily influenced by schooling (e.g., secondary mathematics) (Geary, 1995).

Investigators have posited cultural, contextual, and personal factors as influencing the poor mathematics showing of American children. The differential emphasis given to mathematics in school across cultures seems to reflect the value of mathematical achievement in those cultures (Geary, 1996). Research shows that East Asian teachers spend a greater proportion of time on large-group mathematics activities, whereas American teachers spend less time providing instruction (Stigler et al., 1987). American students engage in a higher proportion of off-task activities during mathematics (Stigler et al., 1987). Chinese and Japanese high school students spend more time attending school than do American students (Fuligni & Stevenson, 1995). Relative to Caucasian American students, Asian American and East Asian students are more likely to (1) believe that success is attained through effort, (2) hold positive attitudes toward mathematics, (3) study diligently, (4) have fewer distractions from schoolwork due to jobs and peer interactions, and (5) have parents who hold high mathematical standards for their children (Chen & Stevenson, 1995).

Motivational processes have been implicated as prime causes of low mathematical achievement of American children. Many students find mathematics learning difficult and hold a low sense of perceived competence for learning and performing well (Kloosterman, 1988; Stipek & Gralinski, 1991). Across Chinese, Japanese, and American cultures, mothers' ratings of their children's abilities and of their own abilities in mathematics vary directly with children's level of mathematical achievement (Uttal et al., 1988). Other research indicates significant differences between Asian American and non-Asian students' beliefs about their mathematical ability, their attributions for success, and their parents' beliefs about their children's mathematical ability (Whang & Hancock, 1994).

In recent years investigators have hypothesized that poor self-regulatory skills also contribute to low motivation and learning in mathematics (Meece & Courtney, 1992; Newman, 1994; Schunk, 1994). *Self-regulation* (or *self-regulated learning*) refers to self-generated thoughts, feelings, and actions that are systematically designed to affect one's learning of knowledge and skills (Zimmerman, 1989, 1990; Zimmerman & Kitsantas, 1996). Self-regulatory processes include attending to and concentrating on instruction; organizing, coding, and rehearsing information to be remembered; establishing a productive work environment; using resources effectively; holding positive beliefs about one's capabilities, the value of learning, the factors influencing learning, and the anticipated outcomes of actions; and experiencing pride and satisfaction with one's efforts (Schunk, 1994).

Self-regulation is assuming increasing importance among educators. Research shows that students are mentally active during learning rather than being passive recipients of information, and that they exert a large degree of control over attainment of their goals (Pintrich & Schrauben, 1992). Educators are realizing the importance of students developing self-regulatory competence in addition to subject-area skills.

In this chapter I discuss the influence of modeling on elementary school students' self-regulation during mathematical skill acquisition. The use of models during mathematics instruction has been shown to promote students' learning and development of positive achievement beliefs (Schunk, 1989). Use of models may be a contextual factor that distinguishes American classrooms from those of other countries and thereby contributes to cross-cultural differences in mathematical achievement. Stigler et al. (1987) found significant cross-cultural differences in the amount of mathematical class time that students worked, observed, and listened together as a whole class (Japan, 74%; Taiwan, 82%; United States, 41%); American students spent the more time working on their own (52%) than involved in whole-class activities. Models (teachers, parents, other adults, or peers) who explain and demonstrate mathematical operations are more prevalent in large-group contexts than when students are engaged in seatwork.

For the past few years I have been conducting research on the acquisition of self-regulatory skills by elementary school children during mathematics instruction. These intervention projects focused on improving children's skills through the use of models. The conceptual focus of these studies is *social-cognitive theory* (Bandura, 1986). The next section discusses the social-cognitive theory of self-regulation including modeling. A key variable in self-regulation and modeling is perceived *self-efficacy*, or learners' beliefs about their capabilities to learn or perform behaviors at designated levels (Bandura, 1986, 1997). I then describe several intervention studies and their effects on students' self-regulation, motivation, and achievement. I conclude by discussing *self-reflective practice*, or the process whereby students further the development of self-regulatory competence through such processes as self-verbalization and self-regulation of achievement beliefs.

SOCIAL-COGNITIVE THEORY OF SELF-REGULATION

Triadic Reciprocality

Bandura (1986, 1993) views human functioning as a series of *reciprocal interactions* between *behavioral, environmental,* and *personal* variables. For example, research shows that self-efficacy (a personal variable) influences achievement behavior (choice of tasks, effort, persistence); efficacious students are more likely to choose to engage in mathematical tasks, expend effort, and persist to overcome obstacles and succeed (Schunk, 1996; Zimmerman, 1995). Behaviors also influence personal variables. As students work on mathematical tasks (behavior) they mentally note their progress (personal variable), which conveys to them that they are capable of learning and raises their self-efficacy (Schunk, 1989).

An example of the influence of environment on behavior occurs when teachers introduce an unusual mathematical formula (environmental variable) and students direct their attention toward it (behavior). Behavior can also affect the environment. If students act bewildered by a teacher's explanation (behavior), the teacher may reteach the material (environmental variable).

Personal and environmental variables also affect one another. When students with high self-efficacy try to solve problems in a distracting environment they may concentrate especially hard (personal variable) to make the environment less distracting. The influence of environment on personal variables is seen when teachers give students verbal feedback (environmental variable) (e.g., "Correct. You're getting really good at math.") that raises their self-efficacy (personal variable).

Subprocesses of Self-Regulation

Social-cognitive theory postulates that self-regulation comprises three sub-processes: self-observation, self-judgment, self-reaction (Bandura, 1986; Kanfer & Gaelick, 1986). *Self-observation* (or *self-monitoring*) refers to deliberate attention to specific aspects of one's behavior. Bandura (1986) and others (Mace, Belfiore, & Shea, 1989) recommend assessing behaviors on such dimensions as quantity, quality, rate, and originality. When self-observation results in perceptions of goal progress, it can motivate one to improve (Schunk & Zimmerman, 1997). Self-observation is assisted with *self-recording*, where instances of behavior are recorded along with their time, place, and frequency of occurrence (Mace et al., 1989). Children working on arithmetic might periodically record how many problems they have solved, which indicates progress.

Self-judgment refers to comparing present performance with a standard. Self-judgments are affected by the type and importance of standards used. Absolute standards are fixed (e.g., student who attempts to finish a math assignment during a class period); normative standards are based on performances of others (e.g., student who attempts to be the first one in the class to finish the math assignment). Standards can be acquired by observing models (Bandura, 1986). Socially comparing one's performances with those of others helps one evaluate behavioral appropriateness. Social comparisons become important in the absence of absolute standards (Schunk & Zimmerman, 1997).

Self-judgments also are affected by the importance of standards. People are more likely to judge their progress for tasks they value and may not attempt to improve their skills at tasks they do not value. Students who have little interest in doing well in math may be concerned with progress only to the level required to pass the course.

Self-reaction involves making evaluative responses to judgments of one's performance (e.g., good/bad, acceptable/not acceptable). The belief that one is making acceptable goal progress, along with the expected satisfaction of goal attainment, enhances self-efficacy and sustains motivation (Schunk, 1996). Negative evaluations will not decrease motivation if students believe they are capable of improving (i.e., by working harder, using a better strategy). Motivation suffers if students think they lack the capability to succeed and that other factors will not help. Self-reactions can be influenced by tangible rewards. Students given free time after completing a problem set may believe they are becoming more competent.

Self-Efficacy

Self-efficacy is hypothesized to influence choice of activities, effort expenditure, persistence, and achievement (Bandura, 1986, 1997; Schunk, 1996;

Zimmerman, 1995). Compared with students who doubt their learning capabilities, those with high self-efficacy for acquiring a skill or performing a task participate more readily, work harder, persist longer when they encounter difficulties, and achieve at higher levels.

Learners obtain information about their self-efficacy from their performances, vicarious (observational) experiences, forms of persuasion, and physiological reactions. Students' own performances offer reliable guides for assessing self-efficacy. Successes raise efficacy, and failures lower it (Zimmerman & Ringle, 1981). Students socially acquire efficacy information by comparing their performances with those of others. Similar others offer a valid basis for comparison (Schunk, 1987). Observing similar peers succeed (fail) at a task may raise (lower) observers' efficacy. From teachers, parents, and others, learners often receive persuasive information that they are capable of performing a task (e.g., "You can do this."). Such information can raise efficacy but can be negated by subsequent performance failure (Bandura, 1997). Students also acquire efficacy information from physiological reactions (e.g., sweating, heart rate). Symptoms signaling anxiety may convey that one lacks skill; lower anxiety may be construed as a sign of competence.

Self-efficacy is not the only influence on achievement. High efficacy will not produce a masterful performance when *knowledge and skill* are lacking. *Outcome expectations* (anticipated consequences of actions) are influential because students engage in activities they believe will lead to positive outcomes (Shell, Murphy, & Bruning, 1989). *Perceived value* (importance of or what use will be made of learning) affects behavior because learners show little interest in activities they do not value.

Self-Efficacy and Self-Regulation

Effective self-regulation depends on feeling self-efficacious for using skills to achieve mastery (Bandura, 1986, 1997; Bouffard-Bouchard, Parent, & Larivee, 1991; Schunk, 1996; Zimmerman, 1989). As students work on a task, they compare their performances to their goals. Self-evaluations of progress enhance self-efficacy and maintain motivation. Students who feel efficacious are apt to use effective strategies, such as concentrating on the task, using proper procedures, managing time effectively, seeking assistance as necessary, and monitoring performance and adjusting strategies as needed (McCombs, 1989; Pintrich & De Groot, 1990; Zimmerman, 1994).

The influential role of self-efficacy in self-regulation is highlighted in the model presented by Zimmerman (Chapter 1, this volume). The model postulates that skillful self-regulators enter learning situations with specific goals and a strong sense of self-efficacy for attaining them. As they work on tasks, they monitor their performances and compare their attainments with their goals to determine progress. Self-evaluations of acceptable progress lead to continued use of effective strategies, motivation for improvement, and positive achievement beliefs. A high sense of self-efficacy for learning in Zimmerman's *forethought* phase becomes realized as self-efficacy for achievement in the *performance* and *self-reflection* phases. The latter, in turn, set the stage for self-efficacy for further learning in this recursive model.

Although low self-efficacy is detrimental, effective self-regulation does not require that self-efficacy be exceptionally high. Salomon (1984) found that a slightly lower sense of self-efficacy led to greater mental effort and better learning than did extreme confidence. In mathematics, students may employ *buggy algorithms,* or incorrect rules that lead to erroneous solutions (e.g., subtracting the smaller from the larger number in each column regardless of whether the larger number is on top) (Brown & Burton, 1978). Because buggy algorithms produce solutions, students may develop unrealistically high self-efficacy. Although very low self-efficacy does not motivate, holding some doubt about success may mobilize effort and effective use of strategies better than feeling overly confident.

Modeling

Modeling refers to the process whereby observers pattern their thoughts, beliefs, strategies, and actions, after those displayed by one or more models (Schunk, 1987). Modeling is an important means for acquiring skills, beliefs, attitudes, and behaviors (Bandura, 1986; Rosenthal & Zimmerman, 1978). Teachers, parents, other adults, and peers serve as powerful models for children (Schunk, 1987).

Observational learning occurs when observers display new behaviors that prior to modeling are not demonstrated even with motivational inducements to do so (Bandura, 1977, 1986; Schunk, 1987). Observational learning through modeling comprises attention, retention, production, and motivation (Bandura, 1986). Observer *attention* to relevant environmental events is necessary for them to be meaningfully perceived. *Retention* requires coding and transforming modeled information for storage in memory, as well as cognitively organizing and rehearsing information. *Production* involves translating mental conceptions of modeled events into actual behaviors. Many actions may be learned in rough form through observation, but practice and feedback are necessary for skill refinement.

Motivation influences observational learning because students who believe that models possess a skill that is useful to know are likely to attend to such models and attempt to retain what they learn. Students do not demonstrate all the knowledge, skills, and behaviors they learn through observation. *Outcome expectations* are important: Students perform actions having functional importance (i.e., those they believe will result in rewarding outcomes) and avoid those they expect to be followed by negative outcomes (Schunk, 1987). Students also perform activities they *value* and avoid those they find dissatisfying.

Observation of models can raise observers' *self-efficacy* (Bandura, 1986, 1997). Seeing a successful model may lead observers to believe that if the model can learn they can as well. As students perform actions and note their learning progress, their sense of self-efficacy is substantiated, which maintains motivation for learning.

Perceived similarity between model and observer is hypothesized to be an important source of information and motivation (Schunk, 1987). Many situations are structured such that the appropriateness of behaviors depends on personal factors (e.g., age, gender, status). In general, the more alike observers are to models, the greater is the probability that similar actions by observers are socially appropriate and will produce comparable results. Similarity is especially influential when observers have little information about the functional value of behaviors. Similarity also enhances motivation. Students who observe peers learning to solve problems may believe that they, too, can be successful. Higher self-efficacy promotes motivation and learning (Schunk, 1989).

Modeling and Self-Regulatory Competence

Models are important sources for teaching self-regulatory skills and for building learners' self-efficacy to employ these skills. The self-regulatory skills mentioned at the outset are subject to teaching by social models: planning and managing time; attending to and concentrating on instruction; organizing, rehearsing, and coding information; establishing a productive work environment; and using social resources (Schunk & Zimmerman, 1997). For example, by observing a teacher engage in effective rehearsal of material to be learned, students may believe that they can learn to rehearse information; this belief creates a sense of self-efficacy for self-regulation and motivates students to engage in rehearsal.

Observational learning through modeling is optimized when social instruction is matched to students' level of regulatory skill on the task. Premature or delayed reliance on self-regulatory processes can retard the speed and course of learning (Schunk & Zimmerman, 1997). Initially, students may need extensive modeling, corrective feedback, and practice. Learners also may need to repeat earlier instructional phases periodically because of setbacks.

Social-cognitive theory predicts that students learn specific tasks under *decreasing levels of social-instructional support* (Schunk & Zimmerman, 1997). At more advanced levels students generally require less assistance from models. When models are used they can teach many components of self-regulation. Thus, learners can acquire academic skills as well as tools for further learning of the skills on their own. For example, they might observe models employing good organizational skills, self-monitoring their learning progress, and using strategies to cope with problems. These skills are further instated as learners engage in self-reflective practice.

INTERVENTION PROGRAM

Instructional Context

In this section I describe a social-cognitive instructional model that has been employed in the intervention studies summarized in the next section. The context is similar to that in which much mathematics instruction takes place in American elementary schools. Different mathematical content has been used in various studies, but all projects share these features: Instruction includes modeled explanation and demonstration of solution strategies; students receive hands-on experience with manipulatives or cutouts and guided practice in solving problems with corrective feedback as needed; and students engage in independent, self-reflective practice that requires application of self-regulatory activities.

The model is portrayed in Table 7.1. Students initially are pretested in a content area (e.g., subtraction, division, fractions). This initial assessment includes a measure of mathematical achievement (e.g., students are given problems to solve that vary in difficulty), as well as a measure of self-efficacy for solving problems (achievement). For this assessment, students are shown sample pairs of problems, each for a period that is too brief to attempt solutions but long enough for them to assess problem difficulty. Students judge their perceived capabilities for correctly solving problems of that type; that is, problems about as easy or difficult as those, with the same format and length. The efficacy problems correspond in form and difficulty to those on the achievement test but they are not the same problems.

Typically students display very low levels of pretest mathematical achievement, because they either have had little exposure to the content to be taught or are having difficulty mastering the operations. Another measure often collected is *persistence* (time spent solving problems). Bandura (1977, 1986) postulates that persistence should increase as students' self-efficacy and skill develop.

Following the pretest, students are assigned to conditions. In some studies a measure of self-efficacy for learning is collected. This assessment is identical to the pretest self-efficacy measure except that students judge their

TABLE 7.1. Social-Cognitive Instructional Model for Mathematics Interventions with Children

Pretest	Intervention	Posttest
Achievement	Modeled demonstrations	Achievement
Self-efficacy for	(cognitive, multiple,	Self-efficacy for
achievement	coping, self)	achievement
Persistence	Guided practice	Persistence
Self-efficacy for	Self-regulatory training	
learning	(verbalization, strategy	
	use, goals)	
	Independent/self-reflective	
	practice (self-monitoring,	
	verbalization, achievement	
	beliefs, self-evaluation)	

perceived capabilities for learning how to solve various types of problems rather than whether they already can solve them. Self-efficacy for learning is hypothesized to relate positively to motivation during instruction (Schunk, 1989).

In a typical intervention session (about 45 minutes), an adult member of the project team begins by giving experimental instructions appropriate for the children's condition, after which he or she verbally explains and demonstrates the relevant mathematical operations by referring to instructional material that children have and by illustrating examples on a board. Variations in models occur during this phase. After this *modeled demonstration* (about 10 minutes), students engage in a hands-on activity with manipulatives and cutouts and solve a few practice problems (*guided practice*, about 10 minutes). The teacher provides corrective feedback and *self-regulatory training* in processes of interest (e.g., goal setting, strategy use). Once the teacher is satisfied that children understand what to do, children solve problems alone during *independent (self-reflective) practice* for the remainder of the session (about 25 minutes). This time is sufficient to allow for demonstration of differences in self-regulatory processes brought about by variations between conditions.

In a typical intervention there are several instructional sessions, because students usually require multiple sessions to begin to acquire skills and because model treatments often are implemented more than once. A day or two after the final instructional session, students receive a posttest that is similar to the pretest but does not include self-efficacy for learning.

This instructional format for teaching mathematical skills reflects several of the assumptions inherent in the National Council of Teachers of Mathematics' (NCTM) *Curriculum and Evaluation Standards for School Mathematics* for kindergarten through fourth grade (NCTM, 1989). For one, this format is conceptually oriented and emphasizes the acquisition of mathematical understanding. For another, it actively involves children in doing mathematics through hands-on activities. Third, it emphasizes the development of children's thinking skills and is intended to build their self-efficacy for learning. Fourth, it stresses application of concepts and principles to real-world problems. Finally, it includes a wide variety of content within a given domain (e.g., fractions).

Objectives and Hypotheses

The research intervention studies had several objectives. One was to determine the influence of models on students' learning, achievement beliefs, and self-regulatory activities. Another was to ascertain how well contexts provide cues that students use to assess their learning progress. Third, in some studies a causal model of achievement was tested to investigate patterns of influence among variables.

Based on social-cognitive theory, several predictions were made regarding the effects of models on students' mathematics learning, achievement beliefs, and self-regulation. Many of the studies employed *cognitive modeling,* which incorporates modeled explanation and demonstration with verbalization of the model's thoughts and reasons for performing actions (Meichenbaum, 1977). The models verbalized statements such as the following explanation of how to solve the problem $276 \div 4$:

> "First I have to decide what number to divide 4 into. I take 276, start on the left and move toward the right until I have a number the same as or larger than 4. Is 2 larger than 4? No. Is 27 larger than 4? Yes. So my first division will be 4 into 27. Now I need to multiply 4 by a number that will give an answer the same as or slightly smaller than 27. How about 5? $5 \times 4 = 20$. No, too small. Let's try 6. $6 \times 4 = 24$. Maybe. Let's try 7. $7 \times 4 = 28$. No, too large. So 6 is correct."

Children then practice applying what they have learned with corrective modeling of any constituent operations they have failed to grasp. It was predicted that cognitive modeling would enhance children's mathematical achievement outcomes and self-regulation better than comparison methods. There is evidence that providing children with explanatory principles and exemplary models is more effective than providing explanatory principles alone (Rosenthal & Zimmerman, 1978).

Some studies investigated the effects of *multiple models.* To the extent that perceived similarity is important in modeling, an advantage of multiple models is that they allow each student to perceive him- or herself as similar to at least one of the models (Schunk, 1987). Thus, relative to a single model it was predicted that multiple models would raise achievement outcomes and promote self-regulation better than a single model.

Another set of hypotheses involved mastery and coping models. *Mastery models* perform competently from the outset. They also may verbalize statements reflecting high confidence and ability and positive attitudes. Mastery models demonstrate rapid learning and make no errors. In contrast, *coping models* illustrate how determined effort and positive self-thoughts can overcome difficulties. At first they demonstrate learning difficulties and possibly fears, but gradually they improve their performances and gain confidence. They might verbalize statements of task difficulty and low confidence, but then verbalize coping statements indicating high effort, persistence, and concentration. Eventually their performances and verbalizations improve to the levels portrayed by mastery models.

Although mastery models teach skills, it was predicted that coping models would be better with students who often encounter learning difficulties. Students with learning problems may view themselves as being more similar to coping models, given the initial difficulties and gradual progress, and may feel that if the models can learn, they can as well.

The final prediction concerns the effect of *self-modeling*, or behavioral change that results from observing one's own behaviors (Dowrick, 1983). Self-modeling represents the highest degree of model–observer similarity, because one is one's own model. A child may be videotaped while learning or performing a task and then views the tape. Observing a self-model tape is a form of review and viewing one's progress in learning or skillful performance conveys that one is capable, which raises self-efficacy and motivation. Relative to conditions not involving self-modeling, it was predicted that self-modeling would better promote learning, achievement beliefs, and self-regulation.

RESEARCH INTERVENTIONS AND RESULTS

A summary of research interventions appears in Table 7.2.

Changes in Achievement Outcomes

A study by Schunk (1981) explored changes in children's mathematical outcomes. Children who demonstrated below-grade-level achievement in mathematics received instruction and practice in solving long division problems. Half of the children received cognitive modeling from an adult model. The other half received didactic instruction, which provided the same instruction and materials but did not include cognitive modeling.

TABLE 7.2. Research Interventions and Results

Study	Intervention variables[a]	Effects[b]
Schunk (1981)	CgM, EF	CgM (A); CgM + EF (self-appraisal)
Schunk & Hanson (1985)	MM, CM, TM	MM, CM (A, M, SE)
Schunk, Hanson, & Cox (1987)	SM, MuM, MM, CM	SM-CM, MuM-CM, MuM-MM (A, SE)
Schunk & Hanson (1989a)	SM, MuM, MM, CAM, CEM	CEM (SE for learning)
Schunk (1982)	SV, SeV	SeV (A, M); SV + SeV (SE)
Schunk & Cox (1986)	CV, DV, EF	CV (A, SE); EF (A, SE)
Schunk & Gunn (1985)	MSU, MAB	MSU (A, M); MSU + MAB (SE)
Schunk & Hanson (1989b)	SfM	SfM (A, M, SE)
Schunk & Gunn (1986)	SVS, SVA, SVE	SVS (A); SVA (SE); SVE (A)
Schunk (1996)	LG, PG, SfE	LG, LG + SfE, PG + SfE (A, M, SE)

[a]Explanation of abbreviations: CAM, coping-alone model; CEM, coping-emotive model; CgM, cognitive modeling; CM, coping model; CV, continuous verbalization; DV, discontinued verbalization; EF, effort feedback; LG, learning goal; MAB, modeled achievement beliefs; MM, mastery model; MSU, modeled strategy use; MuM, multiple models; PG, performance goal; SeV, self-verbalization; SfE, self-evaluation; SfM, self-modeling; SM, single model; SV, strategy verbalization; SVA, self-verbalization of ability; SVE, self-verbalization of effort; SVS, self-verbalization of strategy; TM, teacher model.
[b]The influential variables are listed, followed in parentheses by the outcomes they influenced (A, achievement; M, motivation; SE, self-efficacy).

Within each instructional condition, half of the children received verbal effort attribution feedback for success and difficulty. For example, when a student succeeded on a difficult task the teacher verbalized, "You worked really hard on that one"; after a student experienced difficulty with insufficient effort the teacher stated, "You need to work harder."

Both instructional treatments enhanced division achievement, persistence, and self-efficacy, but cognitive modeling produced greater gains in accuracy. Effort attribution did not raise self-efficacy or skill; however, children who received modeling with attribution feedback displayed the most accurate judgments of their capabilities. Modeling helps to focus students on the requisite operations, provides a concrete set of observable operations tied to abstract principles, and specifies the source and remedy for deficiencies. These children may have perceived the effort attribution as credible and engaged in more self-reflection about their learning progress during independent practice. In the absence of modeling or attributional feedback, students can be swayed by modest successes and may overestimate what they can do.

Schunk and Hanson (1985) compared the effects of peer and adult models. Elementary school children who had experienced difficulties learning to subtract observed either a peer model learn subtraction with regrouping (borrowing) operations, an adult model demonstrate the operations, or no model. Children in the peer model conditions observed either a mastery or a coping model. The *mastery model* solved problems correctly and verbalized statements reflecting high self-efficacy and ability, low task difficulty, and positive attitude. The *coping model* initially made errors and verbalized negative statements, but began to verbalize coping statements (e.g., "I need to pay attention to what I'm doing.") and eventually verbalized and performed as well as the mastery model. All children then received instruction and practice in subtraction.

Mastery and coping models increased self-efficacy, motivation, and subtraction achievement better than the adult model or no model; adult-model children outperformed no-model students. Higher self-efficacy developed through peer observation may have led to better self-regulation of strategy use during subsequent problem solving and resulted in higher achievement. Observation of the adult model may have led children to reflect on whether they were capable of learning the mathematical skills.

The lack of differences between the coping and mastery model conditions may have arisen because the children had previously experienced success with subtraction. They might have reflected on those successes and thought that if the peer could learn to regroup, they could too. Schunk, Hanson, and Cox (1987) further explored the coping–mastery model distinction and found that observing coping models enhanced children's self-efficacy and achievement more than did observing mastery models. Unlike Schunk and Hanson (1985), Schunk et al. (1987) used a task (fractions) with which children had no prior success. Coping models may be more beneficial when students have little task familiarity or have experienced learning difficulties. Schunk et al. (1987) also found that multiple models (coping or mastery) promoted outcomes as well as a single coping model and better than a single mastery model.

Schunk and Hanson (1989a) further explored the effects of peer models. Children observed either single or multiple models learn to solve fraction problems using a same-sex peer mastery, coping-emotive, or coping-alone approach. *Mastery* models learned quickly; *coping-emotive* models initially experienced difficulties learning and verbalized negative emotive statements (e.g., "I don't think I can do this."), but then displayed coping behaviors and eventually performed as well as mastery models; *coping-alone* models performed in identical fashion to coping-emotive models, but never verbalized negative statements. Coping-emotive models produced the highest self-efficacy for learning. Mastery and coping-alone children perceived the model as competent and themselves as equally competent; coping-emotive subjects viewed themselves as more competent than the model. Following instruction and practice on fractions, the three conditions did not differ in self-efficacy or achievement.

Differences in self-efficacy for learning did not affect self-regulatory problem solving during instruction or posttest outcomes, perhaps because most children learned the operations. Coping-emotive children overestimated their learning efficacy, which may not be instructionally desirable if children subsequently encounter difficulty and begin to doubt their competence for learning.

Use of Self-Regulatory Statements

Research attests to the importance of models in fostering students' use of self-regulatory statements during mathematical problem solving. Schunk (1982) identified elementary school children who could not solve long division problems and were in the lowest third of their classes in mathematical achievement. Following a pretest on self-efficacy and division performance, children received modeled instruction and self-directed problem solving. Adult cognitive models verbalized strategy descriptors at appropriate places (e.g., "multiply," "check," "subtract"). During the self-directed practice, some children verbalized the strategy descriptors, others constructed their own verbalizations (e.g., "How many times does 7 go into 22?"), those in a third group verbalized strategies and self-constructions, and children in a fourth group did not verbalize.

Self-constructed verbalizations yielded the highest division achievement and motivation during problem solving. Children who verbalized both strategies and self-constructions demonstrated the highest self-efficacy. Analysis of verbalizations showed that self-constructions typically included the strategies and thus were oriented toward strategic problem solving.

Schunk and Cox (1986) determined how verbalization of subtraction self-regulatory strategies influenced self-efficacy and skill among children with learning disabilities. *Continuous verbalization* students spoke aloud while solving problems, *discontinued verbalization* children spoke aloud during the first half of the instructional program but then were told to discontinue overt verbalizations during the second half, and *no-verbalization* children did not speak aloud. All students either periodically received verbal feedback linking effort with success during the first or second half of the program, or did not receive effort feedback.

Continuous verbalization resulted in the highest self-efficacy and achievement; providing effort feedback enhanced these outcomes more than no feedback. When instructed to discontinue verbalizing aloud, discontinued-verbalization students may have not self-regulated their use of the strategies. For strategies to become internalized, such students may need to be taught to fade verbalizations from an overt to a covert level through a series of stages (i.e., spoken aloud, spoken softly, whispered, spoken internally). During a training session, children could move sequentially through these stages and spend a sufficient amount of time solving problems at each stage.

Development of Strategic Competence

Strategic competence and self-regulated strategy use can be enhanced by models who emphasize the importance of using strategies (Schunk, 1989; Zimmerman & Martinez-Pons, 1992). Schunk and Gunn (1985) conducted an intervention project in which elementary school children lacking long division skills received cognitive modeling and practice over sessions. In one condition, the model verbally emphasized the importance of using task strategies (e.g., following the solution steps in the correct order), in a second condition the model emphasized the importance of positive achievement beliefs (e.g., thinking that one can solve the problems), in a third condition the model stressed the importance of task strategies and achievement beliefs, and in a fourth condition the model cognitively modeled solution steps but did not stress strategies or beliefs. Modeling the importance of using task strategies enhanced students' motivation and skill development. Emphasizing both task strategy use and achievement beliefs led to the highest self-efficacy.

Schunk and Hanson (1989b) found support for the notion that *self-model* tapes highlight progress in learning and help to develop self-regulated strategic problem solving, self-efficacy, and achievement. Children were videotaped solving mathematical problems and later viewed their tapes. The tapes clearly portrayed the children's acquisition of strategic competence as they became more proficient in problem solving over the duration of the tape. Following an instructional program, these children demonstrated higher self-efficacy, motivation, and learning than did students who had been videotaped but did not observe their tapes and those who had not been videotaped.

Relation of Strategies to Achievement Beliefs

Schunk and Gunn (1986) determined how self-regulation of task strategy use and attributions for success during mathematics learning influence self-efficacy and skill. Elementary children lacking division skills received modeled instruction (which included self-regulatory use of task strategies) and practice over sessions. Children verbalized aloud as they solved problems, and use of effective task strategies (i.e., those that lead to successful solutions) was determined. Results of path analysis showed that attributions of success to high ability exerted the strongest influence on self-efficacy. Mathematical achievement was most strongly affected by use of effective task strategies; self-efficacy also was a significant predictor of achievement. Effort attributions for success exerted the largest direct attributional influence on achievement. This study did not explore the influence of children attributing failure to low ability. Other research shows that attributions of failure to low ability relate to low self-efficacy, motivation, and achievement, and can lead to negative affective reactions (Schunk, 1989; Weiner, 1992).

Schunk (1981) employed path analysis to examine the relations among modeled strategy instruction, self-efficacy, persistence, and mathematical achievement. Modeled strategy instruction influenced achievement directly, as well as indirectly through its effects on persistence and self-efficacy. Instruction affected persistence indirectly through self-efficacy, and self-efficacy exerted direct effects on achievement and persistence.

Other research attests to the influence of perceived self-efficacy on mathematical achievement. Using high school students, Pajares and Kranzler (1995) found with path analysis that mathematical ability and self-efficacy strongly affected achievement and that ability affected self-efficacy. Using college students, Pajares and Miller (1994) showed that mathematics self-efficacy was a better predictor of achievement than were mathematics self-concept, perceived usefulness of mathematics, prior experience with mathematics, and gender.

Goal Orientations

Schunk (1996) explored the role of goal orientations in mathematics learning. *Goal orientations* are sets of behavioral intentions that influence how students approach and engage in learning. Of primary interest were *task orientation* (desire to master and understand academic work independently) and *ego orientation* (desire to perform well to please the teacher and avoid trouble).

In two projects, average-achieving children received cognitively modeled instruction on fraction solution strategies and practice opportunities. Students worked under conditions involving either a *learning goal* (learning how to solve problems) or a *performance goal* (solving problems). In the first project, half of the students in each goal condition evaluated their problem-solving capabilities daily. The learning goal with or without self-evaluation and the performance goal with self-evaluation led to higher self-efficacy, motivation, achievement, and task orientation and to lower ego orientation than did the performance goal without self-evaluation. In the second project, all students evaluated their progress in skill acquisition. The learning goal led to higher self-efficacy, motivation, achievement, and task orientation and lower ego orientation than did the performance goal. These results suggest that modeled strategy instruction, learning goals, and opportunities for self-evaluation help to focus children's attention on the task and direct their self-regulation of problem-solving strategies.

SELF-REFLECTIVE PRACTICE

Self-reflective practice allows learners to monitor, evaluate, and adjust their performances during learning. Learners may adjust their strategies based on assessments of their learning progress and determine what activities will best assist them to accomplish their learning goals.

Interventions can teach self-regulatory activities that are useful during self-reflective practice. Some important activities are self-monitoring, self-verbalization, and self-regulation of achievement beliefs.

Self-Monitoring

Schunk (1983) taught children to self-monitor their progress during mathematics learning. Children lacking subtraction skills received modeled instruction and practice over sessions. Some children (self-monitoring) recorded the number of problems they solved during each instructional session, whereas others (external monitoring) had this information recorded by an adult. A third group did not record progress. Results showed that self- and external monitoring led to higher self-efficacy, persistence, and achievement than did no monitoring. The two monitoring conditions did not differ significantly on these measures. A drawback of external monitoring is that it requires teacher assistance, which limits the benefits of self-directed practice. Teaching students a self-monitoring procedure has practical benefits in that it allows students to work independently of teacher direction—a key element of self-regulated learning.

Self-monitoring also can help promote long-term maintenance of self-regulatory strategy use. Much strategy instruction research shows that students may learn and practice strategies that benefit their performances but may discontinue strategy use when no longer required (Pressley et al., 1990). They may believe that the strategy is not useful in improving their performances (Schunk, 1989). Students who continue to monitor and record their use of strategies should be less apt to discontinue their use.

Zimmerman, Bonner, and Kovach (1996) describe a self-monitoring procedure useful for many academic subjects. This procedure uses a form that students complete. For example, to self-monitor study time students might record information such as the date, assignment, time started, time spent, and information about the study context (where, with whom, distractions). To monitor self-efficacy for learning, students might record how well they expect to score on a quiz and their confidence for attaining that score.

Like other self-regulatory procedures, self-monitoring is not performed automatically. Teachers may need to train students in its use and schedule opportunities for self-monitoring. Once self-monitoring becomes more habitual, a prompt by the teacher may be all that is needed to have students engage in it.

Self-Verbalization

Verbalization of self-regulatory strategies can help students learn, apply, and maintain their use. Students who verbalize during self-reflective practice are apt to focus and maintain their attention, which promotes encoding and retention of information and leads to greater subsequent availability. Verbalization is a form of rehearsal, which is beneficial for learning, and it may create in students a strong sense of personal control, which can raise self-efficacy and maintain motivation for learning (Schunk, 1982).

A drawback of verbalization is that it constitutes an additional task and may interfere with performance on the learning task (Zimmerman & Bell, 1972). If children concentrate too much on verbalizing, they may not attend properly to the content of the verbalizations, and learning may suffer. As discussed earlier, children may discontinue use of effective strategies when asked not to verbalize aloud (Schunk & Cox, 1986).

Verbalization seems most beneficial for students who do not normally organize, rehearse, or otherwise properly attend to strategies and operations necessary for successful performance (Denney & Turner, 1979; Schunk, 1982). Their achievement performances may suffer further from self-doubts about their capabilities. Children who have a good grasp of cognitive operations and who typically monitor their performances may not benefit from overt verbalization (Denney, 1975).

Verbalization seems most useful in the early stages of learning when students are acquiring skills and strategies or at any time when they encounter difficulties learning (Schunk, 1982). During self-reflective practice, students might verbalize coping statements as needed, as well as statements indicating self-efficacy for succeeding, effort and ability attributions, and positive attitudes (e.g., "I'm finally catching on to this, and I'm starting to like it."). Self-monitoring also can be employed in conjunction with self-verbalization, as students can be asked periodically to stop and record whether they are verbalizing and whether the verbalizations are task relevant.

Self-Regulation of Achievement Beliefs

Self-reflective practice can be used to develop and maintain positive achievement beliefs. These include beliefs about the value of learning, the uses of learned information, and the factors that contribute to success (e.g., self-efficacy, attributions, attitudes).

Unfortunately, research suggests that achievement beliefs occupy a small part of students' thoughts while engaged in tasks. Schunk and Gunn (1986) found that only 6% of students' verbalization involved achievement beliefs, whereas 94% involved strategic task statements. In Schunk and Gunn's study, students were generally successful at problem solving, so most of the achievement-belief verbalizations were positive. We might expect that such verbalizations would be critically important in situations where students experience difficulty, so that they can self-regulate their task involvement through positive beliefs. Again, students may need to be explicitly prompted to verbalize at critical times by teachers.

Self-reflective practice also provides the opportunity for students to self-evaluate their capabilities or progress in learning. Schunk (1996) found that self-evaluation is most effective under circumstances where students might not otherwise engage in it on their own and when opportunities are frequent and interspersed throughout instructional sessions. Self-evaluation may not bear a strong relation to achievement outcomes when it is used infrequently. As with other self-regulatory activities, students may need to be trained to engage in self-evaluation and urged to seek assistance when they assess their learning progress as inadequate.

CONCLUSIONS

In this chapter I have argued that the use of models during mathematics instruction is an important contextual factor that can promote elementary children's mathematical self-efficacy, motivation, self-regulation, and achievement. Modeling seems to have a limited use in American classrooms given the emphasis on seatwork, and low use of classroom models may help to explain the poor mathematical achievement of American children relative to students in other countries. I have summarized results of several intervention studies showing the benefits of models. In addition to cognitive skills and strategies, models also may verbalize positive achievement beliefs that help students cope with difficulties and maintain task focus. During periods of self-reflective practice, students can apply mathematical problem-solving strategies and other important self-regulatory activities such as self-monitoring of progress and self-enhancement of achievement beliefs. My hope is that American educators will realize the value of models and design curricula and environments to capitalize on their vast potential.

REFERENCES

Bandura, A. (1977). *Social learning theory*. Englewood Cliffs, NJ: Prentice-Hall.

Bandura, A. (1986). *Social foundations of thought and action: A social cognitive theory*. Englewood Cliffs, NJ: Prentice-Hall.

Bandura, A. (1993). Perceived self-efficacy in cognitive development and functioning. *Educational Psychologist, 28*, 117–148.

Bandura, A. (1997). *Self-efficacy: The exercise of control*. New York: Freeman.

Bouffard-Bouchard, T., Parent, S., & Larivee, S. (1991). Influence of self-efficacy on self-regulation and performance among junior and senior high-school age students. *International Journal of Behavioural Development, 14*, 153–164.

Brown, J. S., & Burton, R. R. (1978). Diagnostic models for procedural bugs in basic mathematical skills. *Cognitive Science, 2*, 155–192.

Chen, C., & Stevenson, H. W. (1995). Motivation and mathematics achievement: A comparative study of Asian-American, Caucasian-American, and East Asian high school students. *Child Development, 66*, 1215–1234.

Denney, D. R. (1975). The effects of exemplary and cognitive models and self-rehearsal on children's interrogative strategies. *Journal of Experimental Child Psychology, 19*, 476–488.

Denney, N. W., & Turner, M. C. (1979). Facilitating cognitive performance in children: A comparison of strategy modeling and strategy modeling with overt self-verbalization. *Journal of Experimental Child Psychology, 28*, 119–131.

Dowrick, P. W. (1983). Self-modelling. In P. W. Dowrick & S. J. Biggs (Eds.), *Using video: Psychological and social applications* (pp. 105–124). Chichester, UK: Wiley.

Fuligni, A. J., & Stevenson, H. W. (1995). Time use and mathematics achievement among American, Chinese, and Japanese high school students. *Child Development, 66*, 830–842.

Geary, D. C. (1995). Reflections of evolution and culture in children's cognition: Implications for mathematical development and instruction. *American Psychologist, 50*, 24–37.

Geary, D. C. (1996). International differences in mathematical achievement: Their nature, causes, and consequences. *Current Directions in Psychological Science, 5*, 133–137.

Kanfer, F. H., & Gaelick, L. (1986). Self-management methods. In F. H. Kanfer & A. P. Goldstein (Eds.), *Helping people change: A textbook of methods* (3rd ed., pp. 283–345). New York: Pergamon Press.

Kloosterman, P. (1988). Self-confidence and motivation in mathematics. *Journal of Educational Psychology, 80*, 345–351.

Mace, F. C., Belfiore, P. J., & Shea, M. C. (1989). Operant theory and research on self-regulation. In B. J. Zimmerman & D. H. Schunk (Eds.), *Self-regulated learning and academic achievement: Theory, research, and practice* (pp. 27–50). New York: Springer-Verlag.

McCombs, B. L. (1989). Self-regulated learning and academic achievement: A phenomenological view. In B. J. Zimmerman & D. H. Schunk (Eds.), *Self-regulated learning and academic achievement: Theory, research, and practice* (pp. 51–82). New York: Springer-Verlag.

Meece, J. L., & Courtney, D. P. (1992). Gender differences in students' perceptions: Consequences for achievement-related choices. In D. H. Schunk & J. L. Meece (Eds.), *Student perceptions in the classroom* (pp. 209–228). Hillsdale, NJ: Erlbaum.

Meichenbaum, D. (1977). *Cognitive behavior modification: An integrative approach.* New York: Plenum Press.

National Council of Teachers of Mathematics. (1989). *Curriculum and evaluation standards for school mathematics.* Reston, VA: Author.

Newman, R. S. (1994). Adaptive help seeking: A strategy of self-regulated learning. In D. H. Schunk & B. J. Zimmerman (Eds.), *Self-regulation of learning and performance: Issues and educational applications* (pp. 283–301). Hillsdale, NJ: Erlbaum.

Pajares, F., & Kranzler, J. (1995). Self-efficacy beliefs and general mental ability in mathematical problem-solving. *Contemporary Educational Psychology, 20,* 426–443.

Pajares, F., & Miller, M. D. (1994). Role of self-efficacy and self-concept beliefs in mathematical problem solving: A path analysis. *Journal of Educational Psychology, 86,* 193–203.

Pintrich, P. R., & De Groot, E. V. (1990). Motivational and self-regulated learning components of classroom academic performance. *Journal of Educational Psychology, 82,* 33–40.

Pintrich, P. R., & Schrauben, B. (1992). Students' motivational beliefs and their cognitive engagement in classroom academic tasks. In D. H. Schunk & J. L. Meece (Eds.), *Student perceptions in the classroom* (pp. 149–183). Hillsdale, NJ: Erlbaum.

Pressley, M., Woloshyn, V., Lysynchuk, L. M., Martin, V., Wood, E., & Willoughby, T. (1990). A primer of research on cognitive strategy instruction: The important issues and how to address them. *Educational Psychology Review, 2,* 1–58.

Rosenthal, T. L., & Zimmerman, B. J. (1978). *Social learning and cognition.* New York: Academic Press.

Salomon, G. (1984). Television is "easy" and print is "tough": The differential investment of mental effort in learning as a function of perceptions and attributions. *Journal of Educational Psychology, 76,* 647–658.

Schunk, D. H. (1981). Modeling and attributional effects on children's achievement: A self-efficacy analysis. *Journal of Educational Psychology, 73,* 93–105.

Schunk, D. H. (1982). Verbal self-regulation as a facilitator of children's achievement and self-efficacy. *Human Learning, 1,* 265–277.

Schunk, D. H. (1983). Progress self-monitoring: Effects on children's self-efficacy and achievement. *Journal of Experimental Education, 51,* 89–93.

Schunk, D. H. (1987). Peer models and children's behavioral change. *Review of Educational Research, 57,* 149–174.

Schunk, D. H. (1989). Self-efficacy and achievement behaviors. *Educational Psychology Review, 1,* 173–208.

Schunk, D. H. (1994). Self-regulation of self-efficacy and attributions in academic settings. In D. H. Schunk & B. J. Zimmerman (Eds.), *Self-regulation of learning and performance: Issues and educational applications* (pp. 75–99). Hillsdale, NJ: Erlbaum.

Schunk, D. H. (1996). Goal and self-evaluative influences during children's cognitive skill learning. *American Educational Research Journal, 33,* 359–382.

Schunk, D. H., & Cox, P. D. (1986). Strategy training and attributional feedback with learning disabled students. *Journal of Educational Psychology, 78,* 201–209.

Schunk, D. H., & Gunn, T. P. (1985). Modeled importance of task strategies and achievement beliefs: Effect on self-efficacy and skill development. *Journal of Early Adolescence, 5,* 247–258.

Schunk, D. H., & Gunn, T. P. (1986). Self-efficacy and skill development: Influence of task strategies and attributions. *Journal of Educational Research, 79,* 238–244.

Schunk, D. H., & Hanson, A. R. (1985). Peer models: Influence on children's self-efficacy and achievement. *Journal of Educational Psychology, 77,* 313–322.

Schunk, D. H., & Hanson, A. R. (1989a). Influence of peer-model attributes on children's beliefs and learning. *Journal of Educational Psychology, 81,* 431–434.

Schunk, D. H., & Hanson, A. R. (1989b). Self-modeling and children's cognitive skill learning. *Journal of Educational Psychology, 81,* 155–163.

Schunk, D. H., Hanson, A. R., & Cox, P. D. (1987). Peer model attributes and children's achievement behaviors. *Journal of Educational Psychology, 79,* 54–61.

Schunk, D. H., & Zimmerman, B. J. (1997). Social origins of self-regulatory competence. *Educational Psychologist, 32,* 195–208.

Shell, D. F., Murphy, C. C., & Bruning, R. H. (1989). Self-efficacy and outcome expectancy mechanisms in reading and writing achievement. *Journal of Educational Psychology, 81,* 91–100.

Steen, L. A. (1987). Mathematics education: A predictor of scientific competitiveness. *Science, 237,* 251–252, 302.

Stevenson, H. W., Chen, C., & Lee, S. (1993). Mathematics achievement of Chinese, Japanese, and American children: Ten years later. *Science, 259,* 53–58.

Stigler, J. W., Lee, S., & Stevenson, H. W. (1987). Mathematics classrooms in Japan, Taiwan, and the United States. *Child Development, 58,* 1272–1285.

Stipek, D. J., & Gralinski, J. H. (1991). Gender differences in children's achievement-related beliefs and emotional responses to success and failure in mathematics. *Journal of Educational Psychology, 83,* 361–371.

Uttal, D. H., Lummis, M., & Stevenson, H. W. (1988). Low and high mathematics achievement in Japanese, Chinese, and American elementary-school children. *Developmental Psychology, 24,* 335–342.

Weiner, B. (1992). *Human motivation: Metaphors, theories, and research.* Newbury Park, CA: Sage.

Whang, P. A., & Hancock, G. R. (1994). Motivation and mathematics achievement: Comparisons between Asian-American and non-Asian students. *Contemporary Educational Psychology, 19,* 302–322.

Zimmerman, B. J. (1989). A social cognitive view of self-regulated academic learning. *Journal of Educational Psychology, 81,* 329–339.

Zimmerman, B. J. (1990). Self-regulating academic learning and achievement: The emergence of a social cognitive perspective. *Educational Psychology Review, 2,* 173–201.

Zimmerman, B. J. (1994). Dimensions of academic self-regulation: A conceptual framework for education. In D. H. Schunk & B. J. Zimmerman (Eds.), *Self-regulation of learning and performance: Issues and educational applications* (pp. 3–21). Hillsdale, NJ: Erlbaum.

Zimmerman, B. J. (1995). Self-efficacy and educational development. In A. Bandura (Ed.), *Self-efficacy in changing societies* (pp. 202–231). New York: Cambridge University Press.

Zimmerman, B. J., & Bell, J. A. (1972). Observer verbalization and abstraction in vicarious rule learning, generalization, and retention. *Developmental Psychology, 7,* 227–231.

Zimmerman, B. J., Bonner, S., & Kovach, R. (1996). *Developing self-regulated learners: Beyond achievement to self-efficacy.* Washington, DC: American Psychological Association.

Zimmerman, B. J., & Kitsantas, A. (1996). Self-regulated learning of a motoric skill: The role of goal setting and self-monitoring. *Journal of Applied Sport Psychology, 8,* 60–75.

Zimmerman, B. J., & Martinez-Pons, M. (1992). Perceptions of efficacy and strategy use in the self-regulation of learning. In D. H. Schunk & J. L. Meece (Eds.), *Student perceptions in the classroom* (pp. 185–207). Hillsdale, NJ: Erlbaum.

Zimmerman, B. J., & Ringle, J. (1981). Effects of model persistence and statements of confidence on children's self-efficacy and problem solving. *Journal of Educational Psychology, 73,* 485–493.

CHAPTER 8

A Strategic Content Learning Approach to Promoting Self-Regulated Learning by Students with Learning Disabilities

Deborah L. Butler

Successful learners approach academic tasks strategically (Borkowski, 1992; Butler & Winne, 1995; Pressley, 1986). They analyze task requirements, define criteria for successful performance, and set realistic goals. They select, adapt, or even invent strategic approaches to achieve their objectives, monitor the success of their efforts, and adaptively adjust activities accordingly (Butler & Winne, 1995). In short, proficient learners are self-regulating (Butler & Winne, 1995; Carver & Scheier, 1990; Zimmerman, 1989, 1994).

Educational researchers have devoted considerable effort to defining instructional approaches that promote students' development of self-regulation (e.g., Ellis, 1994; Harris & Graham, 1996; Pressley et al., 1992). This chapter describes research on the efficacy of one such instructional model, the strategic content learning (SCL) approach. The chapter begins with a brief overview of student needs in the context within which SCL has been implemented. Subsequently, the intervention model is outlined, and the relationship between instructional characteristics and students' development of self-regulation is explained. Next, a summary of research findings is provided. The chapter concludes with a discussion of implications of SCL investigations for theory, future research, and practice.

PROMOTING SELF-REGULATION
IN POSTSECONDARY SETTINGS

To date, the SCL intervention model has been adapted for use to support students with learning disabilities in postsecondary contexts. This initial implementation context was selected for two reasons. First, research suggests that students with learning disabilities are often either deficient (Torgesen, 1977) or "actively inefficient" in their strategic approaches to tasks (Swanson, 1990, p. 51). These students have been shown to profit from interventions, like SCL, that support them to approach learning tasks more strategically (e.g., Graham & Harris, 1989; Sawyer, Graham, & Harris, 1992; Schumaker & Deshler, 1992; Wong, Butler, Ficzere, & Kuperis, 1996).

Second, a clear need existed for research on effective interventions for students with learning disabilities in postsecondary settings. With a few notable exceptions (e.g., Policastro, 1993; Schumaker & Deshler, 1992), most of the research on strategic interventions for students with learning disabilities had been conducted with younger students in elementary, intermediate, or secondary contexts. This research provides excellent guidance for how to structure instruction so as to promote children's development of self-regulation. Yet, the strategic deficiencies of students with learning disabilities have been shown to persist into their adult years (Bursuck & Jayanthi, 1993; Deshler, Schumaker, Alley, Warner, & Clark, 1982). Further, increasing numbers of students with learning disabilities are seeking admission to postsecondary institutions and are requesting assistance from campus support agencies (Vogel & Adelman, 1990), and additional research is required to guide service development (Gerber & Reiff, 1991; Vogel & Adelman, 1990).

Like their younger counterparts, postsecondary students with learning disabilities often need assistance to learn how to self-regulate learning more effectively (Policastro, 1993). At the same time, determining the format for SCL service delivery requires sensitivity to the range of student needs in postsecondary settings. For example, postsecondary students with learning disabilities also require assistance to complete immediately pressing assignments for courses in which they are enrolled. Thus, to be maximally efficient, SCL needs to promote students' development of self-regulation while addressing the requirements of classroom-based tasks.

Another constraint on service delivery in postsecondary settings is that support to students with learning disabilities must be individualized. This is partly because the kinds of assignments that a student finds troublesome depend on the courses she[1] is taking and on her unique profile of processing strengths and weaknesses. Students with learning disabilities enrolled in a variety of courses need assistance with multiple variants of reading, listening, writing, and/or math tasks. Further, even when two students target a common task (e.g., reading course textbooks), the difficulties they experience may vary considerably (e.g., one student might get lost in the details and try to memorize every sentence; another might skim the material without ever actually reading). To provide help expediently, SCL instructors need to target the task an individual finds most difficult, and then quickly address the student's unique difficulties with that task.

This chapter summarizes results from four studies conducted to examine SCL efficacy as a model for supporting students with learning disabilities in postsecondary settings. Across the four studies, participants represented a broad cross section of the population of students with learning disabilities who might attend postsecondary institutions. Participants were drawn from both college and university settings. They were enrolled in a variety of academically and/or vocationally oriented programs. Students' reading and writing skills ranged from the fourth grade to university level. Finally, the specific processing difficulties experienced by students as part of their learning disabilities were highly variable, as were the tasks they targeted for assistance. Such a heterogeneous group of participants was included across the four studies to facilitate evaluation of the robustness of the SCL model across students, settings, programs, and tasks.

THE SCL APPROACH

In this section, the theoretical foundations underlying the SCL approach are introduced. Discussion begins with an overview of the cognitive processes central to self-regulation so as to clarify instructional goals and to establish a framework for describing SCL. Next, the SCL instructional sequence is outlined. The section closes with a theoretical analysis of key instructional features and their hypothesized relationships to students' development of self-regulation.

Cognitive Processes Central to Self-Regulation

Figure 8.1 provides an overview of the cognitive processes central to self-regulation (Butler & Winne, 1995; Carver & Scheier, 1990; Corno, 1993; Zimmerman, 1989, 1994). Self-regulated learners engage in this sequence of processes reflectively, flexibly, and recursively. Their learning activities are continually reshaped as they plan, monitor, and modify their engagement in tasks (Butler & Winne, 1995).

To promote students' development of self-regulation, support must assist students to engage flexibly in the sequence of cognitive processes that comprise self-regulated learning. First, students must learn how to analyze

TASK DEMANDS

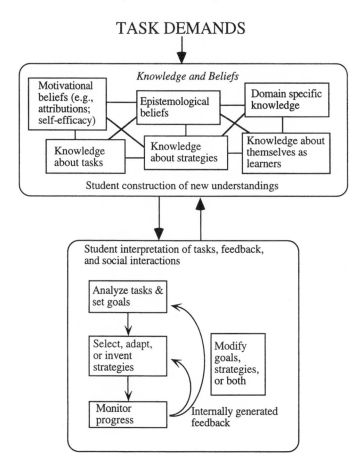

FIGURE 8.1. A model of self-regulated learning.

tasks effectively and to set appropriate task goals. This step in self-regulation is critical, because the goals students select establish the direction for all further learning activities (Butler, 1994; Butler & Winne, 1995; Dweck, 1986). A student's task goals define the outcomes he hopes to achieve and the criteria he uses for selecting or adapting learning strategies. Further, when the student monitors the success of his efforts, he judges his progress, and modifies his efforts, based on his interpretation of task requirements. Unfortunately, students with learning disabilities often have difficulty deciphering task demands. This problem arises because students with learning disabilities often hold inaccurate understandings about tasks (e.g., thinking of reading as decoding words rather than pulling out main ideas) (Baker & Brown, 1984; Campione, Brown, & Connell, 1988; Jacobs & Paris, 1987). Students with learning disabilities also often fail to recognize that interpreting task demands is a key learning activity (Butler, 1994). As a result, promoting self-regulation by students with learning disabilities may require assisting them to construct adequate task understandings, to recognize the importance of analyzing tasks, to learn concrete strategies for interpreting task requirements, and to self-direct learning activities based on the task demands they perceive.

Consider an example from previous SCL research that illustrates the importance of task analysis in shaping students' strategic performance (see Butler, 1992). When studying for an exam in his first year biology course, Bob,[2] a university student with autism, carefully memorized every detail of each research study described in his course text. However, he failed to attend to how sets of studies were interconnected, sequentially testing rival hypotheses to come to some final conclusion. Bob was unsuccessful in his exam preparation, not because he did not try hard or use strategies successfully to memorize details, but because he set inappropriate goals for his studying task. When he better understood task requirements, he was able to self-direct his learning activities more appropriately and to prepare for exams more successfully.

Second, once students understand task requirements, they must implement learning approaches that successfully achieve their objectives. Much research has focused on identifying the types of learning strategies used by effective learners (e.g., Bereiter & Bird, 1985; Dole, Duffy, Roehler, & Pearson, 1991), flaws in strategy use of less proficient learners (e.g., Borkowski, Estrada, Milstead, & Hale, 1989; Englert, Raphael, Anderson, Gregg, & Anthony, 1989; Montague, Maddux, & Dereshiwsky, 1990), and instructional approaches for teaching learning strategies (e.g., Borkowski & Muthukrishna, 1992; Ellis, 1994; Englert, Raphael, Anderson, Anthony, & Stevens, 1991; Harris & Graham, 1996; Palincsar & Brown, 1984; Pressley et al., 1992; Schumaker & Deshler, 1992). This research has shown clearly that many students require support to recognize helpful strategies, implement them effectively, and transfer strategic performance across contexts and time. Further, students with learning disabilities need support to learn how to adapt known strategies flexibly in the face of varying task demands (Swanson, 1990).

Finally, promoting self-regulation requires supporting students to monitor their performance. In a recent review focused on self-regulated processing, Butler and Winne (1995) described monitoring as "the hub of self-regulated task engagement," (p. 275) a pivot around which recursive cycles of self-regulated processing turn. During monitoring, students compare current progress to goals, thereby generating internal feedback about the success of their efforts. This internal feedback comprises students' perceptions of progress that provide the basis for further judgments about how to proceed. In this respect the internal feedback generated during monitoring "is critical in shaping the evolving pattern of a learner's engagement with a task" (Butler & Winne, p. 275).

However, learners often do not monitor their performance successfully, or effectively adapt their approaches to tasks based on the monitoring that they do (Baker, 1984; Bereiter & Bird, 1985; Pressley, Ghatala, Woloshyn, & Pirie, 1990; Swanson, 1990). Students may encounter these difficulties for a number of reasons (Butler & Winne, 1995). For example, if students set inappropriate task goals, the criteria they use to judge performance quality will lead to faulty appraisals. Alternatively, students may make errors when completing the monitoring process, inaccurately comparing performance to goals. Or, students may simply fail to monitor their progress, due to a lack of attention, of knowledge about the importance of monitoring, or of sufficient cognitive resources to manage multiple cognitive activities concurrently.

Researchers acknowledge that students' engagement in self-regulating activities can proceed outside of conscious awareness. For example, often expert readers only become aware of self-monitoring activities when a comprehension failure occurs (Brown, 1980) and when they shift their attention from fluent application of cognitive strategies (e.g., reading for main ideas) to self-reflective direction of learning (e.g., allocating attention to identifying a comprehension problem and implementing debugging strategies) (Bereiter & Bird, 1985). At the same time, the hallmark of effective self-regulation is students' ability to bring automatic processes to conscious awareness when more deliberate processing is called for, for example, in cases when comprehension breaks down during reading, or when facing a task that is difficult or unfamiliar (Butler, in press-b). Additionally, it is students' reflective attempts to identify task requirements and to implement strategies adaptively that are central to strategic processing, not the automatic application of well-learned routines (Brown, 1978; Reeve & Brown, 1985). The implication is that to promote self-regulated learning instructors must not only teach students how to implement task-specific strategies proficiently in the context of familiar tasks, but they must also support students to learn how to orchestrate their strategic activities self-reflectively in the face of fluctuating task demands (Butler, 1995; Harris & Graham, 1996).

It was argued earlier that to promote strategic learning by postsecondary students with learning disabilities support must be individualized. Based on the description of self-regulated learning presented in this section, this argument can be extended. Specifically, individualizing instruction requires assessing students' current self-regulated approaches to tasks and then calibrating instruction to support students' revision of problematic self-regulated processing. For example, in the SCL case described earlier (of the university student with autism), Bob's studying was ineffective because of his misconceptions about task demands. Once he was supported to analyze task requirements and set better goals, Bob needed little additional assistance to identify or implement learning strategies successfully or to self-monitor the success of his studying efforts (Butler, 1992).

Promoting self-regulation requires more than assisting students to engage strategic activities in the context of particular tasks. Students' knowledge and beliefs also mediate they way in which they engage strategic processes. For example, as noted earlier, a student's metacognitive understandings regarding typical task requirements influence her perception of task demands and subsequent self-direction of learning activities. Similarly, a student's confidence in her ability to succeed at a task (i.e., her perception of task-specific self-efficacy) influences the goals she adopts and her task persistence (Bandura, 1993). Therefore, as part of instruction, teachers must support students' construction of knowledge and beliefs that support, rather than undermine, self-regulation (Borkowski & Muthukrishna, 1992; Paris & Byrnes, 1989). Some of the kinds of knowledge and beliefs that influence students' strategic performance are depicted in Figure 8.1 (Alexander & Judy, 1988; Bandura, 1993; Borkowski et al., 1989; Paris & Byrnes, 1989; Schommer, 1990, 1993).

Postsecondary students with learning disabilities generally construct knowledge and beliefs based on a long history of negative and generally frustrating experiences with school; these understandings then interfere with their learning (Wong, 1991b). For example, many SCL participants have initially held inaccurate epistemological beliefs about learning (Schommer, 1990, 1993), convinced for example, that for everyone but them learning is quick and easy. As a result, when they find themselves expending time and effort trying to learn course material, they judge their abilities to be poor and their progress to be unreasonably slow (Butler & Winne, 1995). In these instances, students' misconceptions about the process of learning shape the internal feedback they generate during monitoring and undermine their confidence (Butler & Winne, 1995). Therefore, when individualizing support to postsecondary students with learning disabilities, instructors must recognize and support revision of students' unproductive understandings and beliefs.

An Overview of the SCL Model

In SCL, instructors provide calibrated support to students as the students flexibly and recursively undertake each of the cognitive activities central to self-regulation (i.e., analyzing a task and setting goals; selecting, adapting, or inventing strategic approaches; monitoring progress; and adjusting learning approaches as required; see Figure 8.1). Instructors also engage students in interactive discussions about learning processes to promote construction and/or revision of understandings and beliefs. In this and the next section, SCL instructional activities are described more specifically. To begin, this section provides an overview of the SCL approach as adapted for use in postsecondary settings.

As described earlier, in postsecondary contexts students require immediate help with actual classroom tasks. Therefore, participants in the studies described in this paper were first supported to priorize tasks with which they needed assistance (e.g., reading, studying, writing, math problem solving) and to identify assignments within and across courses where those targeted tasks were required. Next, to guide individualization of instruction, careful observations were made of students' extant approaches to self-regulating learning (i.e., while completing first assignments), without interference or support. Preintervention interviews, questionnaires, and on-line observations were also used to gather information about knowledge and beliefs that influenced students' approaches to tasks.

After preintervention assessments, interventions began. To begin, students were assisted to analyze an assignment, identify task demands, and articulate performance criteria. For many students this step was pivotal. Consistent with previous research (e.g., Graham, Schwartz, & MacArthur, 1993; Winne & Marx, 1982) across the studies described here, preintervention data showed that many students held misconceptions about task demands, misinterpreted assignment directions, and/or did not realize the importance of analyzing tasks as a guide to directing learning activities (Butler, 1994).

Next, students were supported to use task performance criteria to make decisions about learning activities. As a starting point, students were assisted to implement, monitor, and evaluate current strategic approaches and to maintain, abandon, or revise strategies based on the internal feedback monitoring generated. This approach to promoting strategy development was used for several reasons. First, when students' current strategies were shown to be effective, instruction could be efficiently targeted elsewhere. Second, if students recognized the efficacy of current approaches, their competence was highlighted, thereby supporting development of task-specific self-efficacy. Third, revisions to strategies built from what students already knew, thereby supporting construction of new understandings tied to an established knowledge base (see Butler, in press-c). Finally, the strategies developed were personalized. They were founded on students' processing preferences, capitalized on their strengths, circumvented their weaknesses, and responded to their unique difficulties with tasks.

When students had no initial idea of how to approach tasks, they were supported to brainstorm and evaluate possible strategies. Although instructors sometimes provided suggestions or ideas to think about, they never told students how to proceed. Instead, students were consistently required to make all final decisions, while instructors supported students' decision making. For example, from among the range of strategic options discussed, it was the student's role to select an approach and to justify that selection, while the instructor asked questions or made comments that supported the student's judgment. These instructional statements frequently directed students' attention to important decision-making cues (e.g., a strategy quality or performance criteria), or guided students to make systematic comparisons between progress achieved when using a strategy and original learning objectives (see Kamann & Butler, 1996).

Whenever students selected a strategic approach, they were required to articulate the strategy's steps. Their descriptions were transcribed to serve as processing cues, to facilitate systematic strategy evaluation and modification, and to provide evidence of strategy evolution over time. Further, requiring students to define their own strategies contributed to their personalization: Not only did students select the strategies that they would employ, but their strategy descriptions were expressed in their own words.

Finally, in SCL sessions, students were supported to monitor outcomes of strategy implementation and to modify and fine-tune approaches. Engaging students in these kinds of strategic analysis activities (Ellis, 1993) has been linked with the development of metacognitive understandings about strategies and about tasks (Borkowski et al., 1989; Ellis, 1993). Further, when students actively observe the relationship between strategy use and outcomes, they build positive perceptions of self-efficacy (e.g., Schunk & Cox, 1986; Schunk, 1994, 1996) and feel more in control over outcomes. They also recognize the relationship between the effortful use of strategic approaches and successful performance (e.g., Borkowski, Weyhing, & Turner, 1986; Schunk & Cox, 1986). Finally, students learn how to select, monitor, adapt, and even create strategies given their analyses of varying task demands (Butler, 1995).

Within each session, SCL instruction was provided via interactive discussions focused alternately on completing the targeted task (e.g., brainstorming ideas for an essay assignment) and on the process of learning (e.g., the benefits of brainstorming ideas in the writing process). To promote self-reflection, instructors responsively cued students' shifts between these cognitive and metacognitive levels of analysis. Here again instruction had to be individualized. Although some students needed assistance to shift from an exclusive task focus to a more reflective stance, other students were already highly reflective, but lacked focused approaches to tasks. Thus, whereas the former group of students needed to become more reflective; the latter group needed to harness their metacognitive skills to develop concrete, effective, and task-specific strategies.

Finally, between sessions, SCL participants were encouraged to pilot test emerging strategies as they completed actual coursework and to evaluate strategy effectiveness on their own. Students referred to written records of their developing strategies to guide their performance between meetings. Then, during subsequent sessions, students reported back on the success of their efforts and any strategy modifications that they made. These procedures encouraged students both to transfer task-specific strategies across learning contexts and to self-direct learning independently.

Key Instructional Elements

The SCL model was developed based on concurrent analyses of strategy training research, of the cognitive processes underlying self-regulation (e.g., Butler & Winne, 1995; Carver & Scheier, 1990; Paris & Byrnes, 1989; Zimmerman, 1989, 1994) and of mechanisms associated with transfer (e.g., Salomon & Perkins, 1989; Wong, 1991a). The model shares many key features with other instructional models also designed to promote students' development of self-regulation, metacognition, and strategic performance (e.g., Borkowski & Muthukrishna, 1992; Ellis, 1993, 1994; Harris & Graham, 1996; Policastro, 1993; Pressley et al., 1992; Schumaker & Deshler, 1992; Wong et al., 1996).

Structured and Explicit Instruction

A feature SCL shares with many intervention models is that instruction is both structured and explicit. However, in most approaches to strategy training (e.g., Ellis, 1994; Harris & Graham, 1996; Pressley et al., 1992; Schumaker & Deshler, 1992), teaching is initially structured in part by providing direct instruction about and modeling of strategic approaches, followed by guided and then independent practice. In SCL, in contrast, discussions are structured by systematically focusing attention on the sequence of cognitive activities central to self-regulation. Similarly, whereas in most instructional approaches explicitness is initially established through direct explanations about tasks and strategies, in the SCL model explicitness derives from requiring students to articulate developing understandings and by formally recording student strategy descriptions.

Although SCL does not begin with the direct explanation of a set of predefined learning strategies, neither is it a form of discovery learning. Instead, instructors actively employ questions and comments to shape students' on-line decision making. Although direct explanations about specific approaches are sometimes provided, they comprise less than 4% of the instructional statements employed (Kamann & Butler, 1996)

Promoting Knowledge Construction

Like most current intervention models (e.g., Borkowski & Muthukrishna, 1992; Ellis, 1993; Harris & Graham, 1996; Pressley et al., 1992), SCL includes instructional activities designed to promote students' construction of a range of knowledge and beliefs. For example, in many training models, students are required to implement, discuss, and evaluate a range of strategic approaches (e.g., Borkowski et al., 1989; Ellis, 1993), activities that support students' construction of metacognitive understandings about tasks and strategies. Pressley (Pressley et al., 1992, 1995) recently used the term *transactional* to describe the collective understandings students generate about texts while interactively employing strategic approaches during reading. In the SCL model, I have extended Pressley's description to suggest that students also construct transactional understandings about *self-regulation* during interactive discussions about learning (Butler, 1997b, in press-c). That is, in interactive discussions, construction of metacognitive understandings about tasks, strategies, and the process of learning are mutually influenced as participants define common referents for discussing processing and share interpretations of on-line experiences with tasks.

Promoting Transfer

Initial enthusiasm over the success of strategy training interventions in the 1980s was soon tempered by findings of limited maintenance and transfer (Brown, Campione, & Day, 1981; Wong, 1992). As a result, intervention researchers started to identify instructional components specifically designed to promote transfer (Borkowski et al., 1986; Borkowski & Muthukrishna, 1992; Ellis, 1993; Paris, Wixson, & Palincsar, 1986; Wong, 1992). In the SCL model, transfer is promoted in several ways. First, instruction is provided in the context of meaningful classroom-based work (Paris et al., 1986). Second, when students articulate generalized strategy descriptions, they abstract decontextualized principles about strategic processing. Later, students can draw on these understandings when reflectively planning strategic approaches (i.e., "high road transfer"; Salomon & Perkins, 1989; Wong, 1991a). Third, including students in the process of strategy development may also be linked to improved transfer. This is in part because a student is likely to view personalized strategies as useful, if they target that individual's needs. Further, when students are actively involved in the decision-making process underlying strategy construction, they may feel ownership over the strategies developed and so continue to use them. Finally, if students do learn how to self-direct learning activities and to construct and modify strategies for themselves based on an analysis of task demands, they should transfer these competencies across tasks.

Social Interaction

In many instructional models, the role of social interaction in students' development of self-regulation is highlighted. As in these other approaches, in the SCL model interactive discussions provide the medium through which students' approaches to self-regulation are influenced. However, rather than suggesting that students internalize the strategic processing modeled by more capable learners in social environments (e.g., Pressley et al., 1992; Stone, in press), SCL emphasizes individuals' mediation of learning (see Butler, in press-a, for a more complete discussion). It is presumed that each student's understandings are ultimately determined by his interpretation of external input as filtered through existing knowledge and beliefs (Butler & Winne, 1995).

Nonetheless, social interactions provide the external input that learners interpret as they struggle with others to comprehend tasks. Once participants mutually establish common referents for communication, they are able to share ideas with each other and to construct transactional understandings about learning. Across students, emerging understandings therefore share many features, because they include common terms and derive from joint experiences. And, as a result, individuals construct understandings that they might not have come to on their own (Pressley et al., 1992). Ultimately, however, each student constructs new understandings that are in some respects idiosyncratic, because those understandings build from a unique knowledge base modified by an individual's interpretations of group understandings (Butler, in press-a).

RESEARCH ON SCL EFFICACY IN POSTSECONDARY SETTINGS

This section presents a description of research evaluating SCL efficacy in postsecondary settings. To begin, applications of SCL instructional principles in postsecondary settings are further explained. This is followed by an overview of the research design used in a series of parallel studies (Butler, 1992, 1993, 1995, 1996, 1997a, 1997b).

Adapting SCL in Postsecondary Settings

An informal survey of supports typically offered to postsecondary students with learning disabilities identified three general service delivery models: (1) individualized tutoring provided by teachers or learning disabilities specialists, through a counseling department, learning assistance center, or service established for students with disabilities; (2) peer tutoring; and (3) group-based study skills interventions. This chapter summarizes findings from four parallel studies on SCL efficacy as a framework for structuring one-on-one tutoring by teachers or learning disability specialists. Studies evaluating SCL adaptations within the two remaining support models (i.e., peer tutoring and study skills courses) are also planned or are underway.

In each of the studies described here, individualized SCL tutoring was provided to students as an adjunct to regular classroom instruction. Sessions were held at students' home campuses, within the center or department where students with learning disabilities typically accessed assistance. In general, tutors met with students for roughly 3 hours per week, distributed across two to three sessions. The total number of intervention sessions was determined by students' course schedules and individual need. Whenever possible, instruction was provided for at least one semester. In four cases, tutoring was provided for up to 2 years.

Initial meetings with students were devoted to negotiating tasks, collecting background information, describing research procedures, and collecting preintervention data. Once interventions began, students targeted specific assignments to work on during each meeting, based on immediate course needs. During each session, tutors provided calibrated support to promote students' self-regulated completion of classroom assignments, following the instructional procedures outlined earlier. As students progressively took more control over their own learning activities, instructional support was responsively faded.

Research Design

The research design employed in SCL studies was selected based on three overriding objectives. These were (1) to trace the process of students' development of self-regulation while engaged in instructional sessions; (2) to evaluate SCL efficacy in naturalistic contexts using realistic service delivery models; and (3) to evaluate the consistency of SCL efficacy across students, tasks, instructors, and settings.

To achieve these objectives simultaneously, a mixed design was employed. First, within each research project, parallel, in-depth case studies were conducted to trace the progress of individuals (Merriam, 1988; Yin, 1994). Case study data provided an in-depth view of the intervention process and of the interrelationships between instructional activities and effects (Yin, 1994). Second, to facilitate cross-case comparisons, individual case studies were embedded within a pre–post design. During pre- and posttest sessions, parallel questionnaires, observations, and interviews were employed to measure common effects across students (see Butler, 1995).

A REVIEW OF RESEARCH RESULTS

In this section, an integrated overview of findings from four SCL studies is provided (see Butler, 1992, 1993, 1995, 1996, 1997a, 1997b). Across these four studies, 11 instructors provided individualized tutoring to 40 postsecondary students with learning disabilities in college and University settings. Discussion centers first on evidence related to students' development of knowledge and beliefs that mediate self-regulated processing. Subsequently, evidence related to shifts in students' task performance and strategic approaches to tasks is reviewed.

Shifts in Knowledge and Beliefs

Among the most consistent findings across SCL studies were improvements in students' metacognitive understandings about tasks and strategies. In each SCL study, students' metacognitive understandings were assessed at both pre- and posttest via parallel interviews and questionnaires. Across all four SCL studies, consistent improvements from pre- to posttest in students' metacognitive understandings were detected on these measures (see Butler, 1995).

In the three later SCL studies, the criteria for scoring the interview and questionnaire data were fine-tuned to assess more effectively the metacognitive understandings of *adult* students with learning disabilities (MacLeod, Butler, & Syer, 1996). It was observed that adult students frequently could describe strategies prior to intervention, but that they failed to understand how to judge strategy effectiveness or how to match strategic approaches to task requirements. These difficulties reflect problems students experienced in efficiently self-directing their learning in light of task demands. New criteria were established that more effectively assessed the clarity of students' understandings about self-regulated processing across four dimensions: task description (students' perceptions of typical task requirements), strategy description (students' understandings regarding task-specific strategies), strategy focus (the degree to which described strategies were focused, personalized, and connected to task demands), and monitoring (students' descriptions of how they reflect on progress and manage learning activities accordingly) (Butler, 1997a, 1997b; MacLeod et al., 1996).

Analyses of the pooled data from these three SCL studies revealed that when asked to describe approaches to completing targeted tasks students provided better descriptions at posttest than they had at pretest, across all four metacognitive dimensions (effect sizes ranging from 0.50 to 1.10; Butler, 1997b). In addition, when asked to describe approaches across a range of tasks, students' descriptions were also significantly clearer at posttest than they had been at pretest for three of the four dimensions (Butler, 1997b). Taken together, these findings suggest that improvements in students' ability to describe strategic activities can be associated with participating in SCL interventions.

Another consistent finding across SCL studies was a pre- to posttest increase in students' perceptions of task-specific self-efficacy (see Butler, 1995, 1996, 1997a, 1997b). For example, in all four studies analyses revealed that at posttest, SCL participants rated their competence to be higher on task-specific skills (e.g., their ability to organize their ideas while writing). Further, when asked to describe the extent of difficulties they encountered when completing a range of tasks (in the three later studies), students reported significantly less difficulty at posttest than they had at pretest for their selected tasks. Finally, in the latter two SCL projects, a measure of students' confidence in their ability to complete task-specific requirements was added. Significant improvements from pre- to posttest were observed on this measure as well. In these two studies, students also reported significantly less difficulties across a range of tasks. However, no gains were observed on a measure of global self-efficacy.

Some consistent shifts in attributional patterns have also been observed across SCL studies. For example, in the first, third, and fourth SCL studies, students were significantly more likely to associate successful performance with ability at posttest than they were at pretest. Conversely, in the first two SCL studies, students were less likely to blame unsuccessful performance on a lack of ability. These attributional shifts suggest that some students developed a positive attributional bias while participating in SCL studies: at posttest students were less likely to blame failure on a lack of ability, but were more willing to credit ability for success. This latter finding is consistent with the observed increases in students' perceptions of task-specific self-efficacy (Butler, 1993, 1995, 1996, 1997b). Only in the first SCL study did students rate effort as significantly more important to successful performance at posttest than they had at pretest. However, strategy use was perceived as more important at posttest by students in the first, third, and fourth studies. Taken together, these attributional shifts suggest that at least some SCL participants better recognized the role of effort and strategy use in successful performance.

Task Performance and Strategic Processing

To assess changes in students' achievement and strategic approaches to tasks, students' performance during intervention sessions was carefully chronicled. The data collected afforded not only tracing of individuals' progress, but also established relationships between instructional activities and effects (Miles & Huberman, 1994; Yin, 1994). Unfortunately, reproducing the richness of these comprehensive data is not possible in this brief summary. Instead, an overview of trends will be provided. Interested readers can access more complete case study descriptions elsewhere (Butler, 1993, 1997b; Butler, Elaschuk, & Poole, 1997).

To trace changes in students' task performance, two sources of information were accessed: First, when they served as fair measures of the skills worked on during interventions, grades on in-class quizzes or exams were recorded. Second, for all students, samples of task performance completed prior to, during, and after the intervention period were collected. These samples were appropriate to students' selected tasks and most often included copies of written assignments (e.g., essays, letters), written or oral summaries of reading passages, and/or math worksheets. For each type of task and for each individual, criteria were established for evaluating the quality of performance reflected in these samples. For example, for students working on writing tasks, scoring criteria assessed the quality of writing samples across four dimensions: thematic salience, organization, idea flow, and clarity (note that application of these criteria was appropriate to the type of writing assessed). Task performance was judged both for tasks completed during intervention sessions with the aid of tutors and for tasks completed independently (see Butler, 1995, 1997a). Finally, to provide a rough metric for cross-case comparisons, an estimate of the percentage gain during the intervention period was calculated for each individual. Across the four SCL studies, task performance data revealed that 53% of students increased performance by more than 15% (up to 49%); 11% increased performance between 10% and 14%; and 25% increased between 5% and 9%. Only three students failed to make any observable gains, while one student's performance declined slightly. Further, performance gains were observed both on instructed and independently completed tasks.

To characterize development of students' strategic approaches to tasks, several types of records were maintained. First, students' strategy descriptions in each session were recorded. Each strategy step was then categorized as having emerged transactionally out of collaborative discussions or as having been independently constructed by students without instructor assistance. Second, evidence of students' application of strategies to complete targeted tasks in nontraining contexts was collected (i.e., students' self-reports of strategy use; physical traces of strategy implementation). Finally, students' spontaneous descriptions of adapting strategic approaches for *noninstructed* tasks were captured on session audiotapes and transcribed.

This combination of evidence allowed for two types of analyses of changes in each participant's strategic performance over time. In a first set of analyses, copies of each student's strategies were sequenced to trace the evolution of strategies over time. Final strategies were compared across students who experienced varying problems with similar tasks to observe consistencies and dissimilarities in the strategies developed. Finally, the steps included in developing strategies were associated with corresponding achievement outcomes. Taken together, these analyses suggested that students consistently developed personalized strategies responsive to their unique needs (Butler, 1993, 1995, 1996, 1997b). Further, students' strategy development could be directly associated with observed task performance gains.

In a second set of analyses, patterns of students' involvement in independent strategy development and transfer were summarized. Across studies, these data revealed that 83% of students independently contributed to strategy development, 78% of students transferred developed strategies across contexts, and 73% of students spontaneously adapted strategies for use *across tasks*. This latter finding is particularly significant in that it suggests that the majority of students adjusted their strategic approaches across a range of academic tasks (thereby self-regulating more effectively across tasks).

Inspection of patterns in students' strategy development also supported a point made earlier—that although some students need support to reflect on their learning and develop metacognitive awareness, other students were very reflective from the outset. These latter students were actively engaged in strategy development, adaptation, and/or transfer from the first intervention session (Butler, 1996, 1997b). This evidence has implications for conceptualizing the process of promoting self-regulation in adult students with learning disabilities. That is, students do not generally enter instructional contexts as self-regulating "blank slates" (Butler & Winne, 1995). Therefore, rather than teaching self-regulation per se, instruction might be more accurately conceived as shaping students' extant self-regulating approaches to academic tasks.

CONCLUSIONS

Results from the research described here provide convincing evidence of SCL efficacy as a model for providing one-on-one tutoring to postsecondary students with learning disabilities (Butler, 1992, 1993, 1994, 1995, 1996, 1997a, 1997b). Research results suggest that SCL participants develop focused understandings about tasks and strategies, build more positive perceptions of task-specific self-efficacy, and are more likely to attribute successful performance to effort or strategy use. Students also develop personalized strategies that can be associated with improved task achievement. Finally, participants learn to coordinate learning activities in light of task demands. Specifically, they reflectively build strategies for themselves, apply strategic approaches across contexts, and adapt strategies for use across tasks.

In short, SCL appears to support self-reflective practice by students with learning disabilities. What is self-reflective practice? Self-reflective practice can be defined as students' active, reflective, and deliberative orchestration of learning activities in the context of important tasks. In terms of the model of self-regulation articulated earlier (see Figure 8.1), self-reflective practice requires that students analyze task requirements carefully, evaluate and select strategic approaches, monitor the qualities of their performance and the success of the strategies they implement, and then modify goals or learning strategies adaptively based on the progress they perceive (Butler & Winne, 1995; Zimmerman, 1994). SCL is designed to promote self-reflective practice by providing calibrated support to students as they learn how to implement this set of cognitive activities flexibly and recursively. In SCL research, improvements in self-reflective practice have been evidenced by students' gains in metacognitive understandings about tasks, strategies, and monitoring; increased ability to provide focused descriptions of strategies linked to task demands; and independent development, monitoring, and adaptation of strategies across contexts and tasks.

Several practical implications emerge from the SCL research described here. Perhaps most significantly, the description of self-reflective practice advanced in this chapter emphasizes the role of students' reflective decision making as central to strategic performance. It has been argued that students are responsible for making a variety of judgments and decisions when managing their learning activities, including setting goals, selecting strategies, judging performance quality, and deciding how to adapt strategies. It follows that promoting strategic learning requires assisting students to make better decisions as they self-regulate their learning. At the same time, if students are to manage their learning activities independently, they must ultimately recognize for themselves the types of decisions that need to be made. For example, it is not enough that students have metacognitive understandings about particular tasks (e.g., qualities of a compare–contrast essay). They also must recognize that task analysis is a critical activity and that they have to make decisions about performance criteria and goals. Students need to know that they should bring to bear the metacognitive knowledge they have about tasks to make a decision about how to proceed.

Further, the findings underline the importance of targeting all aspects of self-regulated processing comprehensively when promoting strategic learning (see also Harris & Graham, 1996). The implication is that just teaching learning strategies will be insufficient to promote successful performance. For example, the performance of students like Bob may be undermined not by a lack of knowledge about strategies, but by an inadequate understanding of tasks. Similarly, a student may know of effective strategies but not know how to monitor or adapt them to meet immediate needs (Swanson, 1990). Thus, to promote self-reflective practice in the long term, instructors must assist students to learn how to coordinate all aspects of strategic performance in light of task demands (Brown, 1980; Butler, in press-b; Harris & Graham, 1996).

Finally, SCL research raises important theoretical questions regarding the relationship between instruction and students' development of self-regulation. Specifically, many researchers explain that students learn to self-regulate by "internalizing" the cognitive processes observed in social interactions (e.g., Pressley et al., 1992; Stone, in press). Thus, in many approaches to strategy training, students are explicitly taught strategies (with direct explanations and modeling) and then asked to practice them until mastered (i.e., making them their own). However, a question remains regarding exactly what students need to internalize. For example, must internalization entail students' memorization of steps outlined in predefined task-specific strategies? Or, in some cases can instruction focus more broadly on promoting self-reflective practice by assisting students to systematically, flexibly, and adaptively self-regulate their learning activities (and by requiring explicit articulation of individually constructed task-specific strategies as part of that process)?

Another outstanding question concerns the interplay between social influences and individual knowledge construction in students' development of self-reflective approaches to tasks. In early strategy training models, direct instruction and modeling of task-specific strategies proved insufficient to promote strategy maintenance and transfer (Pressley et al., 1995). To redress this problem, most current strategy training models incorporate instructional activities in which social models (e.g., instructors, peers) provide examples of effective learning so that students can imitate and then internalize the cognitive processing first guided by others (thereby moving from other- to self-regulation). However, in tandem with these sociocultural explanations for the development of self-regulation, strategy training researchers also often take a constructivist view, acknowledging that students play an active role in constructing understandings about learning founded on a unique history of experiences with tasks (e.g., Harris & Pressley, 1991; Paris & Byrnes, 1989). Further, the instructional activities that provide opportunities for modeling and social interaction are also optimal for supporting individualized knowledge construction (e.g., by having students try out and discuss strategic approaches). To date, little attention has been paid to characterizing how "internalization" interacts with individual knowledge construction to influence students' self-reflective practice. In response to this problem, an attempt has been made in the SCL model to articulate how students' self-regulated processing may be shaped by a combination of sociocultural and individual influences (see Butler, in press-a). Further research is clearly required to clarify these important relationships.

ACKNOWLEDGMENTS

The research described here was supported in part by a Standard Research Grant (No. 410-95-1102) from the Social Sciences and Humanities Research Council of Canada. I would like to thank Cory Elaschuk, Shannon Poole, Michael Kamann, Barrie MacLeod, Kim Syer, Sandra Jarvis, and the remaining members of my research team for their invaluable assistance on the projects described herein. I am also grateful to Bernice Wong and Phil Winne for their insightful input and moral support. Finally, I would like to thank Dale H. Schunk and Barry J. Zimmerman for their helpful feedback on earlier versions of this chapter.

NOTES

1. To avoid gender bias in descriptions in this chapter, the pronouns "her" and "his" are used alternately.

2. All names used in this chapter are fictional.

REFERENCES

Alexander, P. A., & Judy, J. E. (1988). The interaction of domain-specific and strategic knowledge in academic performance. *Review of Educational Research, 58,* 375–404.

Baker, L. (1984). Children's effective use of multiple standards for evaluating their comprehension. *Journal of Educational Psychology, 76,* 588–597.

Baker, L., & Brown, A. L. (1984). Cognitive monitoring in reading. In J. Flood (Ed.), *Understanding reading comprehension: Cognition, language, and the structure of prose* (pp. 21–44). Newark, DE: International Reading Association.

Bandura, A. (1993). Perceived self-efficacy in cognitive development and functioning. *Educational Psychologist, 28,* 117–148.

Bereiter, C., & Bird, M. (1985). Use of thinking aloud in identification and teaching of reading comprehension strategies. *Cognition and Instruction, 2,* 131–156.

Borkowski, J. G. (1992). Metacognitive theory: A framework for teaching literacy, writing, and math skills. *Journal of Learning Disabilities, 25,* 253–257.

Borkowski, J. G., Estrada, M. T., Milstead, M., & Hale, C. A. (1989). General problem-solving skills: Relations between metacognition and strategic processing. *Learning Disability Quarterly, 12,* 57–70.

Borkowski, J. G., & Muthukrishna, N. (1992). Moving metacognition into the classroom: "Working models" and effective strategy teaching. In M. Pressley, K. R. Harris, & J. T. Guthrie (Eds.), *Promoting academic competence and literacy in school* (pp. 477–501). Toronto, Ontario: Academic Press.

Borkowski, J. G., Weyhing, R. S., & Turner, L. A. (1986). Attributional retraining and the teaching of strategies. *Exceptional Children, 53,* 130–137.

Brown, A. L. (1978). Knowing when, where and how to remember: A problem of metacognition. In R. Glaser (Ed.), *Advances in instructional psychology* (pp. 77–165). Hillsdale, NJ: Erlbaum.

Brown, A. L. (1980). Metacognitive development and reading. In R. J. Spiro, B. C. Bruce, & W. F. Brewer (Eds.), *Theoretical issues in reading comprehension: Perspectives from cognitive psychology, linguistics, artificial intelligence, and education* (pp. 453–481). Hillsdale, NJ: Erlbaum.

Brown, A. L., Campione, J. C., & Day, J. D. (1981). Learning to learn: On training students to learn from texts. *Educational Researcher, 10*(2), 14–21.

Bursuck, W. D., & Jayanthi, M. (1993). Strategy instruction: Programming for independent skill usage. In S. A. Vogel & P. B. Adelman (Eds.), *Success for college students with learning disabilities* (pp. 177–205). New York: Springer-Verlag.

Butler, D. L. (1992). Promoting strategic learning by learning disabled adults and adolescents. *Exceptionality Education Canada, 2,* 109–128.

Butler, D. L. (1993). *Promoting strategic learning by adults with learning disabilities: An alternative approach.* Unpublished doctoral dissertation, Simon Fraser University, Burnaby, British Columbia.

Butler, D. L. (1994). From learning strategies to strategic learning: Promoting self-regulated learning by post secondary students with learning disabilities. *Canadian Journal of Special Education, 4,* 69–101.

Butler, D. L. (1995). Promoting strategic learning by post secondary students with learning disabilities. *Journal of Learning Disabilities, 28,* 170–190.

Butler, D. L. (1996, April). *The strategic content learning approach to promoting self-regulated learning.* Paper presented at the annual meeting of the American Educational Research Association, New York.

Butler, D. L. (1997a, March). *The roles of goal setting and self-monitoring in students' self-regulated engagement in tasks.* Paper presented at the annual meeting of the American Educational Research Association, Chicago.

Butler, D. L. (1997b). *The strategic content learning approach to promoting self-regulated learning: A summary of three studies.* Manuscript submitted for publication.

Butler, D. L. (in press-a). In search of the architect of learning: A commentary on scaffolding as a metaphor for instructional interactions. *Journal of Learning Disabilities.*

Butler, D. L. (in press-b). Metacognition and learning disabilities. In B. Y. L. Wong (Ed.), *Learning about learning disabilities* (2nd ed.). New York: Academic Press.

Butler, D. L. (in press-c). Promoting strategic content learning by adolescents with learning disabilities. *Exceptionality Education Canada.*

Butler, D. L., Elaschuk, C., & Poole, S. (1997). *Strategic content learning in postsecondary settings: A summary of three studies.* Unpublished technical report.

Butler, D. L., & Winne, P. H. (1995). Feedback and self-regulated learning: A theoretical synthesis. *Review of Educational Research, 65,* 245–281.

Campione, J. C., Brown, A. L., & Connell, M. L. (1988). Metacognition: On the importance of understanding what you are doing. In R. I. Charles & E. A. Silver (Eds.), *The teaching and assessing of mathematical problem solving* (Vol. 3, pp. 93–114). Hillsdale, NJ: Erlbaum.

Carver, C. S., & Scheier, M. F. (1990). Origins and functions of positive and negative affect: A control-process view. *Psychological Review, 97,* 19–35.

Corno, L. (1993). The best laid plans: Modern conceptions of volition and educational research. *Educational Researcher, 22*(2), 14–22.

Deshler, D. D., Schumaker, J. B., Alley, G. R., Warner, M. M., & Clark, F. L. (1982).

Learning disabilities in adolescent and young adult populations: Research implications. *Focus on Exceptional Children, 15*(1), 1–12.

Dole, J. A., Duffy, G. G., Roehler, L. R., & Pearson, P. D. (1991). Moving from the old to the new: Research on reading comprehension instruction. *Review of Educational Research, 61,* 239–264.

Dweck, C. S. (1986). Motivational processes affecting learning. *American Psychologist, 41,* 1040–1048.

Ellis, E. S. (1993). Integrative strategy instruction: A potential model for teaching content area subjects to adolescents with learning disabilities. *Journal of Learning Disabilities, 26,* 358–383, 398.

Ellis, E. S. (1994). An instructional model for integrating content-area instruction with cognitive strategy instruction. *Reading and Writing Quarterly: Overcoming Learning Difficulties, 10,* 63–90.

Englert, C. S., Raphael, T. E., Anderson, L. M., Anthony, H. M., & Stevens, D. D. (1991). Making strategies and self-talk visible: Writing instruction in regular and special education classrooms. *American Educational Research Journal, 28,* 337–372.

Englert, C. S., Raphael, T. E., Anderson, L. M., Gregg, S. L., & Anthony, H. M. (1989). Exposition: Reading, writing, and the metacognitive knowledge of learning disabled students. *Learning Disabilities Research, 5,* 5–24.

Gerber, P. J., & Reiff, H. B. (1991). *Speaking for themselves: Ethnographic interviews with adults with learning disabilities.* Ann Arbor: University of Michigan Press.

Graham, S., & Harris, K. R. (1989). Components analysis of cognitive strategy instruction: Effects on learning disabled students' compositions and self-efficacy. *Journal of Educational Psychology, 81,* 353–361.

Graham, S., Schwartz, S. S., & MacArthur, C. A. (1993). Knowledge of writing and the composing process, attitude toward writing, and self-efficacy for students with and without learning disabilities. *Journal of Learning Disabilities, 26,* 237–249.

Harris, K. R., & Graham, S. (1996). *Making the writing process work: Strategies for composition and self-regulation.* Cambridge, MA: Brookline Books.

Harris, K. R., & Pressley, M. (1991). The nature of cognitive strategy instruction: Interactive strategy construction. *Exceptional Children, 57,* 392–404.

Jacobs, J. E., & Paris, S. G. (1987). Children's metacognition about reading: Issues in definition, measurement, and instruction. *Educational Psychologist, 22,* 255–278.

Kamann, M. P., & Butler, D. L. (1996, April). *Strategic content learning: An analysis of instructional features.* Paper presented at the annual meeting of the American Educational Research Association, New York.

MacLeod, W. B., Butler, D. L., & Syer, K. D. (1996, April). *Beyond achievement data: Assessing changes in metacognition and strategic learning.* Paper presented at the annual meeting of the American Educational Research Association, New York.

Merriam, S. B. (1988). *Case study research in education: A qualitative approach.* San Francisco: Jossey-Bass.

Miles, M. B., & Huberman, A. M. (1994). *Qualitative data analysis: An expanded sourcebook* (2nd ed.). Thousand Oaks, CA: Sage.

Montague, M., Maddux, C. D., & Dereshiwsky, M. I. (1990). Story grammar and comprehension and production of narrative prose by students with learning disabilities. *Journal of Learning Disabilities, 23,* 190–197.

Palincsar, A. S., & Brown, A. L. (1984). Reciprocal teaching of comprehension-fostering and comprehension-monitoring activities. *Cognition and Instruction, 1,* 117–175.

Paris, S. G., & Byrnes, J. P. (1989). The constructivist approach to self-regulation and learning in the classroom. In B. J. Zimmerman & D. H. Schunk (Eds.), *Self-regulated learning and academic achievement: Theory, research, and practice* (pp. 169–200). New York: Springer-Verlag.

Paris, S. G., Wixson, K. K., & Palincsar, A. S. (1986). Instructional approaches to reading comprehension. *Review of Research in Education, 13,* 91–128.

Policastro, M. M. (1993). Assessing and developing metacognitive attributes in college students with learning disabilities. In S. A. Vogel & P. B. Adelman (Eds.), *Success for college students with learning disabilities* (pp. 151–176). New York: Springer-Verlag.

Pressley, M. (1986). The relevance of the good strategy user model to the teaching of mathematics. *Educational Psychologist, 21*(1–2), 139–161.

Pressley, M., El-Dinary, P. B., Brown, R., Schuder, T., Bergman, J. L., York, M., & Gaskins, I. W. (1995). A transactional strategies instruction Christmas carol. In A. McKeough, J. Lupart, & A. Marini (Eds.), *Teaching for transfer: Fostering generalization in learning* (pp. 177–213). Mahwah, NJ: Erlbaum.

Pressley, M., El-Dinary, P. B., Gaskins, I. W., Schuder, T., Bergman, J. L., Almasi, J., & Brown, R. (1992). Beyond direct explanation: Transactional instruction of reading comprehension strategies. *Elementary School Journal, 92,* 513–555.

Pressley, M., Ghatala, E. S., Woloshyn, V., & Pirie, J. (1990). Sometimes adults miss the main ideas and do not realize it: Confidence in responses to short-answer and multiple-choice comprehension questions. *Reading Research Quarterly, 25,* 232–249.

Reeve, R. A., & Brown, A. L. (1985). Metacognition reconsidered: Implications for intervention research. *Journal of Abnormal Child Psychology, 13,* 343–356.

Salomon, G., & Perkins, D. E. (1989). Rocky roads to transfer: Rethinking mechanisms of a neglected phenomenon. *Educational Psychologist, 24,* 113–142.

Sawyer, R. J., Graham, S., & Harris, K. R. (1992). Direct teaching, strategy instruction, and strategy instruction with explicit self-regulation: Effects on the composition skills and self-efficacy of students with learning disabilities. *Journal of Educational Psychology, 84,* 340–352.

Schommer, M. (1990). Effects of beliefs about the nature of knowledge on comprehension. *Journal of Educational Psychology, 82,* 498–504.

Schommer, M. (1993). Epistemological development and academic performance among secondary students. *Journal of Educational Psychology, 85,* 406–411.

Schumaker, J. B., & Deshler, D. D. (1992). Validation of learning strategy interventions for students with learning disabilities: Results of a programmatic research effort. In B. Y. L. Wong (Ed.), *Contemporary intervention research in learning disabilities: An international perspective* (pp. 22–46). New York: Springer-Verlag.

Schunk, D. H. (1994). Self-regulation of self-efficacy and attributions in academic settings. In D. H. Schunk & B. J. Zimmerman (Eds.), *Self-regulation of learning and performance: Issues and educational applications* (pp. 75–99). Hillsdale, NJ: Erlbaum.

Schunk, D. H. (1996). Goal and self-evaluative influences during children's cognitive skill learning. *American Educational Research Journal, 33,* 359–382.

Schunk, D. H., & Cox, P. D. (1986). Strategy training and attributional feedback with learning disabled students. *Journal of Educational Psychology, 78,* 201–209.

Stone, C. A. (in press). The metaphor of scaffolding: Its utility for the field of learning disabilities. *Journal of Learning Disabilities*.

Swanson, H. L. (1990). Instruction derived from the strategy deficit model: Overview of principles and procedures. In T. Scruggs & B. Y. L. Wong (Eds.), *Intervention research in learning disabilities* (pp. 34–65). New York: Springer-Verlag.

Torgesen, J. K. (1977). The role of non-specific factors in the task performance of learning disabled children: A theoretical assessment. *Journal of Learning Disabilities*, *10*, 27–34.

Vogel, S. A., & Adelman, P. B. (1990). Intervention effectiveness at the postsecondary level for the learning disabled. In T. Scruggs & B. Y. L. Wong (Eds.), *Intervention research in learning disabilities* (pp. 329–344). New York: Springer-Verlag.

Winne, P. H., & Marx, R. W. (1982). Students' and teachers' views of thinking processes for classroom learning. *Elementary School Journal*, *82*, 493–518.

Wong, B. Y. L. (1991a, August). *On the thorny issue of transfer in learning disabilities interventions: Towards a three-prong solution*. Invited address presented at the Fourth European Conference for Research on Learning and Instruction, University of Turku, Turku, Finland.

Wong, B. Y. L. (1991b). The relevance of metacognition to learning disabilities. In B. Y. L. Wong (Ed.), *Learning about learning disabilities* (pp. 231–256). New York: Academic Press.

Wong, B. Y. L. (1992). On cognitive process-based instruction: An introduction. *Journal of Learning Disabilities*, *25*, 150–152, 172.

Wong, B. Y. L., Butler, D. L., Ficzere, S., & Kuperis, S. (1996). Teaching low achievers and students with learning disabilities to plan, write, and revise opinion essays. *Journal of Learning Disabilities*, *29*, 197–212.

Yin, R. K. (1994). *Case study research: Design and methods* (2nd ed.). Thousand Oaks, CA: Sage.

Zimmerman, B. J. (1989). A social-cognitive view of self-regulated learning. *Journal of Educational Psychology*, *81*, 329–339.

Zimmerman, B. J. (1994). Dimensions of academic self-regulation: A conceptual framework for education. In D. H. Schunk & B. J. Zimmerman (Eds.), *Self-regulation of learning and performance: Issues and educational applications* (pp. 3–21). Hillsdale, NJ: Erlbaum.

CHAPTER 9

Operant Theory and Application to Self-Monitoring in Adolescents

Phillip J. Belfiore
Rebecca S. Hornyak

Ultimately, education is only beneficial when it results in the development of academic independence in students. Academic independence, the ability to maintain and enhance academic performance through self-management, is the result of an established, dynamic history of student success within academic contexts. When students are successful in academic situations, with academic stimuli, those students are more likely to continue in those academic-related situations, and seek out other, similar situations. Although as educators, providing multiple academic situations to all students seems simple to achieve, students are simultaneously presented with, and exposed to, a variety of nonacademic alternatives. Selecting such nonacademic alternatives usually results in a variety of nonschool or nonacademic behaviors. For example, (1) each day 13,076 public school students are suspended, (2) 73% of high school seniors have used alcohol within the past 12 months, (3) 19% of high school seniors have used marijuana/hashish within the past 30 days, (4) 6.1% of all ninth graders felt too unsafe to go to school, (5) almost 22% of all American children are classified as poor, and (6) each day 342 and 359 school-age students are arrested for violent crimes and drug offenses, respectively (Annie E. Casey Foundation, 1996; Children's Defense Fund, 1996; National Center for Educational Statistics, 1996a, 1996b). For schools and communities to prevail in establishing academic success in students, a refocus and prioritization on school and academic performance is imperative.

THE ROLE OF SELF-MANAGEMENT IN ADOLESCENT SCHOOL PERFORMANCE

Initially, academic success is fostered through student interactions with educators (e.g. teachers, parents, caregivers, siblings, local community leaders, peers, other school personnel). Incorporating effective educational interactions that gradually shift responsibility, from teacher delivered to student managed, results in students possessing a set of academic strategies they can utilize across multiple curriculum areas (Belfiore & Hutchinson, 1998). What is required for this shift from teacher directed to student maintained to succeed is (1) teachers providing multiple opportunities for academic achievement in relevant contexts; and (2) students monitoring, reflecting on, and modifying personal performance compared to educational standards of mastery and excellence (as set by the school community and/or the student).

Educators can create a learning environment that results in academic success by delivering effective instruction that challenges students and by promoting self-management in students (see Figure 9.1). Effective instruction requires planning and prioritizing curricular activities, managing the day-to-day classroom context, delivering quality instructional materials, creating and maintaining a motivating environment, and self-evaluating teacher-delivered instruction (i.e., intervention integrity) and student performance. Self-management requires students to master such related skills as self-monitoring, self-instruction, self-evaluation, and self-reinforcement. Also required for self-management are informed decision making and problem solving given contextual cues. Self-reflection through decision making

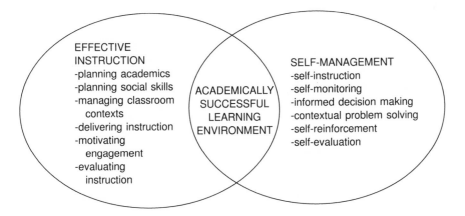

FIGURE 9.1. Instructional variables targeted for learning environment that fosters academic success.

and problem solving adds a dimension of dynamics necessary in teaching and self-management. Students who encounter repeated and consistent success in challenging academic situations while learning to manage their own behavior are more likely to develop academic independence.

When critiquing the development of academic independence in students, emphasis must also be placed on competing behaviors. Nonacademic or nonschool behavior may be viewed as the result of (1) a history of academic failure, and (2) little or no current support for academic behavior(s). For example, a history of school performance resulting in academic punishment (e.g., poor test grades, negative or no feedback, suspension, retention) results in a decrease in future school behavior given academic situations. Similarly, successful academic behaviors previously displayed at school that are ignored by family, peers, media, and the community result in a decrease in future attempts at academics. Students not doing well in academics and receiving little or no support for attempts in academics rarely persist in academics. Students, like everyone else, tend to engage in those activities that result in greater opportunity for reinforcement.

Students may currently engage in nonacademic behaviors because either they have been unsuccessful in the past with the academic materials now being presented to them or they receive little positive feedback when attempting or initiating academic behaviors. For example, a student who demonstrates poor reading skills (word attack skills and comprehension) will also perform poorly in science, English, and social studies because each of those academic subject areas is word/text based. The resulting noncompliance or problem behavior results from a lack of academic achievement in reading. The student may be identified as having "low self-esteem" or "poor self-concept," which is perceived as resulting in a lack of initiative regarding schoolwork, but the self-esteem or self-concept is a teacher-perceived construct that is actually a result of a deficit in reading skills.

Behaviors associated with low self-esteem or poor self-concept are often the result, not the cause, of poor academic performance. Schickedanz (1994) warns not to assume that academic instruction and the resulting academic performance can only occur once social and emotional behaviors are under control. Quality academic performance may result in a better self-concept and higher self-esteem in the student. The target of intervention should be the academics, not the self-esteem or self-concept.

The role of self-regulation in academic independence becomes one of fostering academic achievement, which in turn may result in a better self-concept or higher self-esteem. Creating and maximizing educational situations or contexts that occasion appropriate academic behavior followed by reinforcement (e.g., positive feedback, teacher attention to academics, passing grades, work completion) result in an increase in future academic behavior given similar academic situations. Once a history of success with academics is achieved through classroom instruction, community support, and teacher motivation, students begin to take ownership over their continued learning. Purposeful learning is the result of self-managed academic success.

PURPOSEFUL LEARNING: STUDENTS AT RISK
FOR ACADEMIC FAILURE

Serna and Lau-Smith (1995) consider students at risk to be those adolescents whose potential for academic success in schools, as well as success in home and community, is limited due to specific environmental, behavioral, and social problems. Adolescents who are unsuccessful academically and receive little or no attention for academic behaviors from peers and teachers either withdraw from school-related situations, or engage in some nonacademic behavior to gain attention (Testerman, 1996). Unfortunately, "nonacademic" behaviors (e.g., disruptions, noncompliance, talking out) tend to result in more immediate teacher and/or peer attention than "academic" behaviors (e.g., reading quietly, raising one's hand, writing an essay). Continuing this scenario, as the behavior of students engaged in academics continues to be ignored, those students begin to observe what behaviors do result in attention. Those students not receiving attention for academic behaviors learn to engage in nonacademic behaviors because it is nonacademic behaviors that are receiving reinforcement in the classroom. In an effort to maintain control in the classroom, the teacher has now created a classroom of students at risk for academic failure. Students at risk for failure in school are those students who have neither received effective academic instruction nor learned to self-manage their own academic behavior. The initial problem lies in the inability of the educational environment (e.g., teacher-related, instructional, classroom, and community variables) to establish and maintain academic success.

In light of increasing numbers of students at risk for academic failure, Serna and Lau-Smith (1995) created a self-determination curriculum designed to foster learning with purpose in students. By (1) developing self-management behavior in at-risk students, and (2) systematically teaching those behaviors, the curriculum encourages students to take a proactive role in their academic learning. Domain areas that make up a self-determination curriculum include social skills (e.g., negotiation, problem solving), self-evaluation of present skills and future skills needed, self-direction skills (e.g., goal setting, self-management), networking skills (e.g., seeking advice, developing strategies), collaboration skills (e.g., determining team needs, planning strategies), persistence and risk-taking skills (e.g., problem solving, decision making), and stress management skills (e.g., recognizing feelings, time management) (Serna & Lau-Smith, 1995). From this list of skills a systematic procedure (*PURPOSE*) for teaching self-determination emerges. PURPOSE represents (1) student Preparation, (2) student Understanding, (3) student Rehearsal, (4) Performance of self-checks, (5) Overcoming of performance barriers, (6) Selecting of own performance, and (7) Evaluating of own outcome. In addition, the *Learning with PURPOSE* curriculum includes a strong parent–community component designed to increase family support, communication, and relationship building.

Using task-analytic assessment to indicate a level of self-determination proficiency gives teachers directions for academic programming. More importantly, the outcome of such an assessment gives the student directions necessary for self-management in general, and self-monitoring in particular. The act of recording, monitoring, and reflecting on one's behavior is a critical step in achieving academic success and independence.

CONCEPTUALIZATION

Before any serious discussion on the impact and utility of self-management can be engaged, a brief conceptualization of key components that constitute self-management is in order.

Self-Management

Self-management may be defined simply as "the ability of the individual to interface his or her behavior with the environment [incorporating the] application of behavior analysis principles and procedures [in an effort to] modify the behavior/environment interactions *of* the individual *by* the individual" (Brigham, 1982, p. 49). Similarly, Cooper, Heron, and Heward (1987) define self-management as a personal and systematic application of behavior change strategies that result in the desired alteration of one's own behavior. Self-management establishes a relationship between controlling and controlled responses (Skinner, 1953). Thus, any self-management or self-regulation system must involve at least two responses: (1) the *target response* (i.e., *controlled response*) of the student to be controlled, and (2) the *self-management response* (i.e., *controlling response*) emitted by the student in order to control the target response(s) (Cooper et al., 1987). This relationship must be a functional one, in that the controlling response (posting a note "car to Joe's Garage @ 4:00 P.M.") must occasion the controlled response (driving the car to the garage at 4:00 P.M.). If the change in the controlled response (drive the car to the garage by 4:00 P.M.) does not occur, self-management has not be demonstrated (Cooper et al., 1987). The posted note did not occasion the response. Similarly, if a change in the controlled, or target, response takes place without the controlling, or self-management response, self-management has not been demonstrated (Cooper et al., 1987). The saliency of the relationship of the response to be monitored and the monitoring response establishes the functionality of self-management.

The emphasis of self-management is on the individual's ability to discriminate and modify behavior–environment interactions and contingencies (Brigham, 1982). The ability to discriminate one's response targeted for self-observation is essential to the success of self-management. The ability to modify one's response or the environment is essential for performance to be fluid as situations change. Regardless of the "self" as the change agent responsible for the display of controlled and controlling responses, the management of human behavior continues to be influenced ultimately by the environment.

Seabaugh and Schumaker (1994) suggest the study of self-management includes one or more of the following components; goal setting, self-monitoring, self-instruction, self-evaluation, and self-reinforcement/self-punishment. This package of components allows a student to (1) determine criteria levels or standards to be met, (2) chart improvement and overall performance, (3) initiate and maintain instructional strategies, (4) determine when and if criteria levels or standards have been met, and (5) administer consequences given the relationship between performance and criteria.

Goal Setting, Self-Monitoring, and Self-Evaluation

One fundamental, and sometimes sole component of any self-management system is self-monitoring (Mace & Kratochwill, 1988). In general, self-monitoring involves two steps. Initially, self-monitoring requires the student to discriminate the occurrence of a target response that is to be controlled. This response must be observable to the student. Following discrimination of the target response, self-monitoring requires the student to record some behavioral dimension (i.e., frequency, rate, duration, latency) of that response (Mace, Belfiore, & Shea, 1989). A student may self-monitor the occurrence or the absence of a response (although, technically, the nonoccurrence of a response is replaced by the occurrence of other responses). For example, a student may record on a data sheet (1) homework handed to the teacher at 8:45 A.M. on Monday, as well as (2) no fighting incidents on the playground from 1:00–1:30 P.M. on Monday. To be able to discriminate the occurrence or nonoccurrence of the target response is only one-half of the requirements for self-monitoring. The success of self-monitoring relies on the ability to (1) discriminate when a response has occurred or not occurred, *and* (2) record the result of that discrimination.

Self-monitoring may take the form of a student (1) observing and recording whether their own behavior has occurred or not (e.g., "Am I reading the story silently or not?"), or (2) observing and recording a behavior so as to monitor if performance has met a set criteria (e.g., "Have I completed reading the 37 pages of Chapter 2?") (Webber, Scheuermann, McCall, & Coleman, 1993). Self-monitoring behavior when compared to a set criteria or set standard also involves such self-management components as goal setting and self-evaluation. *Goal setting* involves a standard or criteria set by the student prior to or during self-management, whereas *self-evaluation* involves the comparative outcome between some component of performance and the set standard. When achievement of a predetermined level is part of a self-monitoring program, students must record performance on the steps involved in the act of self-monitoring, as well as target response performance. For example, when teaching students to use the self-monitoring homework routine displayed in Figure 9.2, performance was assessed as to (1) the accuracy of completing the self-monitoring routine (steps 1 through 9), (2) the completion of the daily homework (step 7), and (3) the number of homework assignments turned in per week. Ultimately, students will self-monitor routine accuracy, daily homework completion, and overall homework performance.

STUDENT: _____   DATE: _____
SUBJECT AREA: _____   GRADE: _____
TEACHER: _____

STEPS TO FOLLOW	YES	NO	NOTES
1. Did I turn in yesterday's homework?			
2. Did I write all homework assignments in my notebook?			
3. Is all homework in homework folder?			
4. Are all my materials to complete homework with me?			
5. BEGIN HOMEWORK?			
6. Are all homework papers completed?			
7. Did someone check homework to make sure it was completed?			
8. After checking, did I put all homework back in folder?			
9. Did I give this paper to teacher?			

FIGURE 9.2. Daily self-monitoring checklist for academic-related routine of homework.

Self-Reinforcement

When the component of self-evaluation becomes part of the overall self-management program, the outcome of that evaluation must be addressed. *Self-reinforcement* may be described as a process in which a student, after a standard or criteria has been met or exceeded, "comes into contact with a stimulus following the occurrence of that response that, in turn, results in an increase in the probability of the occurrence of the response subject to the performance standard" (Mace et al., 1989, p. 36). Mace et al. (1989) suggested that their definition of self-reinforcement is descriptive of the process and avoids issues of terminology that set apart the operant view of self-reinforcement from other perspectives.

From the self-monitoring homework example displayed in Figure 9.2, students locate the homework folder and chart steps completed on the self-monitoring checklist. Upon completion of the self-monitoring checklist, students evaluate which steps have been met or which have not. If the total number of steps completed meets or exceeds the standard, students may self-administer predetermined rewards (e.g., board games, computer time, art activities). Those contingencies are not freely accessible, but become available only after homework has been turned in and the self-monitoring checklist has been completed.

Ultimately, control of self-managed behavior is the result of environmentally controlled contingencies, which are self-administered. If behaviors associated with self-management result in greater reinforcement or a more effective method for obtaining reinforcement (Hughes & Lloyd, 1993), those behaviors will continue given similar self-management opportunities in the future.

IMPLEMENTATION

Learning to self-manage requires instructional strategies similar to the learning of any other behavior. Jones and Davenport (1996) stress that self-managed learning is orchestrated by the individual student, but ultimately influenced by the educational environment. When students are initially learning to self-manage, teachers must provide antecedent strategies that clearly explain outcomes, use examples and nonexamples of problem solving, and create multiple opportunities to practice and review. In addition, teachers must provide consequent strategies that reward problem-solving behaviors (i.e., persistence or improvement) (Jones & Davenport, 1996), as well as outcome behaviors (i.e., achievement or performance) and self-monitoring accuracy.

Once self-monitoring strategies have been mastered, fluency is critical for self-management to continue. All target responses that occur must be recorded to ensure discriminability between controlled and controlling behaviors. If a lack of fluency due to novel stimuli (e.g., new concepts, different setting, shorter time interval) is recorded by the student while self-monitoring, the student provides *self-instruction to remediate problems*. If problem solving was taught while the students were learning to self-monitor, the student self-instructs and modifies without the assistance of the teacher. If the student was not exposed to possible problems and potential solutions during initial acquisition, the teacher may have to provide additional support at this time. To enhance and maintain fluent self-monitoring, a feedback mechanism that allows for *self-evaluation* and *self-delivery* of contingencies is created. Evaluations may be made in relationship to the accuracy of self-monitoring behavior (e.g., written checks in boxes, slash marks through page numbers, counting beads on a rope), the progress made from day-to-day, and/or the overall performance level.

Self-Monitoring Routines

One of the most effective methods for creating meaningful self-monitoring is to develop a system that is generic enough for use across educational levels, while allowing for adaptability for the individual student. A promising area that meets this definition is *academic-related routines*. Related routines in academics may be defined as those chains of skills necessary for academic achievement that are not directly related to specific teaching techniques or specific academic curriculum areas (Belfiore & Hutchinson, 1998). For example, a generic note-taking routine includes gathering materials, locating a quiet area, copying notes on an outline template, and comparing key points copied with original notes. Such a related routine, when prepared and displayed on a self-recording sheet, provides the student an effective means of academic self-management (see Figure 9.3). The key to making academic-related routines and self-monitoring more meaningful, and ideally more useful, to the student is to take the generic sequence and individualize the operational steps with input from the student. For example, with the note-taking routine, the student can (1) determine materials necessary for the task, (2) determine a location that will foster note taking, and (3) select a template onto which main ideas are copied. When each self-monitoring step is completed, the student crosses that box on the list. At the end of the note-taking exercise, the student can self-evaluate the accuracy of the self-monitoring and the quality of the note taking by comparing the student-completed note guide and a teacher's copy of a peer-completed model.

STUDENT: _____ DATE: _____
SUBJECT AREA: _____ GRADE: _____
TEACHER: _____

STEPS TO FOLLOW	Mon.	Tues.	Wed.	Thurs.	Fri.	NOTES
1. Get notes, paper, template, pencil						
2. Find a comfortable location						
3. Read notes provided by note taker						
4. Write key points on template						
5. Check notes with copy						
TOTAL COMPLETED						

REVISIONS:

FIGURE 9.3. Weekly self-monitoring checklist for academic-related routine of note taking.

Define and Record

As a general educational strategy, self-monitoring has been shown to be an effective technique for behavior management, as well as leading to generalization of those managed behaviors across settings (Webber et al., 1993). Reid and Harris (1993) reported self-monitoring as an effective strategy for enhancing both attention to academic stimuli and performance in academic situations, when compared to an independent practice study procedure. In addition, self-monitoring has been effective for increasing academic quality and academic performance (Martin & Manno, 1995). In general, the use of self-monitoring as an educational intervention has been shown to be effective across academic performance, academic improvement, and additional academic variables associated with "successful academic performance."

Mace et al. (1989) suggested several common self-monitoring methods that can be developed for defining and recording in educational situations, including narrative self-reports, frequency counts, time durations, and time sampling. Frequency counts are the most common and easiest method for recording some dimension of a targeted behavior. When assessing academic performance and academic attention, several studies (Lee & Tindal, 1994; Lloyd, Bateman, Landrum, & Hallahan, 1989; Reid & Harris, 1993) use a combination of frequency counts to measure academic performance and time sampling to measure academic on-task behavior. Lee and Tindal (1994) and Lloyd et al. (1989) had students record the (1) number of correct mathematics problems completed and, (2) using a momentary time-sampling method, (b) intervals of on-task behavior. Similarly, Reid and Harris (1993) required students to count the number of spelling words correctly practiced and to give a yes/no response to a cued tape message of "Was I paying attention?" Maag, Reid, and DiGangi (1993) required students to monitor not only arithmetic productivity (problems completed), and academic on-task behavior, but also arithmetic accuracy (problems correct).

In self-monitoring studies that require a measure of time spent on the academic task, time intervals are cued to the students via prerecorded tapes or verbally by the teacher. The purpose of the cue and momentary time-sampling procedure is to prompt students to observe what they were doing at the moment of the cue and to record it. At each cue, students are taught to check if they were on the academic task at that moment. To increase the probability of consistent responding when using a momentary time sampling, educators should develop a cued tape or cueing technique using a variable interval schedule (e.g., cues at 1 minute, 5 minutes, 3 minutes, 7 minutes, 2 minutes, 1 minute, etc.). Such a variable schedule will allow students to maintain work on-task, without developing a pattern based on when the cues are forthcoming, which would be the case if all time intervals were of same length (e.g., 2 minutes, 2 minutes, 2 minutes, etc.). Such a time-sampling procedure is effective at the individual and class level, if directions are initially delivered by the teacher, and practice to mastery by the students is required.

For any self-monitoring routine to be effective in behavior change, it must (1) define both the behavior to be controlled (monitored behavior) and the controlling behavior (monitoring behavior), and (2) develop a recording system to ensure self-monitoring accuracy. Rehearsing, modeling, testing, and reviewing are also components necessary when teaching self-management strategies to students.

In a current fieldwork cooperative between Mercyhurst College and an inner city afterschool program (fourth through sixth grades), we augmented an existing homework routine with a component of self-monitoring. Prior to our involvement, one portion of the afterschool program required all students to complete daily homework assignments. We created a self-monitoring homework routine (see Figure 9.2) that would eventually allow students to monitor and evaluate their own progress on homework completion daily and weekly, in the absence of teacher monitoring. Initially students were taught how to (1) determine the outcome for each step of the self-monitoring sheet and (2) evaluate overall accuracy of the completed homework. Data were collected regarding accuracy of the completed self-monitoring sheet (i.e., number of steps completed accurately) and performance (i.e., frequency of homework turned in on time). Later in the academic year additional data were collected on improvement (i.e., change in frequency of homework turned in on time) and accuracy (i.e., number of homework problems performed correctly).

Following classroom instruction, which included teacher modeling and feedback, students maintained homework self-monitoring in the absence of direct teacher intervention. On average students required less than 1 week to record self-monitoring behaviors accurately on the homework routine checklist. Daily homework assignments were placed in individual manila folders, with the self-monitoring homework routine attached to the folder. During homework time, students located their folder, opened it, and followed the steps on the self-monitoring sheet. Upon completion of all steps on the sheets, students were initially required to get a signature from the teacher to verify step accuracy. Eventually, this final, external check will be removed from the homework self-monitoring routine.

In order for self-monitoring to affect attention or performance behavior, the self-monitoring routine must be firmly established in the repertoire of the student, and be independent of teacher-delivered prompts. Behaviors to be monitored and the monitoring behaviors must also be well defined, and a recording system must be in place. Scripted, teacher-delivered instruction (Reid & Harris, 1993); instruction given separately, then reviewed (Maag et al., 1993); and modeling (Martin & Manno, 1995) are some techniques educators can increase the probability that the self-monitoring procedure is learned. The result of initial teacher instruction is student mastery in recording of behavior occurrences and student accuracy in self-monitoring routine procedures. Clearly defined behaviors and recording protocols make the shift from teacher-delivered to student-initiated routines more efficient and permanent.

Self-Instruction and Problem Solving

Once the self-monitoring routine has been taught and mastered, the emphasis turns to shifting immediate control from teacher to student. Training in self-instruction requires steps in which verbal or nonverbal control of behavior is modeled by the teacher and then initiated by the student (Kauffman, 1997). Once the routine is mastered, the student continues to deliver cues that occasion the target response. As a component of self-monitoring, self-instruction assists in (1) solving problems not encountered during training and (2) prompting or enhancing accurate self-monitoring responses.

Serna and Lau-Smith (1995) suggest that problem solving is a key prerequisite skill for self-determination. Problem-solving skills introduced during training of self-management can enhance self-monitoring fluency in the absence of immediate educator control. A lack of problem solving may be defined as a stimulus control problem. For example, the note-taking routine in Figure 9.3 provides an operationally defined sequence of steps (a task analysis), and this sequence, as a stimulus condition, controls the responding of the student to complete the sequence, resulting in some consequence upon completion. This control is established through effective teacher-delivered instruction (see Figure 9.1). When a variation or novelty in the stimulus array occurs, the control sequence is not established. A missing template, misplaced materials, or a seat taken by another student are variables not previously encountered by the student, which may result in a failure to complete the self-monitoring routine. Initial instruction and mastery of the routine must include examples and nonexamples of situations in which problem solving is necessary for routine completion. Students need to know when to problem solve, and when problem solving is not necessary. Students initially taught problem-solving techniques as part of learning to self-manage are better able to self-instruct in the absence of teacher instruction. On encountering a novel situation, students must reflect on past experiences and instruction in order to solve the problem and complete the activity. When faced with novel stimuli arrays, self-instruction as a component of the self-monitoring routine is essential for eventual academic independence.

Solving problems as they arise within a self-monitoring routine is one function self-instruction serves. Additionally, self-instruction may be useful as a means to enhance the control of the discriminative stimulus to occasion the desired behavior. Mace et al. (1989) suggest that additional self-statements, verbal or nonverbal, provide discriminative stimuli that increase the likelihood the target behavior will occur and reinforcement will follow. By following the note-taking routine, the student may verbalize or match symbols to the sequence of self-monitoring steps. The addition of the verbalization or symbol enhances the likelihood the sequence will be accurately followed, which in turn results in self-administered consequences. For example, when instituting a classwide self-monitoring strategy with students identified with emotional handicaps, Grskovic et al. (1994) initially required students to observe, then model, and finally to self-manage the learned strategy in the classroom. While students modeled the steps for accurate self-monitoring, they were taught to self-instruct. Self-instruction required students to count backwards subvocally from 10 to 1 while moving a bead with each exhalation of their breath. The outcome of this self-instruction component, paired with self-monitoring, was a decrease in the likelihood students would be sent to a more restrictive time-out.

With a fluent self-monitoring routine to follow and a mechanism for self-instruction when variations in the routine occur, the student has the necessary components to self-manage eventually with little support from the teacher. To maintain and create a more dynamic self-management system, the student must also learn to self-evaluate.

Self-Evaluation and Self-Administration of Reinforcement

Self-evaluation requires the student to compare some dimension of her or his behavior with that of a set standard or criterion. The standard or criterion may be determined by the educator(s), the student, or a collaboration between educator(s) and student. The dimension to be evaluated by the student may be (1) the accuracy of the self-monitoring, (2) the improvement of performance over time, and/or (3) the overall performance for that instance. As mentioned earlier, for evaluation to be meaningful, accurate descriptions of recording procedures and performance must be in place. For example, following completion of several handwriting samples, Sweeney, Salva, Cooper, and Talbert-Johnson (1993) taught students to self-evaluate their performance across such characteristics as letter size, slant, letter shape, spacing between letters and words, and general letter appearance. Self-evaluation was initially followed by experimenter modeling and feedback, but later no experimenter influence was necessary.

As part of our afterschool homework program, students were initially required to review and evaluate the steps of the self-monitoring homework routine (see Figure 9.2) with a teacher providing feedback. The initial review was a check to assure the teacher that the student understood the self-monitoring steps. Following the review of the routine, student and teacher evaluated how well the student completed all the steps of the homework routine. This initial interaction allowed teachers to model correct step completion and inquire as to the reason for incomplete steps. For example, if students scored "Did I turn in yesterday's homework?" (step 1) as "no," they were asked what the problem was and shown how to remediate the problem. The initial, teacher-directed evaluation gave students information necessary for future self-instruction, problem solving, and self-evaluation. Self-evaluation initially required students to complete all homework, have someone check that all homework was completed (step 7), complete the self-monitoring routine, and obtain a signature from the classroom teacher. Near the end of the school year teachers would occasionally check student recording on the routine and actual steps completed. As students became more fluent with the self-monitoring routine and with self-evaluation, step 7 ("Did someone check homework to make sure it was completed?") was checked as "no" by the students because there was no need for external evaluation. The final step ("Did I give the paper to teacher?") continued to be required so that the teacher would know what student turned in which assignment.

Self-evaluation results in a self-monitoring system that expands and modifies as the learner acquires new skills. In self-instruction, the student enhances or adds saliency to an existing aspect of the self-monitoring system.

In self-evaluation, the student reintegrates information gleaned from evaluation and reorganizes the self-monitoring system to meet future education needs.

Results and Outcomes

In a summary of recent research on the efficacy of self-monitoring, Kauffman (1997) reported general conclusions to include the following:

1. Self-monitoring behaviors associated with academic attention increase time spent on task a majority of the time
2. Self-monitoring behaviors associated with academic attention typically increase academic productivity
3. The beneficial effects of self-monitoring are usually achieved without additional rewards or reinforcers
4. Self-recording is a necessary component of initial instruction, but it can be discontinued once mastery of self-monitoring has been achieved
5. Accuracy of self-monitoring is not critical to effects on performance or attention

Recently, self-monitoring has been shown to be an effective change agent in such academic areas as academic attention, mathematics fact performance, handwriting, story composition, and homework completion, to name only a few (Lloyd et al., 1989; Martin & Manno, 1995, Olympia, Sheridan, Jenson, & Andrews, 1994; Reid & Harris, 1993; Sweeney et al., 1993).

As the first year of our afterschool homework program ended, students had little problem with the definitions of what homework completion was, and what each step on the self-monitoring checklist meant. By using teacher instruction initially, which included teaching examples and non-examples, students rarely required teacher assistance to complete the worksheet or to solve problems that arose. As the students continued to use the checklist, teacher checks of homework completion (step 7) and checklist completion (step 9) decreased, while accuracy and completion remained constant. Homework completion may have served as reinforcement for routine maintenance once the routine was mastered. In such a case, the result of task completion may serve as either positive reinforcement in the form of accomplishment or negative reinforcement in the form of one less activity to complete (Belfiore, Lee, Vargas, & Skinner, 1997). No specific tangible rewards were administered by staff or student. The reactivity of self-monitoring may have occasioned and maintained homework completion in the absence of specific teacher feedback or teacher-delivered tangible rewards. Reactivity in self-monitoring has been suggested (e.g., Kauffman,

1997) and demonstrated (e.g., Belfiore, Browder, & Mace, 1989) numerous times. Accuracy of homework completed was monitored occasionally by peers during homework time or by the classroom teacher after homework was turned in.

DYNAMICS OF SELF-MANAGEMENT: SELF-REFLECTIVE PRACTICE

As responsibility shifts from teacher to student, self-management of academic behavior becomes a more natural part of the student's life. This shift in responsibility is enhanced further and becomes more natural when students take an active role in self-reflection. If good teaching can be characterized by the ability to integrate new information into the overall theme of the presentation without losing sight of the theme, then creating a self-management system that teaches students to do the same is essential. In self-management, this takes the form of self-reflective practice. *Self-reflection* is the ability to comprehend what was observed or monitored, evaluate the outcome as compared to a criterion (self- or teacher imposed), and create a new focus given evaluative information. Students learn to reintegrate and reorganize evaluative information, which in turn gives future direction.

A dynamic self-management system allows for self-reflection because the student must monitor, evaluate, reorganize, and reintegrate, and then monitor again. One mechanism already discussed that aids in self-reflection is problem solving. Without learning how to problem solve, students following a designed self-management system can progress through the system until they are fluent and independent within that system. However, when a novel situation arises in any component of that system, the student may not be able to discriminate the situation while maintaining the integrity of the system in place. As in the homework self-monitoring example a student enters the afterschool program homeroom and finds materials not on the shelf. A student who has not learned problem solving may engage in a variety of behaviors, but probably will not seek teacher assistance. The variation in the system (materials out of location) causes the self-management system to break down. A student who has been exposed to a variety of novel situations while enrolled in the program will more likely find a teacher to secure materials, or seek out the materials on her or his own. This can be considered an example of self-reflection within an existing self-management system. A problem occurred and it was solved; the system remains the same. The action was dynamic, yet static within the existing self-management system, thus it is termed *static quality* (Pirsig, 1974, 1991).

A second way in which self-reflection aids self-management is when the student reorganizes the system to compensate for performance at evaluation.

This may be described as *dynamic quality* (Pirsig, 1974, 1991). For example, when a student in the afterschool program repeatedly forgets her folder at home, as evaluated by the student through self-monitored performance, she modifies the system by keeping the homework folder on a shelf on the teacher's desk after each session is over. In this instance she encounters no variation in the existing system (no materials available on shelf); rather the variation is a result of her self-evaluation of current information, and she reorganizes the self-management system to create a more effective system to meet her needs.

Self-narratives, journals, and portfolios may also act as self-reflective practices that incorporate dynamic quality. Self-statements of personal growth and evaluation are critical components of any academic student portfolio. As part of the chronology of assignments placed into the portfolio, students reflect on past and current performance. They then integrate evaluation information and make decisions about future directions. The overall theme of the portfolio has not altered, but the methodology the students use to achieve goals is modified given new information from self-reflection on work completed. These new directions were not planned for prior to instruction, but because creative problem solving was a component of teaching and self-management, these directions are easily developed. A self-management system that reorganizes and reintegrates new information without losing sight of the overall goal (academic independence) maintains equilibrium.

Pirsig (1974, 1991) suggested that static quality keeps a system in place, whereas dynamic quality allows a system to evolve. A combination of the two may be described as dynamic equilibrium (Iannone, 1994; Pirsig, 1974, 1991). If a goal of education is to establish academic independence in students, and if effective instruction and self-management are means to that end, then the concept of dynamic equilibrium through self-reflection becomes the overall context in which education should occur. The ability to reorganize and reintegrate while maintaining a focus on the goal brings students one step closer to academic independence through self-direction.

CONCLUSIONS

Students who believe they have influence over the management of their academic behavior usually achieve success in academics (Bandura, Barbaranelli, Caprara, & Pastorelli, 1996). As illustrated in Figure 9.1, academically successful learning environments are developed through a combination of initial effective instruction, followed by self-management. In general, effective instruction may be defined as the ability to present challenging, relevant information while responding and modifying responses in light of variations within classroom interactions. Iannone (1994) suggested effective teachers attend to the chaotic nature of the classroom moment by moment. Good teaching creates an educational and community environment rich in motivation, challenges, instructional variations, and academic rewards. From such an environment, students build an ever-expanding history of academic or school success. If academic independence in students is the goal of education, a history of success in academics and school is the foundation. In order to achieve the goal, students must first learn and later become fluent in self-management. Self-management involves components of goal setting, self-monitoring, self-instruction and problem solving, self-evaluation, and self-delivery of feedback or reinforcement.

REFERENCES

Annie E. Casey Foundation. (1996). *Kids count.* Baltimore: Author.

Bandura, A., Barbaranelli, C., Caprara, G. V., & Pastorelli, C. (1996). Multifaceted impact of self-efficacy beliefs on academic functioning. *Child Development, 67,* 1206–1222.

Belfiore, P. J., Browder, D. M., & Mace, F. C. (1989). Effects of experimenter surveillance on reactive self-monitoring. *Research in Developmental Disabilities, 10,* 171–182.

Belfiore, P. J., & Hutchinson, J. M. (1998). Enhancing academic achievement through related routines: A functional approach. In T. S. Watson & F. Gresham (Eds.), *Child behavior therapy: Ecological considerations in assessment, treatment, and evaluation* (pp. 84–98). New York: Plenum Press.

Belfiore, P. J., Lee, D. L., Vargas, A. U., & Skinner, C. H. (1997). Effects of high-preference, single-digit mathematics problem completion on multiple-digit mathematics problem performance. *Journal of Applied Behavior Analysis, 30,* 327–330.

Brigham, T. (1982). Self-management: A radical behavioral perspective. In P. Karoly & F. H. Kanfer (Eds.), *Self-management and behavior change: From theory to practice* (pp. 32–59). New York: Pergamon Press.

Children's Defense Fund. (1996). *Every day in America.* Washington, DC: Author.

Cooper, J. O., Heron, T. E., & Heward, W. L. (1987). *Applied behavior analysis.* New York: Macmillan.

Grskovic, J., Montgomery-Grimes, D., Hall, A., Morphew, J., Belfiore, P., & Zentall, S. (1994, May). *The effects of active response delay training on the frequency and duration of time-outs for students with emotional disabilities.* Paper presented at the annual conference of the Association for Behavior Analysis, Atlanta.

Hughes, C., & Lloyd, J. W. (1993). An analysis of self-management. *Journal of Behavioral Education, 3,* 405–426.

Iannone, R. (1994). Chaos theory and its implications for curriculum and teaching. *Education, 15,* 541–547.

Jones, J. E., & Davenport, M. (1996). Self-regulation in Japanese and American art education. *Art Education, 49,* 60–65.

Kauffman, J. M. (1997). *Characteristics of emotional and behavioral disorders of children and youths.* Upper Saddle River, NJ: Prentice-Hall.

Lee, C., & Tindal, G. A. (1994). Self-recording and goal-setting: Effects on on-task and math productivity of low-achieving Korean elementary school students. *Journal of Behavioral Education, 4,* 459–480.

Lloyd, J. W., Bateman, D. F., Landrum, T. J., & Hallahan, D. P. (1989). Self-recording of attention versus productivity. *Journal of Applied Behavior Analysis, 22,* 315–324.

Maag, J. W., Reid, R., & DiGangi, S. A. (1993). Differential effects of self-monitoring attention, accuracy, and productivity. *Journal of Applied Behavior Analysis, 26,* 329–344.

Mace, F. C., Belfiore, P. J., & Shea, M. C. (1989). Operant theory and research on self-regulation. In B. J. Zimmerman & D. H. Schunk (Eds.), *Self-regulated learning and academic achievement: Theory, research, and practice* (pp. 27–50). New York: Springer-Verlag.

Mace, F. C., & Kratochwill, T. R. (1988). Self-monitoring: Application and issues. In J. Witt, S. Elliot, & F. Gresham (Eds.), *Handbook of behavior therapy in education* (pp. 489–502). New York: Pergamon Press.

Martin, K. F., & Manno, C. (1995). Use of a check-off system to improve middle school students' story compositions. *Journal of Learning Disabilities, 28,* 139–149.

National Center for Educational Statistics. (1996a). *The condition of education.* Washington, DC: Author.

National Center for Educational Statistics. (1996b). *The digest of education statistics.* Washington, DC: Author.

Olympia, D. E., Sheridan, S. M., Jenson, W. R., & Andrews, D. (1994). Using student-managed interventions to increase homework completion and accuracy. *Journal of Applied Behavior Analysis, 27,* 85–100.

Pirsig, R. M. (1974). *Zen and the art of motorcycle maintenance.* New York: Bantam.

Pirsig, R. M. (1991). *Lila.* New York: Bantam.

Reid, R., & Harris, K. R. (1993). Self-monitoring of attention versus self-monitoring of performance: Effects on attention and academic performance. *Exceptional Children, 60,* 29–40.

Schickedanz, J. A. (1994). Helping children develop self-control. *Childhood Education, 70,* 274–278.

Seabaugh, G. O., & Schumaker, J. B. (1994). The effects of self-regulation training on the academic productivity of secondary students with learning problems. *Journal of Behavioral Education, 4,* 109–133.

Serna, L. A., & Lau-Smith, J. A. (1995). Learning with purpose: Self-determination skills for students who are at risk for school and community failure. *Intervention in School and Clinic, 30,* 142–146.

Skinner, B. F. (1953). *Science and human behavior.* New York: Free Press.

Sweeney, W. J., Salva, E., Cooper, J. O., & Talbert-Johnson, C. (1993). Using self-evaluation to improve difficult-to-read handwriting of secondary students. *Journal of Behavioral Education, 3,* 427–444.

Testerman, J. (1996). Holding at-risk students: The secret is one-on-one. *Phi Delta Kappan, 77,* 364–365.

Webber, J., Scheuermann, B., McCall, C., & Coleman, M. (1993). Research on self-monitoring as a behavior management technique in special education classrooms: A descriptive review. *Remedial and Special Education, 14,* 38–56.

CHAPTER 10

Factors Influencing Children's Acquisition and Demonstration of Self-Regulation on Academic Tasks

Andrew Biemiller
Michal Shany
Alison Inglis
Donald Meichenbaum

This chapter concerns the conditions under which most children can engage in verbal task regulation. We believe that this perspective is relevant to any program that seeks to enhance academic achievement through improved student self-regulation of academic tasks.

A basic premise of all projects described in this book is that when students increase their level of self-regulation, the quality of their academic achievement improves. As Zimmerman (1994) and others have summarized, the evidence for this assertion comes both from correlational studies showing that higher-achieving students are more likely to be "self-regulated" (as reported by others or themselves, or as observed), and from experimental studies showing that curricula designed to increase student self-regulation in an academic domain lead to improved achievement.

In this chapter, we present evidence consistent with previous findings showing that in the classroom students with high achievement in a domain make more use of language to regulate their own and especially others' academic tasks in that domain. (E.g., high-achieving students often monitor other students' work and make suggestions for improvement. Also, other students often approach high-achieving students for assistance.) However, we are also going to show that "low"- and "average"-achieving students can similarly use language to regulate academic tasks when they are placed in role and task situations comparable to those experienced by the higher-achieving children.

Much current educational policy appears to be premised on the idea that if we would only treat children the same, they would somehow develop more similarly. Thus we have strident calls for higher standards for all and often for "destreaming" the organization of instruction. In this chapter, we both agree and disagree with the view that students should be treated "the same." The main implication of our findings is that conditions supporting spontaneous verbal task regulation for *all* students should be a normal, ongoing aspect of educational programs. However, creating these conditions often involves finding better matches between task demands and individual students' current skills and planning abilities than is currently common. This implication, evidence consistent with it, and some classroom settings for supporting verbal task regulation are discussed in the final section of this chapter.

We begin with a review of findings regarding individual differences in self-regulation in classrooms. We then turn to a theory about the nature of verbal task and self-regulation, and discuss *why* only a few students are seen to demonstrate much verbal task regulation in school classrooms. We follow this with an illustrative study contrasting children's verbal task regulation in the classroom and in a lab setting designed to foster verbal regulation. Finally, we discuss the implications of this approach for programs intended to foster self-regulation.

SELF-REGULATION ON ACADEMIC TASKS

In this section, we review data on the relationship between self-regulation and academic achievement. We will see that students perceived as being self-regulated demonstrate significantly higher levels of verbal task regulation than peers who are less self-regulated. We will also show that *verbal task regulation* and *self-regulation* are both conceptually and empirically similar.

Indicators of Verbal Task Regulation

Meichenbaum, Burland, Gruson, and Cameron (1985) have summarized a number of approaches to measuring task-regulatory speech. These include *interviews* (regarding task accomplishment), *stimulated interviews* in which subjects are shown videotapes of themselves accomplishing a task and interviewed about their thoughts while doing it, *think-aloud* techniques in which subjects attempt to verbalize thoughts while doing a task, and *inferring metacognitive processes from task performance.* Meichenbaum (1985) and Zimmerman (1994) have reviewed findings using most of these methods, which show that students demonstrating or reporting higher levels of self-regulation have higher academic achievement. Similarly, Biemiller and Richards (1986) demonstrated that elementary children with high teacher ratings of self-regulation in October showed substantially greater gains in academic achievement over the school year than those rated low in self-regulation.

However, most of the research in this area has used observational measures of verbal task regulation. The two main overt indicators of verbal task regulation are speech directed to others about tasks, and *private speech* (audible and not clearly audible speech directed to the self—or at least not to others).

Private Speech and Achievement

The largest body of available research has focused on private speech. Research in this area has been summarized by Zivin (1979), Berk (1992), and Diaz (1992). Both Berk and Diaz conclude that higher observed levels of student private speech (while solving problems) are associated with gains in achievement over time. (Diaz emphasizes that this may not mean better performance on a specific task—private speech is often elicited when moderate difficulties are experienced in accomplishing a task. Private speech is rare when tasks are very difficult for learners.) For example, in a longitudinal study of private speech during math work, Bivens and Berk (1990) reported that those using more private speech showed larger gains in math achievement from first to third grade. Berk (1992) summarizes other shorter-term laboratory studies that also show a positive relationship between using private speech while problem-solving and levels of task achievement.

Task-Regulatory Speech and Achievement

We have studied task-regulatory speech during independent work in two separate studies. In one, we found that children rated by their teachers as "high in self-direction" engaged in twice as much *spontaneous* or self-initiated task-regulatory speech on a variety of elementary school tasks as did children rated "low in self-direction" (Meichenbaum and Biemiller, 1992). Examples of such speech include the following: "Look! You can shake glitter onto glue" (re: own task but directed to other); "You need a period there" (re: other's task and directed to other); "Now I need to add 12 and 2" (re: own task and directed to self). In both groups, about 15% of this spontaneous task-regulatory speech was directed to the *self*, that is, private speech.[1] Thus, the large majority of spontaneous task-regulatory speech was directed to others.

In a second study (Biemiller, Shany, Inglis, & Meichenbaum, 1993), we refined our measure of classroom task-regulative speech, replicated the finding that children perceived as highly self-directed engage in substantially more task-regulatory speech than children perceived as little self-directed, and extended our findings to include achievement data, children receiving "middle" ratings of self-direction, and the use of peers as well as teachers to rate self-direction. We are going to describe this study in more detail in this chapter, both because the measure of task-regulatory speech used provides a good classroom index of this phenomenon, and because this study sheds light on the relationship between classroom academic demands, student ability, and *observed* student verbal task regulation.

Effects of Inducing Self-Regulatory Behavior

Many studies in this book and in previous books and articles have demonstrated that experimentally induced self-regulatory behavior is associated with improved academic achievement. Often, this behavior has been induced in less-advanced students. Examples include Palincsar and Brown's *reciprocal teaching* studies (Palincsar & Brown, 1984; A. Brown & Palincsar, 1989), a recent demonstration by R. Brown, Pressley, Van Meter, and Schuder (1996) of the effectiveness of *transactional strategy instruction*, Deshler and Schumaker's (1988) *Learning to Learn* approach. A majority of chapters in this book cover the same ground, as well as earlier books by the same editors (Schunk & Zimmerman, 1994; Zimmerman & Schunk, 1989) and others (e.g., Pressley, Harris, & Guthrie, 1992; Pressley & Woloshyn, 1995). The paradox is that although self-regulatory approaches can clearly be fostered in a wide range of students, and students benefit from this, the evidence shows that in normal classrooms it is able students who engage in self-regulatory behavior and who presumably benefit from doing so.

Summary

Higher-achieving students make more overt use of task-regulatory speech (including private speech) in the classroom than do lower-achieving students. On the other hand, from Vygotsky to the present time, researchers have viewed verbal regulation of tasks as a normal human phenomenon, not limited to especially able cases. (Berk, 1992, reviews evidence supporting this position.) How do we reconcile this view with the finding that able children demonstrate more task-regulatory speech in the classroom?

WHY ONLY ABLE STUDENTS ARE OBSERVED TO REGULATE TASKS VERBALLY IN CLASS

The Development of Verbal Task Regulation

Regulation of Tasks

Regulation of tasks refers to selecting, planning or modifying ("constructing"), implementing, and evaluating tasks; task regulation also includes interrupting and relinquishing tasks. As Vygotsky (1978, pp. 20–24) notes, much behavior and problem solving obviously does not involve "higher mental processes" or verbal control—all animals "behave" and virtually all "solve problems" to some degree. However, Vygotsky also points out that bringing behavior under verbal control vastly increases humans' power to plan, by drawing on past experience and anticipating new situations. Verbal control of behavior also makes possible the role of human culture in shaping behavior.

Verbal Regulation of Tasks

Early in development, others' speech begins to regulate or control infants' tasks (sometimes!), while infants often use speech (or vocalization) to control others' behavior. For example, an infant's cries will cause a mother to drop what she is doing (relinquish a task) and attend to the child. As speech and gestural communication improves, infants use others as "tools" in their own tasks (Case, 1985, pp. 137–141). Thus a child might ask to be lifted up (e.g., "Up!"), an example of directing others. At the same time, the child might wave "bye-bye" when told to do so, an example of being verbally directed by another. Students of private speech also note that by 2 or 3 years of age, children sometimes carry on monologues while engaged in tasks. These monologues partially describe their activities as they perform them. (Berk, 1992; Henderson & Cunningham, 1994; Vygotsky, 1987).

Self-Regulation

Somewhat later in development (3–5 years), children are observed to give themselves overt verbal instructions. Kopp (1982) and Diaz, Neal, and Amaya-Williams (1990) distinguish between *controlling* verbalizations—which essentially are imitations of adult commands (e.g., "Teacher says, 'Don't mix the paints!' ")—versus *regulating* verbalizations in which new task-regulating language is generated by the child (e.g., "Oops, I forgot to carry the 2."). In our observations, we find that at about the point at which children begin to generate self-regulatory language (typically after the fifth birthday), they also begin to advise others on the performance of the other person's task.[2]

Self-Regulation and Learning

We suggest that this is not only a *developmental* sequence in which older children come to regulate their behavior verbally, but also a *learning* sequence, in which children (and adults) normally move from: (1) being verbally regulated by others on a novel task (e.g., instruction and guidance from a teacher so that students can acquire new skills or strategies); to (2) being able to perform the task with some verbal guidance or "hints" (Vygotsky, 1978) (e.g., typical independent schoolwork or drill during which students consolidate learned skills and strategies with some scaffolded teacher or peer assistance available); to (3) reaching a level of internalization or mastery (Wertsch, 1993) in which the former learners can now verbally regulate others (and incidentally themselves) in the performance and construction of similar tasks (e.g., some "authentic" school activities, situations in which students consult or collaborate).[3]

Note that when regulating another's activity, a person is assuming a leading or dominant role, at least temporarily. In a sense, one is doing the same thing when regulating one's own task (rather than seeking assistance from others). One must have confidence to proffer advice or direction to others or oneself.

The Relationship between Other-Regulation and Self-Regulation

This analysis suggests that *other-regulation* (regulation of others' tasks) and *self-regulation* (regulation of one's own tasks) are closely related processes. Empirically, we will describe evidence that elementary students who are perceived by teachers or peers to be self directed engage in higher levels of both other-regulatory and self-regulatory speech. Theoretically, Vygotsky's, Wertsch's, and others' accounts of becoming self-regulated suggest that regulating others may precede self-regulation and certainly accompanies it. Stone (in press); Wertsch (1991); Wertsch, Minick, and Arns (1984); and others particularly stress the importance of *shared* or *joint* task regulation for learners' understanding of new tasks and procedures. At any rate, we hypothesize that many students gain much of their experience and competence at verbally regulating tasks through the regulation of others' tasks. We will describe observational data consistent with this interpretation.

The *Surplus Capacity* Hypothesis

A limiting factor in the early development of verbal task regulation may be developed cognitive capacity, particularly in working memory and verbal processing. Robbie Case has suggested that the operations of *comprehending* and *generating* speech may *each* require up to a unit of working memory or "M-space" in infancy (1985, pp. 141–146). Similar constraints operate in the preschool period with respect to comprehending and generating multiword utterances (Case, 1985, pp. 169–175). Generating and comprehending speech *simultaneously* as in self-dialogue (and probably true dialogue with others)—the condition required for true self-regulation—probably requires more capacity than either generating or comprehending speech. When these cognitive demands are combined with the attentional demands of any specific task (e.g., nonverbal aspects of solving a problem as outlined in Case, 1985, 1992), it may be only rarely that children under 4 or 5 years of age will be able truly to self-regulate activity. After this point in development, the total cognitive load of a task may determine the degree to which self-regulation is possible. Findings by Gutentag (1984); Gutentag, Ornstein, and Siemens (1987); Paas and Van Merrienboer (1994); and Pressley, Carigia-Bull, Deane, and Schneider (1987) are all consistent with the view that excessive cognitive load interferes with verbal regulation of tasks. For practical purposes, *cognitive load* refers to the number of variables that must be considered simultaneously while addressing a problem (Case, 1985; Halford, Wilson, & Phillips, in press). From this, we may hypothesize that self-regulation will typically be more likely on tasks that involve skills or strategies that were taught some time in the past than on tasks involving skills and strategies that are just being learned.

The practical implication of this *surplus capacity* theory is that if children (and adults) are to have some experience self-regulating tasks in academic domains, they will probably need to do tasks involving lower cognitive loads than tasks that have just been learned. For example, we shall see that more fourth-grade children can verbally regulate second-grade math work than can verbally regulate fourth-grade math work.

Why High-Achieving Students Use More Task-Regulatory Speech in School

We argue that normal variations in student readiness or cognitive development and experience are magnified by the *interaction* of academic task demands and students' developed capacity. Less advanced students gain little school experience verbally directing tasks because classroom tasks often demand skills or task planning strategies that they lack, and/or because they have insufficient surplus cognitive capacity available to regulate verbally while performing assigned tasks. Teachers and more able students provide assistance with academic tasks, helping less advanced students to complete assignments. However, by the time at which many of these less advanced students might begin to regulate verbally their own and others' tasks, the teacher moves on to new curriculum content. Also, the average and less-advanced students rarely have anyone who *needs* their assistance. Thus they rarely assume the role of assistant, tutor, or "consultant" with respect to academic skills and tasks.

Because they are rarely in a position to provide verbal direction of tasks, less advanced students do not gain experience and practice in using task-regulatory speech, nor do they often find themselves in a dominant or leadership role in relation to academic tasks—being called upon by the teacher to give explanations of tasks is not the same thing as spontaneously doing so, or being asked to help a peer. These students essentially come to see academic work as an area in which they are normally *subordinate*, requiring the assistance of others to accomplish assignments successfully. Thus, average and less-advanced students get little practice in verbally regulating academic tasks, and have little opportunity to experience themselves as academic leaders rather than followers.

We hypothesize that if the less-advanced students are to experience themselves as competent independent learners and users of academic skills as do their more advanced peers, they will need some of the experiences that advanced students now receive in the classroom. This means occasionally working on tasks at which one is quite competent and has some surplus capacity. This also means sometimes functioning in a consulting or assisting role, assisting others less competent than oneself.

Many curriculum guides and advisors have stressed the desirability of working on academic skills slightly above those one presently possesses. There is also evidence that instruction building on current levels of student achievement is effective in leading to the acquisition of new skills Gutierrez & Slavin, 1992; Mosteller, Light, & Sachs, 1996; Slavin, 1987). However, few researchers or teachers have considered the importance of working sometimes on academic content that does *not* exceed current skills or planning strategies, that is, "easy" tasks. Paradoxically, this is a situation that most academic high achievers frequently experience. What we are proposing is the possibility that providing average and below-average students with moderate-difficulty (for them) and assisting experiences similar to those of advanced students would allow these others the opportunity to function like advanced students. Improving the match between task demands and student ability should result in higher levels of verbal task-regulatory behavior and, over time, in increased effectiveness on tasks requiring self-regulation (e.g., problem solving, and constructive tasks).

A STUDY OF THE INTERACTION OF TASK DEMANDS AND STUDENT CAPACITY ON TASK REGULATION

We undertook a study (Biemiller et al., 1993) to show that most students can generate task-regulatory speech in an academic context. Our goals were as follows:

1. To replicate our original classroom findings regarding task-regulatory speech and perceived student self-regulation under more controlled conditions, and
2. To test our hypothesis that a very substantially larger proportion of children can demonstrate high levels of task-regulatory speech *in the same domains in which they look "low" in the classroom*, when they are operating on domain tasks at a level of task difficulty that they *can* handle successfully and they are operating in a role context that calls for them actively to verbalize task functions (specify, plan, monitor, evaluate).

This study was conducted in a laboratory school serving an middle to upper-socioeconomic-status population. Three groups of second-to fourth-grade children were selected for study: (1) children perceived as low in task regulation by peers, (2) children perceived as somewhat task regulated (median ratings by peers), and (3) children perceived as highly task regulated. Peer perceptions were elicited with four questions:

1. Which child in your class would you like to work with on a math project?
2. If someone in your class had a problem with a math project, who would be good to turn to for help?
3. Who is the child in your class who understands very quickly what to do in math?
4. Which child has lots of good and new ideas for things to do in math?

We totaled the number of times each child in a class was named. Those in the top quarter were eligible for the high-self-regulation group, those in the bottom quarter for the low-self-regulation group,[4] and those nearest the median number of nominations in a class were eligible for the middle group. We selected groups rated low, middle, and high in self-regulation, with six children in each group. Each of these groups included two second-grade, two third-grade, and two fourth-grade children.

These peer-selected groups proved to differ significantly in achievement with mean scores of 26 (low self-regulated), 39 (middle), and 42 (high) on a math problem-solving test. The children also differed significantly on an

IQ test (Wechsler Intelligence Scale for Children) with mean scores of 106 (low), 115 (middle), and 129 (high). In both cases, analysis of covariance were significant at the .01 level.[5]

Observing Task-Regulatory Speech

Each child was observed during independent work on math (carrying out math assignments) for an average of 40 minutes. Observations were not made if the teacher was providing direct instruction to the whole class or a group containing the target child. Observers wrote down everything that was said by and to the target children. Observers also recorded the nature of the math activity and any behavioral observations necessary to make analysis of transcripts easier (providing context for speech).

In this study, task-regulatory speech is made up of (1) spontaneous statements uttered by a target child related to the child's own math work (whether directed to self or other), (2) statements made in response to another's request for help, and (3) spontaneous statements made about another's math work. Such speech indicates that a child can and will verbalize goals and plans and can verbally monitor and regulate task progress for him- or herself and others. The observed child's requests for help and responses to help or comments from others (solicited and unsolicited) were not included as evidence of task-regulatory speech. We considered help seeking as just that—seeking rather than giving task regulation. We ignored responses to help in the grounds that such language was not spontaneous and would not have occurred in the absence of the help. (We have included responses to others' requests for help, since such responses are clearly task-regulatory.)

The Appendix at the end of this chapter summarizes coding procedures. Sentences were identified and coded, and the results were adjusted to sentences per hour to provide a common measure across children. Coders, blind to target children's self-regulatory status, achieved 80% agreement in coding task-regulatory speech.

Classroom Results: High-Achieving Students Engage in Task-Regulatory Speech

When the children were observed during independent work in math, we found much higher levels of task-regulatory speech among the high-rated students. Overall, the low-self-regulation children surprisingly averaged 16 task-regulatory sentences per hour ($SD = 9$), the middle-self-regulation children averaged only 8 task-regulatory sentences per hour ($SD = 7$), whereas the high-self-regulation children averaged 57 sentences per hour (SD = 25). These differences were significant, $F(2,15)$ = 15.82, p < .01, thus replicating our earlier findings relating task-directive speech to rated self-direction.

Peer Assistance Sessions: All Children Engage in Task-Regulatory Speech

Our goal was to observe children operating under what we considered to be the circumstances that advanced children frequently experience in their own classroom; to wit, working on a task at which the child is competent, and in a role that requires the child to express his or her competence in words (what we call a *consulting role*). We arranged to have children work in pairs with an older child (older by one grade level) acting as a math helper for a younger child. These pairs worked in the lab on math word-problems. Each pair of children was given a set of problems that started with two or three that could be solved by the younger child, followed by seven or eight increasingly more difficult problems with which the younger child needed help, and at which the older child was competent (based on prior test performance). These conditions were met in about 75% of cases. In the others, the younger children proved more capable than expected, either because the test underestimated their skill, or because they had increased their skill since the initial testing.

An experimenter (M. S. or A. I.) was present during the assistance session, but did not participate in the work, and intervened only if there were behavioral problems or the older child was stuck. Children were reminded of classroom practices regarding assistance ("Don't tell the answer.") and were encouraged to proceed. Laboratory sessions ranged from 10 to 38 minutes in length, averaging 20 minutes. All sessions were videotaped. Videotapes were then coded for task-regulatory speech, as described previously.

Given a task they could do, and a role that called for explaining the task, the older children's behavior in the lab was dramatically different from that observed in the classroom. The peer-rated low-self-regulation children produced an average of 177 task-regulatory sentences per hour (SD = 97), or over 10 times the rate observed in the classroom. The middle-self-regulation children produced 199 sentences per hour (SD = 81), while the high-self-regulation children produced 222 sentences per hour (SD = 143). In the lab condition, there were no significant differences between groups; for overall task-regulatory speech, $F(2,15)$ = 0.25, p < .78. Figure 10.1 contrasts task-regulatory speech in the classroom and laboratory situations.

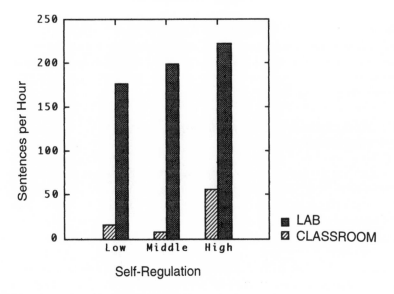

FIGURE 10.1. A comparison of high-, medium-, and low-self-regulation children's total spontaneous task-regulatory sentences per hour in classroom and assistance-giving conditions.

Summary

Clearly, given a chance, the low- and middle-self-regulation children could produce task-regulatory language. Differences in the rate of task-regulative speech observed in classrooms are caused by the demands of tasks relative to student skills and by the roles that students assume, rather than basic differences between the children in task-regulatory potential.

CONDITIONS SUPPORTING SELF-REGULATION

Teaching for self-regulation is not just a question of teaching strategies and modeling self-regulation. It also involves creating valid opportunities for exercising verbal task regulation. In many ways, these results may appear patently obvious. Children who do not use much task-regulatory language in the classroom can be verbally fluent about their tasks *if* we make tasks easy enough and give them a reason to talk! Obvious though this may appear, it remains the case that the situation we created is a very unusual one for children in the bottom quarter of classroom performance *and* for middle children. It may also come as a surprise to some that middle children are not in the middle when it comes to generating task-regulatory speech in the classroom.

The point of this illustrative study is neither that cross-age tutoring is good per se nor that the task-regulatory speech generated in this laboratory context was necessarily effective. The point is that the low and average students in this study were *capable* of generating task-regulatory speech when given easier tasks and a responsibility to talk about the tasks. Making that speech effective remains an educational responsibility.

Note that when tasks are very easy, there may be little need to talk to others or oneself about them. What is crucial to eliciting task-regulatory speech is the combination of a task within the student's area of competence *and* a role that necessitates explaining the task.

This book contains chapters on self-regulation in writing, reading, mathematics, computing, and other areas of instruction. In each chapter, self-regulation of strategies for planning tasks and of overall task focus or attention are included. Our point is that if students are to maintain an active self-regulated approach to their academic tasks, they will not only need effective strategies to use in specific contexts (e.g., visualization and summarizing in reading; goal setting, monitoring progress, and revising in writing), but they will also need tasks at which they can succeed while using these strategies (e.g., books they can read on their own or with appropriately scaffolded assistance; writing objectives they can meet), and *role contexts* in which they can legitimately and successfully assume leadership in providing verbal guidance to others' tasks.

Many successful programs with the goal of self-regulation overtly include *regulation of other* contexts. Perhaps best known is the *reciprocal teaching* of Palincsar and Brown (1984; A. Brown & Palincsar, 1989) in which students assume "teacher" roles, generating questions and summaries for their classmates. Similarly, Aronson's *jigsaw* approach (1979) explicitly creates roles in which each student is an "expert," responsible for teaching other students about his or her area of expertise. A. Brown and Campione's *Community of Learners* program (1994) builds on both reciprocal teaching and jigsaw methods. Pressley, El-Dinary, et al.'s (1992) *transactional strategy instruction* approach to reading comprehension similarly emphasizes dialogue as a route to self-regulation:

> Each student is presumed to benefit from participating in the group process. Long-term participation in such a group is hypothesized to result in internalization of the "executive" activities of the group. That is, the types of decisions once made by and in the group are eventually made by the individual participant when he or she reads alone. (Pressley, El-Dinary, et al., 1992, p. 516)

It is through engaging in these group *transactions* or verbal discussion of tasks that comprehension strategies shift from being teacher taught and teacher instigated to being student initiated.

However, having recognized that situations calling for partial regulation of others' tasks are a common component of programs leading to successful self-regulation, it becomes important to create contexts in which this can legitimately occur. In-class assistance is one such context, but it provides consulting roles to relatively few students, while reinforcing subordinate roles in others. Cross-age assistance (or tutoring or "buddy" activities) provides another such context, but requires more preparation and organization than we commonly see. (Note that accepting assistance from an older student may have psychologically better consequences than accepting assistance from a same-grade classmate.) *Cooperative learning* activities (broadly defined as approaches in which two or more students work on a task with a single product) theoretically provide plenty of opportunities for task-regulatory speech. However, unless much attention is given to the relative skills and roles of children in cooperative groups, often only a few gain what we would describe as consulting experiences (Johnson & Johnson, 1975).

Consulting/Reflecting Roles

In essence, the kinds of roles that give students extensive verbal regulatory experience are those in which the student is a legitimate authority (or equal collaborator) and is called on to generate verbal task directions, guidance, and/or evaluation. We call these *consulting* or *reflecting* roles. These roles occur when one child assists another, when two or more collaborate on a project, when a child reviews (or "edits") another's work and provides constructive advice, and when a child reviews or edits her own work with the goal of current or future improvement. There are a number of different ways in which students can consult or reflect on others' and their own work:

1. *As constructors, and markers* of other students' tasks and products. Students can generate worksheets, math problems, math games, word searches, story starters, etc., for other (often younger) students to use. Students can also mark the other students' work. We recommend that when students generate materials for others, they work in small groups and edit materials jointly before they are used by others. In our view, these assignments work best with students for whom the skills in question are not a problem.

2. *As helpers, assistants, or tutors.* Students must be taught how to *assist,* not "do for." (Note that spontaneous assistance in regular classrooms often takes the "do for" form.[6]) Students may also assist by marking younger students' work and attempting to determine patterns of problems with which they or the teacher might help. We have normally included a self-reflective

component in such work, in which the helper reviews his or her own effectiveness in helping.

3. *As collaborators in constructing tasks or complex products*. For example, students can be asked to construct a guidebook for next year's class on possible problems or "procedural bugs" the class should be alert to. In doing so, students must reflect on problems they and others have experienced. Students may also be asked to collaborate with fellow students on joint projects. For true collaboration, abilities must be similar or complementary.

4. *As participants in structured cooperative learning roles, which may be rotated as in jigsaw and reciprocal teaching*. In these and other cooperative learning modes, each student has a defined subtask responsibility within the overall task.

5. *As editors*. Students may be assigned to copy-edit or content-edit other students' written work. If this editing leads to helpful dialogue with the other students, a consultation setting is created.

6. *As "reflectors" after accomplishing individual and collaborative tasks*. Students can be asked to review their own work and comment on it orally or in print. To a large extent, reflection amounts to self-editing and self-evaluation. If this process is focused on improvement rather than criticism, it can be a positive self-consulting experience.

We are sure that this is not an exhaustive list, and that creative teachers have generated and will continue to develop many other effective consulting roles for students.

Preliminary Evidence Regarding the Effects of Experience in a Consulting Role

Two of the authors (A. I., A. B.) are currently completing a research project in which inner city fourth-grade children with low achievement in math assist second-grade children in math (Inglis & Biemiller, 1997). The purpose of this study was to examine the effects of extended consulting experience on the older children's own mathematics achievement.

In addition to providing cross-age tutoring experiences in math, one of us (A. I.) provided training in how to be a "good helper." Data that we had collected in the lab during the study demonstrated that although children of varying ability levels could generate task-regulatory speech sufficiently to act as helpers, they did not all demonstrate good helping skills. For example, we noticed that some of the children were inattentive, somewhat rude, easily frustrated, too directive, not directive enough, and/or too rushed. Good helping skills were adapted from the scaffolding and strategic instruction literature (see Bruer, 1993; McGilly, 1994; Pressley & Woloshyn, 1994;

Pressley et al., 1990; Wood, 1988) and the vast literature on peer and cross-age tutoring (see Goodlad & Hirst, 1989, 1990; Mavrogenes & Galen, 1978; Rekrut, 1994).

Inglis provided a mixed training and helping sequence of 15–20 sessions of 30–45 minutes each. There were usually two sessions per week, and 10–15 sessions involved directly helping younger children. The training program included a focus on five strategies. The children were taught to (1) Look and Listen to see who needs help and when; (2) Ask Questions to find out what kind of help is needed; (3) Give Hints instead of answers, so that the other person can work out answers on their own; (4) Give Pats on the Back to encourage the other person; and (5) Check It Out to see if work has been done correctly, and whether "I did a good job helping."

Following participation in the training and helping sessions, 31 helpers showed a mean gain of six items on a modified version of Canadian Test of Basic Skills math problem-solving segment.[7] During the same time interval, 38 control children had a mean gain of three items. An analysis of covariance, using pretest scores as covariate, was significant at the .01 level. In short, participating in a consulting role over several months resulted in children becoming more effective at *using* math skills to solve math problems. It should be noted that math helpers worked with younger students on a variety of math activities, very few of which were problem based. Therefore, gains in math problem solving cannot be attributed simply to practice gained in the helping experience. Gains were also not attributable to increases in computational ability, as there were no differences between the training and control groups in initial or final computational ability.

The Place of Consulting in School Programs

We view the cross-age tutoring program not as a specific self-regulation program in math, but rather as an example of a consulting program component that ought to be as much a part of classroom activities as are teacher-led instruction, small group discussion, and independent work. Although logistically it is not practical to provide consulting roles for all students in all academic domains on the same day or week, we suggest that most students should have a consistent, well-designed consulting role in at least one major academic domain at any one time, and should have such roles in all domains in the course of every academic year. Frankly, we think that the emphasis now being placed on the more able students helping the less able within grades offers increased task-regulatory competence to the more able and a lot of learning "how to get others to think for you" for the less able. (E.g., having able children help others is recommended in Pressley et al., 1992, and Brown & Campione, 1994.)

CONCLUSIONS

Early in this chapter, we suggested that we both "agree and disagree" with the idea that by treating children the same, we can obtain more similar (and, it is implied, higher-level) outcomes. In closing, let us return to that paradox.

We agree with the view that a similar curriculum—in the sense of skills covered and opportunities to develop self-regulation and expertise—should be provided to most students. (We suspect that 10–15% of students at each end of the achievement distribution will probably require modified curricula.) Effective instruction and practice of skills and problem-solving strategies, assisting other students, and collaborative learning should be available or useful to most students, rather than just to advanced students. This means that most students should experience sometimes (not always!) being in small-group situations (two to four children) in which they are the most competent members of the group. We hypothesize that following this approach might lead to many more children, as opposed to the usual one-third, achieving high levels of self-regulation in elementary academic tasks.

We disagree with the view that providing the same or similar opportunities to all students means providing those opportunities at the same point in time (Biemiller, 1993). We do not think that this will lead to optimal outcomes for all. Insisting that all students cover the same curriculum at the same time is roughly equivalent to insisting that all people with 100 hours of skiing experience ski the same slope.

The implications appear clear. If we genuinely want to see the majority of children become effective self-regulators, it is not enough to provide children with strategy instruction and other effective approaches to initiate self-regulation. We must also create and maintain ongoing working conditions in which students can successfully exercise their task-regulatory potential with others and with themselves on a regular basis.

APPENDIX: A MEASURE OF TASK-REGULATORY SPEECH

Children were observed during "independent math work" (carrying out assignments) for an average of 40 minutes each. Observers wrote down everything the target child said (to others and self). In addition, they wrote down other information necessary to code speech including (1) the task being discussed, (2) clear affect (e.g., smiles, frowns), and (3) to whom comments were directed. Observers watched lessons preceding independent work, and provided a description of the nature of the assignment children were working on.

The coding system was a simplified version of the one described in Meichenbaum and Biemiller (1992). All of the target child's language was grouped into one of four categories:

1. *Social talk*: *Not* related to either speaker's *current* tasks—for example, "How did you like the Blue Jays (baseball team) last night?" or "Are you going to play with me at recess?"

2. *Verbal products*: Result of *reading* words or numbers out loud, *saying* an answer (or "product") out loud—for example, "She had six eggs left over!"

3. *Task negotiation*: Discussion in which a child negotiates with a teacher to reduce the difficulty of a task (or in one case, to increase it)—for example, "Do I have to write out the answers?"—or in which the child negotiates with another child regarding "turns"—for example, "Now you measure, and I'll write the answers."

4. *Task-related speech*: Speech directed to others or self that either *states* a task function or *questions* a task function. Task functions include the following:

   a. *Specifications* of task, procedures, objects—defining the task, stating goals or problems (e.g., "This is called editing.");

   b. *Planning functions*—stating what comes next or the sequence of actions (e.g., "Now I need to. . . . "); and

   c. *Implementing/monitoring/evaluating functions*—noting progress, noting necessary conditions present or absent (e.g., "I haven't got a red sticker."), or evaluating procedure or task (e.g., "That's done." or "I made a good butterfly.").

For the purposes of the present study, all *task-related* speech was broken into three main categories:

1. *Spontaneous statements regarding one's own task*. This category includes private speech, but in reality, most statements about one's own task appeared to be directed at others, for example, "I've finished problem 7." This category also includes *self*-directed questions.

2. *Giving assistance to others regarding their tasks*. This includes comments on others' tasks, spontaneous assistance, questions intended to help the other person (e.g., "Did you forget something?"), and responding to others' requests for assistance.

3. *Requesting assistance and responding to received assistance*. This includes soliciting assistance and responding to both solicited and unsolicited help.

Task-regulatory speech is indexed by the frequency of sentences coded as "spontaneous–own task" and "giving assistance." Numbers of observed sentences are adjusted to represent sentences per hour. This is done by multiplying the observed number of sentences by 60 ÷ number of minutes of observation.

ACKNOWLEDGMENTS

We wish to thank the children and staff of the Laboratory School of the Institute of Child Study, and of Park, Regent's Park, and Spruce Court Schools within the Toronto Board of Education, without whose cooperation the research reported here could not have been done. We also wish to thank the Social Science and Humanities Research Council of Canada which supported the research reported in this chapter. Last, but not least, we wish to thank Marcie Scherer who transcribed and coded much of the data.

NOTES

1. We did not include the "inaudible mutterings" that are noted in many studies of private speech.

2. We are not sure when children begin to use language to regulate emotion or temperament in others or themselves (e.g., "Calm down," or "That's okay."). We suspect that this happens fairly early in the preschool years.

3. This learning sequence represents part of what Vygotsky (1978, p. 84ff.) meant by the "zone of proximal development"—the difference between new to-be-learned tasks and procedures and those performed independently. (The other aspect of the zone relates to capacity limitations that render some tasks unlearnable at particular points of development.)

4. Children receiving zero or one nominations were excluded on the assumption that these individuals might be socially rejected, and hence yield inconsistent results.

5. Note that the "low" children have "average" IQs. Readers may wonder if less cognitively advanced children might provide less task-regulatory speech. However, in the cross-age tutoring study briefly described later in this chapter (Inglis & Biemiller, 1997), we found that economically disadvantaged children who were performing well below grade level were nonetheless able to provide effective assistance, using task-regulatory speech.

6. At the same time, it may be appropriate to provide "do for" assistance with *skills* on tasks where the goal is to improve student task "construction" or planning (e.g., reading comprehension, writing text, etc.). See, for example, Shany and Biemiller's (1995) work on assisted reading, in which providing extended reading practice with word identification assistance led to markedly improved comprehension of more advanced passages as well as increased sight vocabulary in context. Such assistance is an aspect of scaffolding (Biemiller & Meichenbaum, in press; Stone, in press).

7. Modifications of the test involved using open response rather than multiple choice, and reading items for students when necessary. Items were selected to reflect increases in difficulty based on national norms.

REFERENCES

Aronson, E. (1979). *The jigsaw classroom.* Beverly Hills, CA: Sage.

Berk, L. E. (1992). Children's private speech: An overview of theory and the status of research. In L. E. Berk & R. Diaz (Eds.), *Private speech: From social interaction to self-regulation* (pp. 17–54). Hillsdale, NJ: Erlbaum.

Biemiller, A. (1993). Lake Wobegon revisited: On diversity and education. *Educational Researcher, 22*(9), 7–12.

Biemiller, A., & Meichenbaum, D. (in press). The consequences of negative scaffolding for students who learn slowly: A commentary on C. Addison Stone's "The metaphor of scaffolding: Its utility for the field of learning disabilities." *Journal of Learning Disabilities*.

Biemiller, A., & Richards, M. (1986). *Project Thrive: Vol. 2. Individualized intervention to foster social, emotional, and self-related functions in primary programs.* Toronto, Ontario: Ministry of Education.

Biemiller, A., Shany, M., Inglis, A., & Meichenbaum, D. (1993, August). *Enhancing self direction in "less able" learners.* Paper presented as part of an invited symposium on Issues and Directions in Research on Children's Self-Regulated Learning and Development at the annual conference of the American Psychological Association, Toronto, Ontario, Canada.

Bivens, J. A., & Berk, L. E. (1990). A longitudinal study of the development of elementary school children's private speech. *Merrill-Palmer Quarterly, 36*, 443–463.

Brown, A., & Campione, J. (1994). Guided discovery in a community of learners. In K. McGilly (Ed.), *Classroom lessons: Integrating cognitive theory and classroom practice* (pp. 229–272). Cambridge, MA: MIT Press.

Brown, A. L., & Palincsar, A. S. (1989). Guided, cooperative learning and individual knowledge acquisition. In L. B. Resnick (Ed.), *Knowing, learning, and instruction: Essays in honor of Robert Glaser* (pp. 393–451). Hillsdale, NJ: Erlbaum.

Brown, R., Pressley, M., Van Meter, P., & Schuder, T. (1996). A quasi-experimental validation of transactional strategies instruction with low-achieving second-grade readers. *Journal of Educational Psychology, 88*, 18–37.

Bruer, J. T. (1993). *Schools for thought: A science of learning in the classroom.* Cambridge, MA: MIT Press.

Case, R. (1985). *Intellectual development: Birth to adulthood.* Orlando, FL: Academic Press.

Case, R. (1992). *The mind's staircase: Exploring the conceptual underpinnings of children's thought and knowledge.* Hillsdale, NJ: Erlbaum.

Deshler, D. D., & Schumaker, J. B. (1988). An instructional model for teaching students how to learn. In J. L. Graden, J. E. Zins, & M. J. Curtis (Eds.), *Alternative educational delivery systems: Enhancing instructional options for all students* (pp. 391–411). Washington, DC: National Association of School Psychologists.

Diaz, R. M. (1992). Methodological concerns in the study of private speech. In L. E. Berk & R. Diaz (Eds.), *Private speech: From social interaction to self-regulation* (pp. 55–81). Hillsdale, NJ: Erlbaum.

Diaz, R. F., Neal, C. J., & Amaya-Williams, M. (1990). the social origins of self-regulation. In L. C. Moll (Ed.), *Vygotsky and education: Instructional implications of sociohistorical psychology* (pp. 127–154). New York: Cambridge University Press.

Goodlad, S., & Hirst, B. (1989). *Peer tutoring: A guide to learning by teaching.* London: Kogan Page.

Goodlad, S., & Hirst, B. (1990). *Explorations in peer tutoring.* London: Blackwell Education.

Gutentag, R. E. (1984). The mental effort requirement of cumulative rehearsal: A developmental study. *Journal of Experimental Child Psychology, 37*, 92–106.

Gutentag, R. E., Ornstein, P. A., & Siemens, I. (1987). Children's spontaneous rehearsal: Transitions in strategy acquisition. *Cognitive Development, 2*, 307–326.

Gutierrez, R., & Slavin, R. E. (1992). Achievement effects of the nongraded elementary school: A best evidence synthesis. *Review of Educational Research, 62*, 333–376.

Halford, G. S., Wilson, W. H., & Phillips, S. (in press). Processing capacity defined by relational complexity: Implications for comparative, developmental, and cognitive psychology. *Behavioral and Brain Sciences.*

Henderson, R. W., & Cunningham, L. (1994). Creating interactive socio-cultural environments for self-regulated learning. In D. H. Schunk & B. J. Zimmerman (Eds.), *Self-regulation of learning and performance: Issues and educational applications* (pp. 255–282). Hillsdale, NJ: Erlbaum.

Inglis, A., & Biemiller, A. (1997). *Fostering self-direction in grade four tutors: A cross-age tutoring program.* Manuscript submitted for publication.

Johnson, D. W., & Johnson, R. T. (1975). *Learning together and alone.* Englewood Cliffs, NJ: Prentice-Hall.

Kopp, C. B. (1982). Antecedents of self-regulation: A developmental perspective. *Developmental Psychology, 18,* 199–214.

Mavrogenes, N. A., & Galen, N. D. (1978). Cross-age tutoring: Why and how? *Journal of Reading, 22*(4), 344–353.

McGilly, K. (1994). *Classroom lessons: Integrating cognitive theory and classroom practice.* Cambridge, MA: MIT Press.

Meichenbaum, D. (1984). Teaching thinking: A cognitive-behavioral perspective. In S. F. Chipman, J. W. Segal, & R. Glaser (Eds.), *Thinking and learning skills: Vol. 2. Research and open questions* (pp. 407–426). Hillsdale, NJ: Erlbaum.

Meichenbaum, D., & Biemiller, A. (1992). In M. Pressley, K. Harris, & J. Guthrie (Eds.), *Promoting academic competence and literacy in school* (pp. 3–56). New York: Academic Press.

Meichenbaum, D., Burland, S., Gruson, L., & Cameron R. (1985). Metacognitive assessment. In S. R. Yuson (Ed.), *The growth of reflection in children* (pp. 3–30). New York: Academic Press.

Mosteller, F., Light, R. J., & Sachs, J. A. (1996). Sustained inquiry in education: Lessons from skill grouping and class size. *Harvard Educational Review, 66,* 797–842.

Paas, F. G. W. C., & Van Merrienboer, J. J. G. (1994). Variability of worked examples and transfer of geometrical problem-solving skills: A cognitive load approach. *Journal of Educational Psychology, 86,* 122–133.

Palincsar, A. S., & Brown, A. L. (1984). Reciprocal teaching of comprehension-fostering and comprehension-monitoring activities. *Cognitive Instruction, 1,* 117–175.

Pressley, M., Cariglia-Bull, T., Deane, S., & Schneider, W. (1987). Short-term memory, verbal competence, and age as predictors of imagery instructional effectiveness. *Journal of Experimental Child Psychology, 43,* 194–211.

Pressley, M., El-Dinary, P. B., Gaskins, I., Schuder, T., Bergman, J. L., Almasi, J., & Brown, R. (1992). Beyond direct explanation: Transactional instruction of reading comprehension strategies. *Elementary School Journal, 92,* 513–555.

Pressley, M., Harris, K. R., & Guthrie, J. T. (Eds.). (1992). *Promoting academic competence and literacy in school.* New York: Academic Press.

Pressley, M., & Woloshyn, V. (1995). *Cognitive strategy instruction that really improves children's academic performance* (2nd ed.). Cambridge, MA: Brookline Books.

Pressley, M., Woloshyn, V., Lysynchuk, L. M., Martin, V., Wood, E., & Willoughby, T. (1990). A primer of research on cognitive strategy instruction: The important issues and how to address them. *Educational Psychology Review, 2*(1), 1–58.

Rekrut, M. D. (1994). Peer and cross-age tutoring: The lessons of research. *Journal of Reading, 37*(5), 356–362.

Schunk, D. H., & Zimmerman, B. J. (Eds.). (1994). *Self-regulation of learning and performance: Issues and educational applications*. Hillsdale, NJ: Erlbaum.

Shany, M., & Biemiller, A. (1995). Assisted reading practice: Effects on performance for poor readers in grades 3 and 4. *Reading Research Quarterly, 30*, 382–395.

Slavin, R. E. (1987). Ability grouping and student achievement in elementary schools: A best evidence synthesis. *Review of Educational Research, 57*, 293–336.

Stone, C. A. (in press). The metaphor of scaffolding: Its utility for the field of learning disabilities. *Journal of Learning Disabilities*.

Vygotsky, L. S. (1978). *Mind in society: The development of higher psychological processes*. Cambridge, MA: Harvard University Press.

Vygotsky, L. S. (1987). Thinking and speech. In R. W. Rieber & A. S. Carton (Eds.), *The collected works of L. S. Vygotsky: Vol. 1. Problems of general psychology* (pp. 39–288). New York: Plenum Press.

Wertsch, J. V. (1991). Meaning in a sociocultural approach to mind. In A. McKeough & J. L. Lupart (Eds.), *Toward the practice of theory-based instruction* (pp. 31–49). Hillsdale, NJ: Erlbaum.

Wertsch, J. (1993). Commentary. *Human Development, 36*, 168–171.

Wertsch, J. V., Minick, N., & Arns, F. J. (1984). The creation of context in joint problem-solving. In B. Rogoff & J. Lave (Eds.), *Everyday cognition: Its development in social context* (pp. 151–171). Cambridge, MA: Harvard University Press.

Wood, D. (1988). *How children think and learn*. London: Basil Blackwell.

Zimmerman, B. J. (1994). Dimensions of academic self-regulation: A conceptual framework for education. In D. H. Schunk & B. J. Zimmerman (Eds.), *Self-regulation of learning and performance: Issues and educational applications* (pp. 3–21). Hillsdale, NJ: Erlbaum.

Zimmerman, B. J., & Schunk, D. H. (Eds.). (1989). *Self-regulated learning and academic achievement: Theory, research, and practice*. Hillsdale, NJ: Erlbaum.

Zivin, G. (Ed.). (1979). *The development of self-regulation through private speech*. New York: Wiley.

CHAPTER 11

Conclusions and Future Directions for Academic Interventions

Dale H. Schunk
Barry J. Zimmerman

The chapters in this volume make it clear that in the past few years academic self-regulation has made dramatic advances in theory, research, and educational applications. Although the authors differ in many ways including theoretical perspective, choice of methodology, academic content, use of technology, and type of learner studied, their interventions reflect the operation and subprocesses of self-regulation discussed by Zimmerman (Chapter 1, this volume).

In this concluding chapter we initially recap the history of academic self-regulation from its theoretical beginnings to the present. We then discuss common components of self-regulation interventions, followed by issues where authors diverge in their thinking. We offer suggestions for future research, and we conclude with ideas for facilitating change in educational settings.

ACADEMIC SELF-REGULATION: PAST AND PRESENT

A central objective of our initial volume on academic self-regulation was to ensure that the emerging research was solidly grounded in theory (Zimmerman & Schunk, 1989). Accordingly, authors discussed self-regulation from various theoretical perspectives: operant, phenomenological, social-cognitive, volitional, Vygotskian, constructivist. These accounts all dealt with five key issues or questions.

1. What motivates students to self-regulate during learning?
2. Through what process or procedure do students become self-reactive or self-aware?
3. What are the key processes or responses that self-regulated students use to attain their academic goals?
4. How does the social and physical environment affect student self-regulated learning?
5. How does a learner acquire the capacity to self-regulate when learning?

Answers to these theoretical issues or questions guided research efforts during the ensuing years.

Much initial research on academic self-regulation focused on *testing theoretical predictions and specifying self-regulation components and processes*. For example, Zimmerman and Martinez-Pons (1990) identified self-regulated learning strategies among students in grades 5, 8, and 11; determined whether these varied as a function of grade level, sex, and giftedness; and related strategy use to perceptions of self-efficacy (perceived competence). Pintrich and De Groot (1990) examined relations between self-regulated learning strategies, motivation, and academic performance among seventh graders in science and English classes. Meece, Blumenfeld, and Hoyle (1988) investigated in science classes the operation of fifth and sixth graders' cognitive engagement activities (analogous to self-regulated learning strategies), goals, and motivational patterns.

Other researchers focused on the development of self-regulation, and especially on how instructional and contextual factors affected self-regulation. For example, Schunk and Rice conducted a series of studies with students who possessed reading-skill deficiencies (Schunk & Rice, 1987, 1992, 1993), which showed that strategy modeling and feedback on strategy effectiveness combined to enhance students' self-efficacy, self-regulated strategy use, and reading achievement. Graham and Harris (1989a, 1989b) found that teaching students with learning disabilities a self-regulatory writing strategy improved their self-efficacy and writing performance and that gains were maintained after instruction and generalized to other settings and content. Cognitive modeling was used: Models explained and demonstrated the strategy while applying its steps to write stories, and they conveyed to students that strategy use would help students attain their learning goals. Other components of the procedure were self-monitoring of writing performance and self-evaluation of goal progress.

As researchers began to integrate their results from this first wave of studies with those of other investigators, some confusion began to occur. Often overlapping variables were labeled differently because of diverse theoretical preferences, such as metacognition, cognitive engagement, and planning. In other cases, distinctive processes could affect a common dimension of self-regulation, such as goal setting and self-efficacy beliefs influencing students' motivation.

Our second edited volume (Schunk & Zimmerman, 1994) sought to identify common underlying dimensions of self-regulation and present research showing which processes were most influential regarding each dimension. Being a gifted learner did not insure academic success unless commensurate motivation and behavioral practice accompanied effective strategy choices. Collectively, these studies revealed that successful students displayed personal initiative and self-regulatory control regarding their (1) sources of motivation, (2) choice of learning methods, (3) forms of behavioral performance, and (4) use of social and physical environmental resources.

The present volume moves beyond fundamental theories and basic research identifying key attributes and processes underlying self-regulated learning to consider larger-scale interventions whose effects were broader in scope and assessed over lengthy periods of time. Rather than studying a limited number of processes under highly experimental conditions, researchers collaborated with practitioners to integrate self-regulatory instruction as part of the regular academic curriculum. Additionally, studies were designed to promote long-term maintenance and generalization of these instructional effects. Although the results are promising, most of these instructional models are in the beginning phases of their development.

COMMON COMPONENTS OF
SELF-REGULATION INTERVENTIONS

These chapters discuss several common features of academic self-regulation that link to theory and prior research. Among the techniques most widely used by the contributors to this book are strategy teaching, practice, feedback, monitoring, social support, withdrawal of support, and self-reflective practice.

Strategy teaching is considered a key means of promoting self-regulated learning. Students who learn a systematic approach for working on academic material are able to apply it independently. Strategy learning also raises motivation, because students who believe they can apply an effective strategy are apt to feel more efficacious about succeeding, which raises self-efficacy (Schunk, 1991). In this volume, strategy teaching is central to many interventions (Belfiore & Hornyak, Chapter 9; Graham, Harris, & Troia, Chapter 2; Hofer, Yu, & Pintrich, Chapter 4; Pressley, El-Dinary, Wharton-McDonald, & Brown, Chapter 3; Schunk, Chapter 7). Further, Lan (Chapter

5) taught students a self-monitoring procedure, and in other studies described herein (Butler, Chapter 8; Winne & Stockley, Chapter 6) students constructed strategies based on interactions with teachers.

Two other key elements are *practice of self-regulatory strategies* and *feedback on strategy effectiveness*. These components enhance learning and motivation by conveying learning progress, and they also promote strategy transfer and maintenance. All of the interventions described in this volume include a healthy amount of student practice and feedback from others.

A fourth component is *monitoring*, which all interventions stress. It is imperative that students monitor their application of the strategy, its effectiveness in solving task demands, and ways to modify it to fit different aspects. Monitoring also is involved in determining one's progress in skill acquisition, as a means for enhancing self-efficacy and motivation (Schunk, 1991).

A fifth common component across interventions is *social support* from others as students learn and acquire skills. Social support often comes from teachers, but many interventions in this volume include peer support (Biemiller, Shany, Inglis, & Meichenbaum, Chapter 10; Butler; Hofer et al.; Lan; Pressley et al.).

Linked with social support is the notion of *withdrawal of support* as students become more competent. Graham et al. (this volume) describe one means of withdrawing support: *scaffolding*, where needed instructional supports for learning are provided but eventually are withdrawn. Schunk (this volume) describes an instructional sequence that proceeds from *teacher modeling to guided practice and finally to independent practice*. Pressley et al. note that teacher instruction is gradually replaced with *prompting* as needed. Belfiore and Hornyak discuss how teacher support is replaced with *self-management*, and Butler describes a process for *fading* instructional support.

Finally, across interventions we see an emphasis on *self-reflective practice*, where students practice skills and reflect on their performances. Self-reflective practice often is incorporated into the instructional regimen with independent practice or periods of self-reflection. In the Hofer et al. project, self-reflective practice occurs during students' journal writing, and Belfiore and Hornyak note that their self-management training includes time for self-reflection.

DIVERGENT ISSUES

Along with these many commonalities, there are a few issues where authors diverge in their thinking. Three prominent issues are (1) the relative importance to self-regulated learning of social models and self-constructions, (2) the role of motivation, and (3) the uses of self-reflective practice.

Modeling and Self-Constructions

Social models constitute an important means of transmitting skills and strategies (Bandura, 1986; Rosenthal & Zimmerman, 1978; Schunk, 1987), and models frequently are employed in strategy instruction (Graham & Harris, 1989a, 1989b; Schunk & Rice, 1987, 1992, 1993; Schunk & Swartz, 1993). In the present volume, social models are employed by Belfiore and Hornyak, Graham et al., Hofer et al., Lan, Pressley et al., and Schunk.

Alternatively, strategy instruction can be less formally structured such that students play a greater role in constructing strategies. Student strategy construction is employed in the interventions described herein by Butler and by Winne and Stockley. The teacher's role is to provide support and assistance where needed. This approach, which forces students to take more responsibility for learning, fits well with the literature on reciprocal teaching (Palincsar & Brown, 1984) and collaborative peer-learning groups (Cohen, 1994; Slavin, 1995).

Future research should explore the relative efficacy of modeling and self-constructed self-regulated learning strategies. Their effectiveness may well depend on such factors as the type of research participants and the need for precision in strategy learning. In domains where different strategies are equally effective, self-constructions may work well and have the added benefit of giving the students a greater sense of control over their learning. Conversely, where one or a few strategies will be effective and students may construct erroneous ones, then strategy modeling may be best. We might also expect that strategy modeling would be most effective during initial learning when participants' ability to construct strategies is limited, but that as students acquire competence they might be capable of determining effective alternatives on their own.

Role of Motivation

Self-regulation instruction historically has focused on the teaching of cognitive procedures (e.g., organizing, monitoring, rehearsing) and adaptive behaviors (e.g., self-management, environment structuring, help seeking). These procedures are important, but they do not fully explain the range of self-regulative patterns displayed by students. To engage in self-regulation requires that students possess a level of willingness to learn, often over lengthy periods. The latter involves motivation. It is encouraging that many of the interventions described in this book include such motivational factors as self-efficacy, attributions, perceived control over learning, self-reinforcement, and perceptions of competence (Belfiore & Hornyak; Graham et al.; Hofer et al.; Lan; Schunk).

Central to the role of motivation is its potential importance beyond the instructional context. For example, students may learn a strategy but not continue to use it if they believe that other factors (e.g., hard work) are more important for success (Pressley et al., 1990; Schunk & Swartz, 1993). Providing information about strategy value serves a valuable motivational function (Schunk & Rice, 1992). Additional research is needed on effective ways to incorporate motivational processes into instruction.

Self-Reflective Practice

This is a critical component of self-regulated learning, but to date minimal efforts have been made to integrate it systematically with interventions. Ideally, self-reflective practice allows students to assess their learning progress and the effectiveness of strategies, alter their approach as needed, and make adjustments to environmental and social factors to establish a setting highly conducive to learning.

The need for self-reflective practice may be greater in some settings than in others. Self-reflective practice may be less important where feedback is provided regularly and self-assessment is straightforward. In less structured environments, student self-reflection may play a more valuable role. Systematic *forethought,* such as adopting a learning goal orientation prepares a student for optimal forms of self-reflection, such as a strategy instead of an fixed ability attribution. Thus, self-reflection can be systematically developed by training in forethought and performance or volitional control. Teachers have much latitude in designing instruction. We recommend that self-reflective processes be assessed during practice efforts and when dysfunctional patterns, such as unreasonable self-evaluational criteria, are detected, the instructors should intervene at the outset of the self-regulatory cycle.

SUGGESTIONS FOR FUTURE RESEARCH

We have provided several suggestions for future research in the preceding section. Here we wish to add three educationally important areas where academic self-regulation research is lacking and that have theoretical and educational importance: the role of out-of-school factors, the uses of technology, and the influence of classroom inclusion.

Out-of-School Influences

The chapters in this volume describe programs that were conducted in actual learning settings. This is desirable because programs are woven into academic content and effects have greater generalizability compared with projects conducted in laboratory settings.

At the same time, research increasingly is showing the impact of *out-of-school factors* on school achievement. For example, in Steinberg, Brown, and Dornbusch's (1996) longitudinal research with adolescents, a central finding is that such nonacademic factors as peer groups, families, and part-time employment strongly affect school achievement. The effects of in-school factors (e.g., curriculum, teaching) often are exceeded by those of out-of-school variables. Brody, Stoneman, and Flor (1996) have found that parental monitoring of their children's activities and standard setting regarding their children's performance were very predictive of the children's academic as well as behavioral self-regulation. There is recent research on immigrant students' academic achievement indicating that parents' and peers' emphasis on the value of education, homework, and academic grades is more influential than the families' social class or use of English as a second language (Fuligni, 1997).

We recommend that self-regulation researchers extend their focus to factors beyond those centered in schools. In particular, it seems useful to determine how the family and peer cultures contribute to or detract from students' development of self-regulatory competence. We suspect that such research will be longitudinal in nature, and we believe that the contributions to the literature will be of great value.

Technology

Much has been written about the uses of technology in education (Bork, 1985; Hirschbuhl, 1992; Kozma, 1991). Computer learning has received the greatest attention, and there is evidence that computers promote academic outcomes (Clements, 1995). In the present volume, the procedures by Pressley et al. and by Winne and Stockley include computer-based work.

An area that lends itself well to self-regulation is *distance learning*, where instruction originates at one site and is transmitted to students at distant sites. The practical benefits of distance learning are many, but research is needed that explores the effects on learning. Self-regulation seems critical due to the high degree of student independence deriving from the instructor's physical absence. In particular, we recommend research on the type of self-regulatory strategies that allow good distance learning. For example, comprehension monitoring would seem to be important, as well as forming peer collaborations among members of the student cohort.

Another area where technology can play a key role in self-regulation involves *self-observation*. Learners are often in a poor physical position to be self-observant without special tools, such as a mirror or a taped or filmed record. It is axiomatic that students' ability to self-regulate their functioning directly depends on the quality of their self-observations. Biofeedback research has shown that when given precise feedback regarding blood pressure, head tension, or gastric secretions, individuals can learn to control even autonomic nervous system processes (Holroyd et al., 1984). There is extensive evidence that without specialized instruments for self-observing, students are relatively poor judges of their academic readiness for tests (Ghatala, Levin, Foorman, & Pressley, 1989) as well as their reading comprehension (Glenberg, Wilkinson, & Epstein, 1982). Self-assessment and self-recording methods that can ensure accuracy have the potential for greatly improving students' quality of self-regulatory control and subsequent achievement (Zimmerman & Kitsantas, 1997). As Winne and Stockley noted in Chapter 6, the use of computers as a medium for learning can provide detailed feedback about one's learning efforts and has the potential for raising self-observation to new levels.

Inclusion

The inclusion movement in education focuses on increasing participation of students with disabilities in regular education classes. Inclusion presents challenges for teachers, who cannot rely on preparing a single lesson plan for use with the entire class but rather must tailor instruction to individual differences in learning capacities.

Some of the interventions described in this volume deal with students with disabilities and learning problems (Belfiore & Hornyak; Butler; Graham et al.; Hofer et al.; Pressley et al.; Schunk); however, research on inclusive classes is needed. Thus, we might ask what types of self-regulatory activities work best in learning environments where there are wide ranges in abilities and interests. Self-regulation also benefits teachers, because they will gain time to devote to students requiring individual assistance.

OVERCOMING BARRIERS TO CHANGE

The programs described in this volume and similar ones have intuitive appeal and are based on theory and research, but they are not always easy to implement. There exist many impediments to change in schools: lack of time and space, insufficient funding, need for parental consent, and the belief in some quarters that students do not require self-regulation because achievement-test scores are already high. In addition, the beliefs and instructional practices of teachers can be a barrier to the success of self-regulatory training even when interventions are conducted by outside sources of change, such as tutors or special classes. Instructors in content area courses vary greatly in their organization of the curriculum. Those who give clear instructional goals, who provide content-related learning strategies, and who evaluate frequently and objectively can assist students' efforts to self-regulate. Teachers who are less well organized or who subjectively evaluate course outcomes increase the difficulty of self-regulation for their students.

At the institutional level, universities may not count toward graduation credits from study skills courses, which will preclude some students in need of self-regulatory skills from taking these courses. When courses in self-regulation are labeled or viewed as "remedial," universities are especially reluctant to grant credit for the course. An alternative approach for gaining credit is to expand the scope of self-regulation courses by providing theory and research as well as study techniques and by including students of varying achievement levels. We know of cases where high-achieving undergraduate college students have enrolled in courses on self-regulation in order to prepare for graduate school. Although these students felt their study skills were sufficient for their current coursework, they felt they needed more proficient study skills to succeed at the graduate level.

Academic researchers traditionally have shunned publicly espousing benefits of their programs, feeling instead that these programs speak for themselves. In difficult times, this strategy is ineffective. An excellent way to facilitate change is to take advantage of media exposure and sharpen our presentation skills. It helps to have data in hand showing effectiveness of programs with students of different levels (e.g., gifted, average, remedial).

Another means of facilitating change is to become partners in collaboration with school practitioners. School and university professionals can design and implement programs, patterned along lines of the Professional Development Schools model (Griffin, 1996). School-based collaborations provide ownership across all levels, which is beneficial for implementation and continuation of the program.

Finally, schools will be more receptive to interventions that incorporate self-regulation into regular academic instruction. Special add-on programs take extra time that few schools can provide. Linking self-regulation with academic content also should enhance transfer of self-regulatory skills beyond the training setting. Zimmerman, Bonner, and Kovach (1996) have provided a model for how such training can be implemented by middle and high school teachers are part of the regular curriculum.

CONCLUSIONS

As we complete this third volume, we are gratified by the initial progress in implementing academic self-regulation models in applied instructional settings and are excited about the future prospects. The field contains many talented researchers and dedicated practitioners at all levels, from the elementary school to college. In the next few years, we anticipate continued efforts to expand the scope of self-regulatory intervention models to include additional features of instructional practice. We look forward to addressing such policy issues as the types of institutional reform necessary to enhance students' regulation of their own learning processes.

REFERENCES

Bandura, A. (1986). *Social foundations of thought and action: A social cognitive theory.* Englewood Cliffs, NJ: Prentice-Hall.

Bork, A. (1985). *Personal computers for education.* New York: Harper & Row.

Brody, G. H., Stoneman, Z., & Flor, D. (1996). Parental religiosity: Family processes and youth competence in rural, two-parent African American families. *Developmental Psychology, 32,* 696–706.

Clements, D. H. (1995). Teaching creativity with computers. *Educational Psychology Review, 7,* 141–161.

Cohen, E. G. (1994). Restructuring the classroom: Conditions for productive small groups. *Review of Educational Research, 64,* 1–35.

Fuligni, A. J. (1997). The academic achievement of adolescents from immigrant families: The roles of family background, attitudes, and behavior. *Child Development, 68,* 351–363.

Ghatala, E., Levin, J. R., Foorman, B. R., & Pressley, M. (1989). Improving children's regulation of their reading PREP time. *Contemporary Educational Psychology, 14,* 49–66.

Glenberg, A. M., Wilkinson, A. C., & Epstein, W. (1982). The illusion of knowing: Failure in the assessment of comprehension. *Memory and Cognition, 10,* 597–602.

Graham, S., & Harris, K. R. (1989a). Components analysis of cognitive strategy instruction: Effects on learning disabled students' compositions and self-efficacy. *Journal of Educational Psychology, 81,* 353–361.

Graham, S., & Harris, K. R. (1989b). Improving learning disabled students' skills at composing essays: Self-instructional strategy training. *Exceptional Children, 56,* 201–214.

Griffin, G. A. (1996). Realizing community in schools through inquiry. In D. R. Dillon (Ed.), *Cultivating collaboration: Proceedings from the first Professional Development Schools Conference* (pp. 15–39). West Lafayette, IN: Purdue University School of Education.

Hirschbuhl, J. J. (1992). Multimedia: Why invest? *Interactive Learning International, 8,* 321–323.

Holroyd, K. A., Penzien, D. B., Hursey, K. G., Tobin, D. L., Rogers, L., Holm, J. E., Marcille, P. J., Hall, J. R., & Chila, A. G. (1984). Change mechanism in EMG biofeedback training: Cognitive changes underlying improvements in tension headache. *Journal of Consulting and Clinical Psychology, 52,* 1039–1053.

Kozma, R. B. (1991). Learning with media. *Review of Educational Research, 61,* 179–211.

Meece, J. L., Blumenfeld, P. C., & Hoyle, R. H. (1988). Students' goal orientations and cognitive engagement in classroom activities. *Journal of Educational Psychology, 80,* 514–523.

Palincsar, A. S., & Brown, A. L. (1984). Reciprocal teaching of comprehension-fostering and comprehension-monitoring activities. *Cognition and Instruction, 1*, 117–175.

Pintrich, P. R., & De Groot, E. V. (1990). Motivational and self-regulated learning components of classroom academic performance. *Journal of Educational Psychology, 82*, 33–40.

Pressley, M., Woloshyn, V., Lysynchuk, L. M., Martin, V., Wood, E., & Willoughby, T. (1990). A primer of research on cognitive strategy instruction: The important issues and how to address them. *Educational Psychology Review, 2*, 1–58.

Rosenthal, T. L., & Zimmerman, B. J. (1978). *Social learning and cognition.* New York: Academic Press.

Schunk, D. H. (1987). Peer models and children's behavioral change. *Review of Educational Research, 57*, 149–174.

Schunk, D. H. (1991). Self-efficacy and academic motivation. *Educational Psychologist, 26*, 207–231.

Schunk, D. H., & Rice, J. M. (1987). Enhancing comprehension skill and self-efficacy with strategy value information. *Journal of Reading Behavior, 19*, 285–302.

Schunk, D. H., & Rice, J. M. (1992). Influence of reading-comprehension strategy information on children's achievement outcomes. *Learning Disability Quarterly, 15*, 51–64.

Schunk, D. H., & Rice, J. M. (1993). Strategy fading and progress feedback: Effects on self-efficacy and comprehension among students receiving remedial reading services. *Journal of Special Education, 27*, 257–276.

Schunk, D. H., & Swartz, C. W. (1993). Goals and progress feedback: Effects on self-efficacy and writing achievement. *Contemporary Educational Psychology, 18*, 337–354.

Schunk, D. H., & Zimmerman, B. J. (Eds.). (1994). *Self-regulation of learning and performance: Issues and educational applications.* Hillsdale, NJ: Erlbaum.

Slavin, R. (1995). *Cooperative learning.* Boston: Allyn & Bacon.

Steinberg, L., Brown, B. B., & Dornbusch, S. M. (1996). *Beyond the classroom: Why school reform has failed and what parents need to do.* New York: Simon & Schuster.

Zimmerman, B. J., Bonner, S., & Kovach, R. (1996). *Developing self-regulated learners: Beyond achievement to self-efficacy.* Washington, DC: American Psychological Association.

Zimmerman, B. J., & Kitsantas, A. (1997). Developmental phases in self-regulation: Shifting from process to outcome goals. *Journal of Educational Psychology, 89*, 29–36.

Zimmerman, B. J., & Martinez-Pons, M. (1990). Student differences in self-regulated learning: Relating grade, sex, and giftedness to self-efficacy and strategy use. *Journal of Educational Psychology, 82*, 51–59.

Zimmerman, B. J., & Schunk, D. H. (Eds.). (1989). *Self-regulated learning and academic achievement: Theory, research, and practice.* New York: Springer-Verlag.

Author Index

Abbott, R., 37
Abbott, S., 37
Adelman, P. B., 161
Afflerbach, P., 42–44, 46, 127
Alexander, P. A., 38, 166
Alley, G. R., 161
Amaya-Williams, M., 207
Ames, C., 3, 72, 115
Anderson, J. R., 124
Anderson, L. M., 164
Anderson, M., 26
Anderson, R. C., 45
Anderson, V., 50
Andrews, D., 198
Annie E. Casey Foundation, 184
Anthony, H. M., 164
Arns, F. J., 208
Aronson, E., 215
Atwell, N., 26
Austin, J. T., 123

B

Baker, L., 163, 165
Bandura, A., 3, 6–8, 14, 70–71, 90, 139–144, 166, 200, 229
Barbaranelli, C., 200
Bateman, D. F., 86, 193
Baxter, G. P., 65, 108
Beaugrande, R. de, 20
Belfiore, P. J., 15, 140, 185, 189, 192, 198–199, 227–229, 232
Bell, J. A., 154
Bell, R. Q., 46
Bennett, Z. H., 8
Bereiter, C., 20–21, 164–165
Bergman, J. L., 45
Berk, L. E., 205–207
Berninger, V., 37
Biemiller, A., 4, 8, 15, 109, 205–206, 211, 217, 219, 221, 228

Biggs, J., 57
Bird, M., 164–165
Bivens, J. A., 205
Blumenfeld, P. C., 226
Bonner, S., 10, 153, 233
Bork, A., 231
Borkowski, J. G., 13, 47–48, 60, 72, 80, 160, 164, 166, 168–170
Bouffard-Bouchard, T., 141
Boyle, R. A., 61, 111
Bradley, L., 92
Bransford, J. D., 53, 67
Brigham, T., 188–189
Brody, G. H., 231
Browder, D. M., 199
Brown, A. L., 12, 53, 67–68, 163–165, 170, 178, 206, 215, 218, 229
Brown, B. B., 231
Brown, J. S., 142
Brown, R., 13, 45–46, 49, 54, 206, 227
Brozo, W. G., 101
Bruer, J. T., 217
Bruner, J. S., 47
Bruning, R. H., 141
Bryan, T., 87
Buel, B. J., 86
Burke, J. G., 86
Burland, S., 204
Burnham, S., 20
Burrell, K., 57, 80
Bursuck, W. D., 161
Burton, R. R., 142
Butler, D. L., 14, 68–69, 109–113, 160–178, 228–229, 232
Byrnes, J. P., 166, 169, 178

C

Calderhead, J., 62
Cameron, R., 204

Campione, J. C., 12, 53, 67, 163, 170, 215, 218
Caplan, N., 1
Caprara, G. V., 200
Cariglia-Bull, T., 209
Carr, M., 48, 72, 80
Carver, C. S., 4, 160, 162, 169
Case, R., 207, 209
Cauraugh, J. H., 4
Cazden, C. B., 52
Charness, N., 11
Chen, C., 137–138
Children's Defense Fund, 184
Choy, M. H., 1
Clark, F. L., 161
Clements, D. H., 231
Cohen, E. G., 229
Cohen, J., 96
Coleman, M., 190
Collins, C., 50
Collins, R., 25
Connell, M. L., 163
Connolly, T., 7
Cooper, J. O., 188–189, 197
Corno, L., 3, 8, 37, 65, 67–68, 99, 162
Courtney, D. P., 138
Covington, M. V., 69
Cox, B., 63
Cox, P. D., 148–150, 154, 168
Coy-Ogan, L., 45–46
Cunicelli, E. A., 45
Cunningham, L., 207

D

Danoff, B., 22
Davenport, M., 191
Day, J. D., 12, 170
Deane, S., 209
Deci, E. L., 3, 7
De Groot, E., 7, 13, 60, 65–67, 94, 141, 226
De La Paz, S., 22, 25
Delclos, V. R., 86
Dempster, F. N., 128
DeNisi, A., 128
Denney, D. R., 154
Denney, N. W., 154
Dereshiwsky, M. I., 164
Deshler, D. D., 12, 161, 164, 169, 206
Diaz, R. M., 205, 207
Diener, C. I., 87

DiGangi, S. A., 86, 194
Dole, J. A., 164
Dornbusch, S. M., 231
Dowrick, P. W., 147
Duffy, G. G., 46, 164
Durkin, D., 43–44
Dweck, C. S., 5, 7, 10, 70, 72, 87, 93, 163

E

Earley, P. C., 7
Eccles, J. S., 7, 64
Echevarria, M., 44
Eisenberger, R., 114–116, 119
Ekegren, C., 7
Elaschuk, C., 174
Elbers, E., 48
El-Dinary, P. B., 13, 45, 48, 215, 227
Elliot, E., 93
Elliot, T., 61, 63
Ellis, E. S., 101, 160, 164, 168–170
Englert, C. S., 164
Epstein, W., 232
Ericsson, K. A., 11, 107, 115
Estrada, M. T., 164

F

Ferrara, R. A., 53, 67
Festinger, L., 5
Ficzere, S., 161
Field, D., 114, 117
Fisher, R. P., 128
Flavell, J. H., 67
Fler, C., 101
Flor, D., 231
Flower, L., 20–21
Foesterling, F., 72
Foorman, B. R., 9, 232
Foos, P. W., 128
Fuligni, A. J., 137, 231

G

Gaelick, L., 140
Galen, N. D., 218
Garcia, T., 8, 13, 60, 65–67, 69, 71–72, 81
Garfield, C. A., 8
Gaskins, I. W., 45–46, 48, 52–53, 61, 63
Gast, D., 34
Geary, D. C., 137
Gerber, P. J., 161
Ghatala, E. S., 9, 86–87, 165, 232

Givon, T., 116
Glenberg, A. M., 232
Globerson, T., 34–35, 116
Glover, J. A., 128–129
Goodlad, S., 218
Grabowski, J., 20
Graham, S., 4, 12, 20–23, 25–26, 30–31, 36–38, 109, 160–161, 164–165, 167, 169, 177–178, 226–229, 232
Gralinski, J. H., 138
Gregg, S. L., 164
Greenberg, D., 69
Griffin, G. A., 233
Grskovic, J., 196
Gruson, L., 204
Gunn, T. P., 148, 151, 155
Gupta, L., 109
Gutentag, R. E., 209
Guterman, E., 116
Guthrie, J. T., 206
Gutierrez, R., 210
Guzdial, M., 109, 133

H

Hadwin, A. F., 108–109, 111–113, 132
Hale, C. A., 164
Halford, G. S., 209
Hallahan, D. P., 86, 89, 193
Hamby, R., 25
Hammill, D., 27, 31
Hancock, G. R., 138
Hanson, A. R., 148–149, 151
Harpster, L., 71
Harrington, C., 86
Harris, K. R., 4, 20–23, 25–26, 30–31, 36–38, 48, 60, 86, 109, 160–161, 164–165, 169, 177–178, 193, 195, 198, 206, 226–227, 229
Hativa, N., 107
Hattie, J., 57–59, 61
Hayes, J., 20–21
Heckhausen, H., 3
Heins, E. D., 89, 102
Henderson, R. W., 207
Henk, W. A., 101
Herman, J. L., 107
Heron, T. E., 188
Herzog, A., 87
Heward, W. L., 188
Hidi, S., 71
Hill, K., 71

Hirschbuhl, J. J., 231
Hirst, B., 218
Hofer, B., 79, 81, 227–229, 232
Holroyd, K. A., 232
Hornyak, R. S., 15, 227–229, 232
Howard-Rose, D., 108, 132
Hoyle, R. H., 226
Huberman, A. M., 174
Hughes, C., 191
Hutchins, E., 46
Hutchinson, J. M., 185, 192
Hynd, C., 57

I

Iannone, R., 200–201
Inglis, A., 4, 109, 206, 217, 221, 228
Iran-Nejad, A., 48

J

Jackson, D., 65
Jacobs, J. E., 163
Jayanthi, M., 161
Jenson, W. R., 198
Johnson, D. W., 216
Johnson, R. T., 216
Jones, J. E., 191
Judy, J. E., 166

K

Kamann, M. P., 168–169
Kanfer, F. H., 140
Kauffman, J. M., 195, 198
Kazin, A., 37
Kellogg, R., 20
King, A., 119, 128, 130
Kitsantas, A., 5, 7, 9–10, 138, 232
Kloosterman, P., 138
Kluger, A. N., 128
Kopp, C. B., 207
Kovach, R., 10, 153, 233
Kozma, R. B., 231
Krampe, R. T., 107
Kranzler, J., 152
Kratochwill, T. R., 99, 189
Kuhl, J., 3, 8, 87, 89
Kuperis, S., 161

L

Lan, W. Y., 13, 92, 100, 227–229
Landrum, T. J., 86, 193

Larivee, S., 141
Larsen, S., 27, 31
Latham, G. P., 3
Lau-Smith, J. A., 187–188, 195
Lee, C., 193
Lee, D. L., 198
Lee, S., 137
Leggett, E. L., 70, 72
Lepper, M. R., 86
Lesgold, A., 107
Levin, J. R., 4, 9, 232
Light, R. J., 210
Lin, Y. G., 13, 60, 101
Lipson, M. Y., 66
Lloyd, J. W., 86, 89, 191, 193, 198
Locke, E. A., 3
Lummis, M., 137
Luria, A. R., 12

M

Maag, J. W., 86, 194–195
MacArthur, C. A., 21, 25, 167
Mace, F. C., 99, 140, 189, 191, 193, 196, 199
MacLeod, W. B., 173
Maddux, C. D., 164
Maehr, M., 72
Mahoney, M. J., 87
Malone, L. D., 86
Manno, C., 193, 195, 198
Marks, M. B., 45, 48, 60
Marshall, K. J., 101
Martin, K. F., 193, 195, 198
Martinez-Pons, M., 3, 5, 8, 67, 69, 93–94, 151, 226
Marx, R. W., 61, 111, 127, 167
Masterson, F. A., 115
Mastropieri, M. A., 86
Matlin, M., 77
Mavrogenes, N. A., 218
Mayer, R., 66–68, 73
McCall, C., 190
McCombs, B. L., 141
McCurdy, B. L., 86
McCutchen, D., 20, 22
McDermitt, M., 115
McElroy, K., 25
McGilly, K., 217
McKeachie, W. J., 13, 60, 63–66, 68, 79–80, 101
McKoon, G., 111, 114, 124

Meece, J. L., 7, 93, 138, 226
Mehan, H., 52
Meichenbaum, D., 4, 12, 15, 109, 146, 204–206, 219, 221, 228
Mendez-Berrueta, H., 80
Merriam, S. B., 172
Midgley, C., 72
Miles, M. B., 174
Miller, M. D., 152
Miller, P. H., 116
Milstead, M., 164
Minick, N., 208
Mistretta-Hampson, J., 44
Molloy, D., 21
Montague, M., 164
Morgan, C., 71
Morgan, M., 120–121, 123
Morrow, L. W., 86
Mosteller, F., 210
Murphy, C. C., 141
Muthukrishna, N., 164, 166, 169–170

N

National Center for Education Statistics, 184
National Council of Teachers of Mathematics, 145
Neal, C. J., 207
Nesbit, J. C., 109
Newman, R. S., 11, 69, 138
Nicholls, J. G., 9, 93
Nist, S., 57
Norman, D. A., 112

O

Olympia, D. E., 198
Ornstein, P. A., 209
O'Sullivan, J. T., 47

P

Paas, F. G. W. C., 209
Pagano, R. P., 89
Pajares, F., 152
Palincsar, A. S., 164, 170, 206, 215, 229
Papert, S., 107
Parent, S., 141
Paris, S. G., 66–67, 163, 166, 169–170, 178
Parr, G., 92
Pastorelli, C., 200
Patterson, C. J., 86

Pauk, W., 75, 77
Paulsen, A. S., 8
Pearl, R., 48, 87
Pearson, P. D., 164
Perkins, D. N., 62–64, 108, 111, 169–170
Perry, N. E., 108
Phillips, S., 209
Pintrich, P. R., 7–8, 13, 60–61, 63–72, 77, 79–81, 94, 101, 108, 111, 138, 141, 226–227
Pirie, J., 165
Pirsig, R. M., 199–200
Plimpton, G., 20, 37
Policastro, M. M., 161, 169
Pressley, M., 4, 9, 13, 42–49, 52, 57, 59–60, 63–64, 66, 80, 86–87, 107, 113, 127, 153, 160, 164–165, 169–171, 178, 206, 209, 215, 217–218, 227–232
Purdie, N., 57

R

Raphael, T. E., 164
Ratcliff, R., 111, 114, 124
Reeve, R. A., 165
Reid, R., 25, 193–195, 198
Reiff, H. B., 161
Rekrut, M. D., 218
Rellinger, E. A., 48, 80
Rice, J. M., 226, 229–230
Richards, M., 205
Ringle, J., 7, 87, 141
Risemberg, R., 8, 20–21
Rocha, J., 4, 8
Roehler, L. R., 164
Roit, M., 50
Rosenblatt, L. M., 46
Rosenthal, T. L., 8, 142, 146, 229
Ross, G., 47
Rumelhart, D. E., 112
Rutherford, R. B., 86

S

Sabornie, E. J., 101
Sachs, J. A., 210
Sagotsky, G., 86
SAIL Faculty and Administration, 45
Salomon, G., 34–35, 62–64, 108, 111, 116, 142, 169–170
Salva, E., 197
Sansone, C., 71

Satlow, E., 45
Sawyer, R. J., 25, 161
Scardamalia, M., 20–21
Schank, R., 107
Scheier, M. F., 4, 160, 162, 169
Scheuermann, B., 190
Schickedanz, J. A., 186
Schiefele, U., 71
Schneider, W., 13, 47, 57, 60, 64, 66, 209
Schommer, M., 81, 111, 166
Schrauben, B., 60, 65, 71, 80–81, 138
Schuder, T., 45, 49, 206
Schumaker, J. B., 12, 161, 164, 169, 189, 206
Schunk, D. H., viii, 1, 4, 7, 10–12, 14, 57, 60, 70–72, 86, 102, 107, 120–123, 138–143, 145–155, 168, 206, 225–230, 232
Schwartz, S. S., 21, 25, 167
Seabaugh, G. O., 189
Seier, W. L., 116
Serna, L. A., 187–188, 195
Sexton, M., 26, 30
Shany, M., 4, 109, 206, 221, 228
Shapiro, E. S., 86, 90, 99
Shea, M. C., 140, 189
Shell, D. F., 141
Sheridan, J., 45
Sheridan, S. M., 198
Siemens, I., 209
Simpson, M., 57–58. 60, 62–64, 80
Singer, R. N., 4
Skinner, B. F., 188
Skinner, C. H., 198
Slavin, R. E., 210, 229
Smith, B. D., 101
Smith, D. A. F., 65, 67, 77
Snow, R. E., 65, 108
Sokolov, A. N., 12
Stahl, N. A., 101
Steen, L. A., 137
Stein, S., 45
Steinberg, L., 11, 231
Stevens, D. D., 164
Stevenson, H. W., 137–138
Stigler, J. W., 137–138
Stipek, D. J., 138
Stockley, D. B., 14, 228–229, 231–232
Stoddard, B., 25
Stone, C. A., 171, 178, 208, 221
Stoneman, Z., 231

Swanson, H. L., 161, 164–165, 177
Swartz, C. W., 229–230
Sweeney, W. J., 197–198
Sweller, J., 124–125
Syer, K. D., 173

T

Talbert-Johnson, C., 197
Tanhouser, S., 25, 30
Tao, L., 80
Tawney, J., 34
Tesch-Römer, C., 107
Testerman, J., 187
Thoresen, C. E., 87
Tindal, G. A., 193
Torgesen, J. K., 161
Troia, G., 4, 31, 34, 109, 227
Turner, L. A., 168
Turner, M. C., 154

U

Underwood, V. L., 60, 63, 65, 80
Uttal, D. H., 137–138

V

Vancouver, J. B., 123
Van Merrienboer, J. J. G., 209
Van Meter, P., 49, 206
Vargas, A. U., 198
Vogel, S. A., 161
Voth, T., 25
Vygotsky, L. S., 8, 12, 207–208, 221

W

Warner, M. M., 161
Webber, J., 190, 193
Weiner, B., 5, 9, 72, 152
Weinstein, C. E., 60, 63, 65–69, 73, 80, 107, 132

Weir, C., 71
Wertsch, J. V., 208
Weyhing, R. S., 72, 168
Whang, P. A., 138
Wharton-McDonald, R., 13, 44, 227
Whitaker, D., 37
Whitmore, J. K., 1
Wigfield, A., 7, 64, 71
Wile, D., 45
Wilkinson, A. C., 232
Willoughby, T., 101
Wilson, W. H., 209
Winne, P. H., 4, 14, 68–69, 102, 107–115, 117, 120, 127, 132–133, 160, 162–165, 167, 169, 171, 176–177, 228–229, 231–232
Winograd, P., 67
Wittrock, M. C., 48
Wixson, K. K., 66, 170
Woloshyn, V., 59–60, 63, 80, 165, 206, 217
Wolters, C. A., 60, 65, 72, 80, 108
Wong, B. Y. L., 36, 161, 166, 169–170
Wood, D., 218
Wood, E., 101
Wood, S. S., 47
Wyatt, D., 42

Y

Yin, R. K., 172, 174
Yu, S., 60, 79, 227

Z

Zellermayer, M., 116
Zimmerman, B. J., viii, 1–5, 7–12, 20–21, 37, 57, 60, 67–69, 86–87, 92–94, 107, 138–143, 146, 151, 153–154, 160, 162, 169, 177, 203, 205–206, 225–227, 229, 232–233
Zivin, G., 205

Subject Index

Academic independence, 184, 186, 201
Academic-related routines, 192
Adaptation, 4–8, 127–132
Adolescents, 184–201
Anxiety, 71
At-risk students, 187
Attention, 3, 142
Attributions, 4–6, 9–10, 72

B

Barriers to change, 232–233
Buggy algorithms, 142

C

Chaos, 201
Challenge seeking, 93, 96–97
Cognitive capacity and task demands,
   211
Cognitive strategies, 67–69, 167
Comprehension, 42–47
   nature of, 42–44
   instruction, 44–45
   in classrooms, 44–45
   strategies, 45–47
   teaching of, 45–47
Computer technology for students,
   106–133
Conditional knowledge, 115
Cross-age tutoring, 213, 216 (see also
   Peer assistance)

D

Decision making, 185
Dynamic equilibrium, 200
Dynamic quality, 200

E

Effort, model of, 114
Epistemological beliefs, 81, 111

F

Fluency, 192
Forethought processes, 2–7

G

Goals, 109, 111, 119–122
Goal orientation, 3, 72, 152–153
Goal setting, 2–3, 76, 190
Good strategy use, 45–47, 53–54, 60

H

Homework routine, 197

I

IF–THEN rule, 108, 111–112
Imagery, 4, 6, 8
Inclusion movement, 232
Information processing, 75, 109–114
Interest, 71–72
Instruction
   integrated versus adjunct, 61–63, 80
   intrinsic, 3–7
Intrinsic motivation, 94, 97

K

Knowledge organization, 94–95, 97
Knowledge telling, 21–22

L

Learned industriousness, 115–116, 118–119
Learning disabilities, 161, 163–164, 171–172
Learning in statistics, 86–102
Learning to Learn course, 14, 58, 65–82

M

Mastery learning, 93, 96–97
Mathematics, 137, 145, 193, 211–214
    instruction, 144–151
    achievement outcomes, 147–150
Means–end tactic, 124
Metacognition, 47, 67–69, 166
Mindfulness, 35–36
Modeling, 142–144
    reading, 46–49
    and self-constructions, 229
Models, 138, 143–144
    coping, 147, 149
    mastery, 147, 149
    multiple, 146
    self, 147
Motivation, 138, 141, 229–230
Motivational beliefs, 3, 111
Motivational strategies, 69–72

N

Note taking, 75, 192

O

Observational learning, 140–143
Operant theory, 184–187
Outcome expectations, 141
Out-of-school influences, 230–231

P

Peer assistance, 210, 213, 216
Performance control processes, 3–9
Planning, 37
Portfolios, 200
Positive reinforcement, 198
Postsecondary learning contexts, 161–162
Private speech, 205–206
Problem solving, 195–196
Purposeful learning model, 15, 187–201

R

Reactivity, 198
Reading instruction, 42–56

S

Saliency, 189
Self-determination, 187
Self-direction, 170, 173
Self-efficacy, 3, 70–71, 140–143
Self-evaluation, 4–5, 190, 197
Self-generated questions, 127–129
Self-instruction, 4,
    and problem solving, 195–197
Self-judgment, 94, 97, 140
Self-management, 185–187, 199
Self-monitoring, 4, 86, 89–100, 140, 153–154, 189–190, 194, 196–198
    forms, 90, 100, 190
    outcomes, 198–199
    proximity, 90
    regularity, 90
    routines, 192–199
    and self-reflection, 99
Self-monitoring instructional model, 13–14, 86–102
Self-observation, 140
Self-reaction, 5, 140
Self-reflection, 2–5, 9–10, 86, 98–100, 199
Self-reflective practice, 230
    with adolescents, 199–200
    in mathematics, 139, 145, 153–155
    in reading, 53–54
    in writing, 34–36
Self-regulated learners
    skillful versus naive, 6–10
    teaching college students, 58–65
Self-regulated learning (SRL), 108–109
    computer technologies for, 106–133
    divergent issues, 228–230
    integrated versus adjunct course design, 61–63
    intervention, 65–79
    phase cycle, 2–5, 110–112, 114–142
    subprocesses, 6–10
Self-regulated learning strategies, 92–93, 96, 101
Self-regulated strategy development
    model, 12, 20–38
    case studies, 26–34
    instructional stages and characteristics, 23–26

Self-regulation, 87, 138, 162, 164, 169–
  170, 178, 204, 207
  and achievement beliefs, 151–155
  consulting versus reflecting roles, 216–
    218
  definition, 1, 58
  development of, 10–12, 226
  dimensions of, 227
  indicators, 204–205
  interventions, 227–228
  instructional models of, 12–16
  key questions, 225–226
  and learning, 142, 208
  phases, 2–5
  and self-efficacy, 141–142
  subprocesses of, 6–10, 138, 140
  and supporting conditions, 214
Self-reinforcement, 191
Self-reports, 193
Self-verbalization, 154 (*see also* Self-
  instruction)
Social-cognitive theory 14, 139–144
  instruction program, 144–155
Spacing effect, 128
SRL-as-aptitude, 108
SRL-as-event, 109
Static quality, 199
Strategic content learning
  and knowledge construction, 169–170
  model, 14–15, 160, 162–172
  research results, 172–176
  and social interaction, 170–171
  transfer, 170
Strategic learning, 165, 172
Strategic planning, 3
Strategies, 150–152
  cognition and regulatory, 66
  general, 59
  instruction, 42–48

self-knowledge and motivational, 69–72
  writing, 28
Statistics course, 87–102
STUDY software system, 14, 117–119, 122–
  123, 125–127, 130
Studying time, 99
"Surplus capacity" hypothesis, 209

T

Tactics, 110–119, 123–127
Task demands, 209–210
Task-regulatory speech, 205–206, 211–212,
  219–220
  measure of, 219–220
Technological opportunism, 108
Technology, 231–232
Test taking, 75–76
Testing effect, 128
Time management, 76–77
Transactional strategies instruction model,
  13, 48–54
  validations of, 49–51
  implementation, 51
Transfer, 63, 80–81
Triadic reciprocality, 139

V

Values, 37, 141
Verbal protocol analyses, 43–44
Verbal task regulation model, 15, 207–224
Verbalization, 150, 154
Volition control, 2

W

Writing, 20–38
Writing strategy use, 28–34